# PARENTS WITH INTE
## DISABILITIES

'*Parents with Intellectual Disabilities: Past, Present and Futures* is essential reading for anyone interested in the lives of parents with intellectual disabilities, and it is recommended reading for everyone in the broader field of developmental disabilities. It provides a synthesis of current research and practice, along with a clear picture of the challenges ahead. Its contents are both comprehensive and compassionate. The international authorship provides an important global perspective.'

**Dr Dick Sobsey, University of Alberta, Canada**

'The birth of a new child tends to be a happy event, but if parents are intellectually disabled, it is likely to be associated with "danger" and a case for child protection agencies. The point of departure of this book, however, is the 2006 UN Convention on the Rights of Persons with Disabilities, Article 23, on the elimination of discrimination related to marriage and family. The book discusses the experiences of parents with intellectual disabilities and their children, and also supports such parental training and the role of extended families. It is a very welcome contribution to a topic that tends to be negatively oversimplified.'

**Jan Tøssebro, Ph.D., Norwegian University of Science and Technology**

# PARENTS WITH INTELLECTUAL DISABILITIES
## Past, Present and Futures

### Edited by

**Gwynnyth Llewellyn**
*University of Sydney*

**Rannveig Traustadóttir**
*University of Iceland*

**David McConnell**
*University of Alberta*

**Hanna Björg Sigurjónsdóttir**
*University of Iceland*

**WILEY-BLACKWELL**
A John Wiley & Sons, Ltd., Publication

This edition first published 2010
© 2010 John Wiley & Sons Ltd

Wiley-Blackwell is an imprint of John Wiley & Sons, formed by the merger of Wiley's global
Scientific, Technical, and Medical business with Blackwell Publishing.

*Registered Office*
John Wiley & Sons Ltd, The Atrium, Southern Gate, Chichester, West Sussex, PO19 8SQ, UK

*Editorial Offices*
The Atrium, Southern Gate, Chichester, West Sussex, PO19 8SQ, UK
9600 Garsington Road, Oxford, OX4 2DQ, UK
350 Main Street, Malden, MA 02148-5020, USA

For details of our global editorial offices, for customer services, and for information about how to
apply for permission to reuse the copyright material in this book please see our website at
www.wiley.com/wiley-blackwell.

*Library of Congress Cataloging-in-Publication Data*

Parents with intellectual disabilities: past, present, and futures / edited by
Gwynnyth Llewellyn. . . [et al.].
     p. cm.
   Includes index.
     ISBN 978-0-470-77295-9 (cloth) – ISBN 978-0-470-77294-2 (pbk.)     1. Parents with mental
disabilities—Cross-cultural studies.    2. Parenting—Cross-cultural studies.
I. Llewellyn, Gwynnyth.
   HQ759.912.P363 2010
   306.874087′4—dc22

                                                                                    2009044656

A catalogue record for this book is available from the British Library.

Typeset in 10/12pt Minion by Aptara Inc., New Delhi, India.
Printed in Singapore by Markono Print Media Pte Ltd

1    2010

*We dedicate this book with great gratitude to our friends, mentors and colleagues Tim and Wendy Booth*

# Contents

# List of Contributors

**Marjorie Aunos,** PhD, is a psychologist and counselor to the coordination of ultra-specialized services in two rehabilitation centers for persons with intellectual disabilities (CRDI) in the province of Québec. She obtained her doctorate in 2003 from the University of Québec in Montreal (UQAM) and has numerous publications reporting research data and clinical approaches when working with parents with intellectual disabilities. Her thesis results and recommendations became the foundation for the implementation of a specialized service for parents with intellectual disabilities. Through her involvement with the CRDI and Brock University, she continues to do research in the area of parents with intellectual disabilities and service delivery.

**Sue Candy,** Doctorate in Clinical Psychology, currently works in private practice providing expert witness testimony to the courts. She specializes in assessments of parenting capacity and attachment. She previously worked for many years in the National Health Service providing therapy, assessment, and research in learning disability, mental health, and parenting. She was formerly a Senior Tutor at Plymouth University.

**Jytte Faureholm** has a PhD and Masters in educational psychology and has worked for a number of years as a psychologist for the Ministry of Social Affairs and the Ministry for Refugees, Immigrants, and Integration (Denmark). This includes clinical work and consultation, as well as research, evaluation, and nationwide development projects. As a regional director of psychology she headed a research project with parents with intellectual disabilities and their children. This project, which became her PhD research, has resulted in a number of professional activities with these families in Denmark and other Scandinavian countries and has been the basis for development projects and new ways of working with these families.

**Maurice Feldman,** Professor and Brock Distinguished Researcher, serves as Director at the Centre for Applied Disability Studies, Brock University. Maurice is one of the leading research-practitioners in the area of parents with intellectual disabilities. He established one of the first programs, the *Parent Education Program*, which has been operating for 28 years, specifically for these families. The intervention model he and his associates developed and evaluated has been emulated worldwide. He also conducts specialized parenting capacity assessments and serves as an expert witness. In addition to his work with parents with intellectual disabilities, his other research projects include (1) teaching human rights protection and self-advocacy skills to adults with intellectual disabilities and (2) early detection and intervention of behavioral and developmental problems in young children with developmental delay and/or autism.

**Marie Gustavsson** is a Research/Research and Development Coordinator in the Department for Studies of Social Change and Culture, Linköping University, Sweden. Marie has been conducting research in the areas of disability, parenthood, and family life for over ten years. She finished her doctoral studies in 2002 at Linköping University. Her dissertation focused on disabled parents, their children, and family life. Currently Marie works more broadly with welfare issues and local authorities in Swedish municipalities.

**Gwynnyth Llewellyn** is Professor and Dean of the Faculty of Health Sciences, University of Sydney, and Director of the Australian Family and Disability Studies Research Collaboration. Her research areas are in family and disability studies. Spanning two decades, Gwynnyth is an international leader in the field of parenting with an intellectual disability with her work leading to the world's first national strategy – *Healthy Start: A National Strategy for Children of Parents with Learning Difficulties* (www.healthystart.net.au). Gwynnyth also leads international work on families with children with disabilities, particularly focusing on family perspectives on their everyday lives.

**Rachel Mayes** is a Postdoctoral Research Fellow in the Faculty of Health Sciences, University of Sydney. Rachel has worked in the disability field for over 10 years, primarily in research. Her doctoral work explored becoming a mother for women with intellectual disabilities and what this meant to them. Rachel has published in the areas of women with intellectual disabilities who are mothers and families caring for a child with disabilities.

**David McConnell,** Professor in the Department of Occupational Therapy, Faculty of Rehabilitation Medicine, University of Alberta, has been conducting research in the field of parents and parenting with intellectual disabilities for over 15 years. His recent work has focused on child protection practice and child welfare court proceedings, and building systems capacity to support parents with intellectual disabilities and their children. Formerly Executive Director of the Australian Family and Disability Studies Research Collaboration, University of Sydney, David is now expanding his research program in Canada.

**Sue McGaw** is a Consultant Clinical Psychologist and has been providing specialist assessments, interventions, and support services for parents with learning disabilities for over 22 years. She founded the Special Parenting Service in 1988 in Cornwall; this service was designed specifically to support parents with learning disabilities. She is regarded as a leading expert in this field having completed a PhD on enabling parents with learning disabilities to parent in 1994. She is the British Psychological Society's (BPS) spokesperson on this topic and was awarded the BPS's Award for Distinguished Contributions to Professional Psychology in 2000. She is an active researcher and the author of many articles and chapters, including the *Parent Assessment Manual* (Trecare NHS Trust, 1998).

**Brigit Mirfin-Veitch,** PhD, has been conducting research in the area of intellectual disability for 15 years. Her research has focused on topics such as deinstitutionalization, women's health, and family relationships. For the past decade she has been conducting research and education in the area of parenting by adults with intellectual disabilities. Brigit has a strong commitment to ensuring that parents with intellectual disabilities receive the support they need to care successfully for their children.

**Katherine Moxness,** PhD, is a renowned psychologist, Director of Professional Services and Quality of the West Montreal and Lisette-Dupras readaptation center, and Adjunct Professor at McGill University. Her research interests are mostly around autism and best practices in service delivery. Her clinical vision has led her to support many innovative evidence-based service delivery initiatives.

**Laura Pacheco,** MSW, has completed her master's thesis on parents with intellectual disabilities. She is currently working as a social worker at the West Montreal and Lisette-Dupras readaptation center in the specialized program for parents with intellectual disabilities. She has recently been accepted as a doctoral candidate in the University of Alberta, under the supervision of Associate Professor David McConnell. Her doctoral work will include an exploration of the impact of culture on the experiences of mothers with intellectual disabilities.

**Hanna Björg Sigurjónsdóttir** is an Assistant Professor at the University of Iceland where she teaches about research methods and disability and does research with people with disabilities. She has worked with people with intellectual disabilities for many years, as an advocate, researcher, and an assistant in a parent group. Her doctoral thesis was centered on family support services and parents with learning disabilities. Together with Rannveig Traustadóttir she has published two books in Icelandic, *Contested Families: Parents with Intellectual*

*Disabilities and Their Children* (University of Iceland Press, 1998) and *Invisible Families: Mothers with Intellectual Disabilities and Their Children* (University of Iceland Press, 2001).

**Beth Tarleton** is a Research Fellow at the Norah Fry Research Centre, University of Bristol, UK. Beth has over 10 years' experience in social research and has special interests in the support needs of adults with learning difficulties, especially the provision of easy information and the provision of positive support for parents with learning difficulties. Beth coordinates the Working Together with Parents Network, which aims to improve policy and practice in supporting parents with learning difficulties in the UK.

**Steven J. Taylor,** PhD, is Centennial Professor of Disability Studies and Director of the Center on Human Policy at Syracuse University. He has published widely on disability policy, the sociology of disability, and qualitative research methods. His 10 books include *Introduction to Qualitative Research Methods* (3rd edition), *The Social Meaning of Mental Retardation,* and *Acts of Conscience: World War II, Mental Institutions, and Religious Objectors.* He also serves as the Editor of *Intellectual and Developmental Disabilities.* He has been the recipient of the Research Award from the American Association on Mental Retardation (1997), the Syracuse University Chancellor's Citation for Exceptional Academic Achievement (2003), and the first annual Senior Scholar Award from the Society for Disability Studies (2008).

**Rannveig Traustadóttir** is Professor and Director of the Centre for Disability Studies in the School of Social Sciences, University of Iceland. Much of her research in disability studies has examined the intersection of disability and gender, as well as other categories of inequality, such as social class, race/ethnicity, age and sexuality, and how these create multiple layers of discrimination and social exclusion in disabled people's lives. She has been one of the leaders in developing disability studies as a scholarly field in the Nordic countries and is the former president of the Nordic Network on Disability Research (NNDR).

**Linda Ward,** Professor of Disability and Social Policy at the Norah Fry Research Centre, University of Bristol, UK, has researched and published widely in the field of learning disability. She was co-author of *Finding the Right Support? A Review of Issues and Positive Practice in Supporting Parents with Learning Difficulties and Their Children* (Baring Foundation, 2006) and is Chair of the UK Taskforce on Working Together with Parents with Learning Disabilities. Linda acted as specialist adviser to the Parliamentary Joint Committee on Human Rights' Inquiry on Human Rights and Adults with Learning Disabilities – its report was published as *A Life Like Any Other?* (2008). She is co-author of a review, "Access to Independent Advocacy: An Evidence Review," commissioned by the Government's Office of Disability Issues (ODI) on access to independent advocacy, including advocacy for disabled parents (ODI, 2009).

# Foreword

Should adults with intellectual disabilities be permitted to be parents? In most countries, the answer to this question was clear until relatively recent years: No, they should not. The dramatic growth in the populations of public institutions in the late 18th and early 19th centuries in the United States of America and elsewhere was fueled by the fear that the "feebleminded" would pollute society with their defective genes if allowed to reproduce. In 1890, New York State held a ceremony to dedicate the official opening of Newark State Custodial Asylum for Feebleminded Women, an institution intended for females in their child-bearing years. Segregation was viewed as the simplest way to prevent people with intellectual disabilities from having children, and even institutions housing both men and women separated them in different buildings. It was not the only way. Laws were passed in some states and localities restricting sexual relations with people defined as feebleminded or epileptic. Involuntary sterilization was practiced in a number of countries up until the 1970s and beyond. The 1927 United States Supreme Court case *Buck* v. *Bell* ("Three generations of imbeciles are enough") is widely cited as illustrating the extremes of what was called the eugenics movement, but eugenic sterilization was widely practiced in countries as diverse as Sweden, Finland, and Japan. Citing eugenics literature from the USA and elsewhere, Nazi Germany murdered hundreds of thousands of people with intellectual and other disabilities as part of its so-called "euthanasia program."

Not long ago, a book on parents with intellectual disabilities would have been written to arouse popular opinion and stimulate political action against the presumed social menace posed by procreating "defectives." Today, the hysteria surrounding marriage and procreation of people with intellectual disabilities has waned, although eugenics sentiments persist, if usually unstated. The more common concern is whether people with intellectual disabilities are fit to be parents. Parents with intellectual disabilities are much more likely than other parents to experience intervention by child welfare agencies on the grounds of suspected abuse and neglect. To be sure, some people with intellectual disabilities are unsuitable to be parents. So are some non-disabled people. More often than not, removal of children from the homes of parents with intellectual disabilities is an unnecessary and drastic measure that could be prevented by offering families the supports, resources, and services they need to be successful.

Although public policy in most countries no longer prevents people with intellectual disabilities from having children, many barriers stand in the way of enabling them to bear and raise children. Parents and guardians can exert subtle and not so subtle pressures on people to be sterilized, willingly or unwillingly. The controlled living situations of many people with intellectual disabilities in residential facilities prevent them from enjoying the freedoms that other people take for granted. People cannot have sexual relationships if they are under the constant supervision and control of others. It does not always take a law or public policy against people with intellectual disabilities having children to prevent them from expressing human sexuality.

The contributors to this edited volume, *Parents with Intellectual Disabilities, Past, Present, and Futures*, ask different questions than whether people should be permitted to be parents. Their focus is on the experiences and perspectives of people with intellectual disabilities who are parents and on ways to support them in this role. Four features of this volume make it stand out.

First, the contributors to this volume are committed to the human rights of people with intellectual disabilities and their equal participation in society. Their stance is consistent with the 2006 United Nations Convention on the Rights of Persons with Disabilities, which calls upon states to eliminate discrimination against people with disabilities with regard to marriage and parenthood and to provide them with assistance in the performance of child-rearing responsibilities. The idea that marriage and parenthood are fundamental human rights of people with intellectual and other disabilities challenges prejudicial and stigmatizing policies and practices that have been found in many countries.

Second, this volume is international in scope. The contributors come from Australia, Denmark, Iceland, New Zealand, North America, and the United Kingdom. Too often, researchers, policy makers, and professionals ignore the lessons that can be learned from other countries. Readers of this volume will benefit from learning about the perspectives and experiences of parents with intellectual disabilities from a range of countries.

Third, the chapters in this volume are based on rich qualitative case studies of parents with intellectual disabilities and those around them. Qualitative researchers sometimes make a distinction between *knowing about* people and *knowing* them. To know about parents with intellectual disabilities is to have information about their ages, incomes, number of children, and similar things. To know parents with intellectual disabilities is to identify with them as fellow human beings who have hopes, dreams, fears, disappointments, and inner struggles. By getting to know people we can learn about how they view the world and their experiences.

Finally, the contributors to this volume are not only interested in understanding the experiences of parents with intellectual disabilities. They also aim to improve policies and practices regarding this population. Many of the chapters in the volume provide practical strategies on how to support mothers and fathers with intellectual disabilities and their children. The volume is filled with sound advice. It is fitting that the volume concludes with a set of excellent recommendations from the Special Interest Research Group on Parents and Parenting with Intellectual Disabilities of the International Association for the Scientific Study of Intellectual Disability.

The question of whether adults with intellectual disabilities should be permitted to be parents is the wrong question to ask. As a matter of respecting human rights, societies should not attempt to restrict the ability of any adult to become a parent and to raise children merely on the basis of disability. As a practical matter, they have never been able to prevent people with intellectual disabilities from becoming parents. The contributors to this volume ask the right questions about parenthood and intellectual disabilities and provide some sound answers to these questions.

*Steven J. Taylor, PhD*
*Syracuse University*

# Acknowledgments

We present this first international volume on parents with intellectual disabilities with enthusiasm and pride. We offer it as a part of the growing scholarship around the world on families headed by people with intellectual disabilities. Many individuals, organizations, and institutions have made this book possible. We are grateful to all of them. Most important, however, are the parents who have participated in our research projects, collaborated with us, and generously shared their lives and experiences with us. This research and collaboration, which has taken place over a period of almost two decades, made it possible to create this book. We also want to thank all those who have contributed chapters to this volume for their willingness to work with us on this exciting project.

While editing this book we have lived in different parts of the world, in Australia, Canada, and Iceland. Meeting to work together has therefore required extensive travel. Our universities have provided the support that has enabled us to do this. The University of Iceland awarded Hanna Björg and Rannveig research semesters and travel grants to travel to Canada and Australia in 2007. The Icelandic Centre for Research (RANNÍS) and the University of Iceland Research Fund provided Hanna Björg and Rannveig with research grants for their research with parents with intellectual disabilities. The University of Sydney provided travel grants to supplement support from the International Association for the Scientific Study of Intellectual Disabilities (IASSID) for Gwynnyth's participation in the 2nd European Congress of the International Association for the Scientific Study of Intellectual Disabilities, Maastricht, The Netherlands, and to travel to Iceland, in June 2009.

We also want to acknowledge our colleagues in the Special Interest Research Group (SIRG) on Parents and Parenting with Intellectual Disabilities. This SIRG is part of IASSID, the International Association for the Scientific Study of Intellectual Disabilities, and has been an encouraging and stimulating context for this book. In similar vein we wish to acknowledge Wiley-Blackwell and IASSID for allowing us to publish "Parents Labeled with Intellectual Disability: Position of the IASSID SIRG on Parents and Parenting with Intellectual Disabilities" (2008) within the concluding chapter of this book.

Our final thanks go to Gabrielle Hindmarsh of the Australian Family and Disability Studies Research Collaboration at the University of Sydney for her tireless efforts in the final preparation of the manuscript for submission.

## Chapter 3 Acknowledgments

The research projects that provide the basis for this chapter were supported by grants from RANNÍS, the Icelandic Centre for Research, and the University of Iceland's Research Fund. We are grateful for their support of our research. We also want to thank the parents whose stories are presented in this chapter for their assistance in putting the stories together.

## Chapter 7 Acknowledgments

The research projects that provide the basis for this chapter were supported by grants from RANNÍS, the Icelandic Centre for Research, and the University of Iceland's Research Fund. We are grateful for their support of our research. We also want to thank all the parents who have collaborated with us in these research projects.

## Chapter 10 Acknowledgment

Thanks to the Baring Foundation for permission to quote extensively from *Finding the right support? A review of issues and positive practice in supporting parents with learning difficulties and their children* (Baring Foundation, 2006).

## Chapter 14 Acknowledgment

Thanks to Mencap for permission to quote extensively from *Providing the Right Support for Parents with a Learning Disability* (Mencap, 2007).

# Introduction

## Gwynnyth Llewellyn, Rannveig Traustadóttir, David McConnell, and Hanna Björg Sigurjónsdóttir

In September 1996, in Snekkersten, a small town north of Copenhagen in Denmark, an historic event took place with the convening of the first international conference on parenting with intellectual disabilities. A small group of distinguished academics from eight different countries gathered to present their research findings about the lives of parents with intellectual disabilities. This conference, convened by the Danish Ministry of Social Affairs and supported by the European Union, initiated a train of events which led to the genesis of this book. The then Danish Minister of Social Affairs, Karen Jespersen, provided the preface to the conference report on *Parenting with Intellectual Disability*. She noted that the issue of parenting by people with intellectual disabilities was taken up by the media on regular occasions, and that there was much debate in Denmark and in other countries about the right to marry and have a family, going on to say "that there is nothing unusual in the fact that some intellectually disabled individuals want to have children, and to many of them this is part of leading a normal life" (Danish Ministry of Social Affairs, 1996, p. 6).

Over a decade and a half later this statement remains true, with an increasing number of people with intellectual disabilities having children and establishing their own families. This is due to deinstitutionalization, the banning of sterilization in many countries, and the embedding of the principles of normalization and anti-discrimination in legislation. This has resulted in most adults with intellectual disabilities living in the community with many of them developing relationships and starting a family. Parenting by people with intellectual disabilities has been acknowledged in the research literature since Mickelson's

*Parents with Intellectual Disabilities: Past, Present and Futures*   Edited by Gwynnyth Llewellyn, Rannveig Traustadóttir, David McConnell, and Hanna Björg Sigurjónsdóttir   © 2010 John Wiley & Sons, Ltd

early work in 1947. Despite this early start in research, it is only recently and only in some countries that people with intellectual disabilities are becoming accepted as full citizens and able to enjoy the freedom to have a child if they so desire.

## Why a Book about Parenting with Intellectual Disabilities?

Parenting by people with intellectual disabilities is a new field of study. At the outset empirical studies were few and far between and provided a pessimistic and medicalized view of parents with intellectual limitations and their children (e.g., Brandon, 1957; Gillberg & Geijer-Karlsson, 1983). It is only since the late 1980s that research with a social and human rights-based approach has begun. Today there is a growing interest in this group of parents, but the research is placed within many different disciplines and is not always easily accessible. In spite of that, this is a topic of increasing interest to professionals in the fields of disability, family support, child protection, and social services, as well as researchers and scholars in disciplines such as disability studies, sociology, psychology, social work, education, and the health sciences.

This book is the first international publication to bring together research findings from several countries and across many disciplines to provide an informative pan-disciplinary compendium on the topic of parents with intellectual disabilities and their children. The ideas behind the book are quite straightforward. In line with the United Nations The Standard Rules on the Equalization of Opportunities for Persons with Disabilities (United Nations, 1993) and the United Nations Convention on the Rights of Persons with Disabilities (United Nations, 2006), the underlying theme of the book is about equal participation for disabled people, in this case parents with intellectual disabilities. The UN Convention affirms the right of persons with disabilities to marry and found a family in Article 23 (para 1). Further, in Article 23 (para 1 and 2) states are bound to "take effective action and appropriate measures to eliminate discrimination against persons with disabilities in all matters relating to marriage, family, parenthood and relationships..." and "render appropriate assistance to persons with disabilities in the performance of their child-rearing responsibilities."

Universally, becoming a parent and creating a family of one's own is a highly valued social role. For people with intellectual disabilities who become parents, however, there are many barriers to their equal participation in this role. Many countries now have policy statements and best practice guidelines; for example, in the United Kingdom, the *Good Practice Guidance* is designed to improve support for parents with intellectual disabilities (Department of Health/Department for Education and Skills, 2007). Despite these efforts,

significant challenges face people with intellectual disabilities who wish to become parents and those who already are parents. As the first international
volume on the topic, this book brings together the most up-to-date knowledge
about parenting with intellectual disabilities with all the joys and challenges
that this entails. Our sincere hope is that this book will provide readers with
knowledge and insights that encourage them to support parents with intellectual disabilities and their children in ways which create and sustain happy and
successful families.

Until recently, there has been little attention given to the topic of parents
with intellectual disabilities in the training and education of social welfare
workers and health services professionals, or in continuing education or post-
professional graduate programs. Currently there is limited knowledge about
parenting by people with intellectual disabilities among health and social service professionals. This book therefore comes at a time when many practitioners
internationally are seeking guidance in how to work with parents with intellectual disabilities in ways that recognize family strengths and promote child and
family well-being.

## Parents with Intellectual Disabilities: Who Are They?

Parents with intellectual disabilities broadly speaking constitute three groups.
First, there are people with intellectual disabilities who, although previously
institutionalized, now live in the community and have developed relationships
and taken up the rewarding but challenging task of parenthood. The second
group is made up of parents who were never institutionalized but have received
services for people labeled with intellectual disability more or less continuously
for most of their lives. The third group consists of women and men with intellectual disabilities who become parents and are part of what Edgerton (2001)
refers to as the "hidden majority" – persons with intellectual disabilities who
have mild to borderline cognitive limitations. Typically, these individuals have
been labeled as being "slow," having developmental delay, learning difficulties,
or intellectual disability while at school. On leaving school, they manage with
varying degrees of success to live ordinary lives in the general community with
few or no specialized supports. As young adults they desire to be independent
and to be treated no differently from their peers. It is only when they make the
transition to parenthood, and confront the steep learning curve that parenting
presents for everyone, that their cognitive capacity comes into focus and is again
questioned. This questioning has led to several discriminatory outcomes well
recognized in the research literature, the main focus of which is an extraordinary
over-representation of these parents in care and protection proceedings (Booth,
Booth, & McConnell, 2005a, 2005b; McConnell, Llewellyn, & Ferronato, 2002;
Taylor et al., 1991).

## Parenting in Context

Parents with intellectual disabilities and their children do not exist in isolation. They are a part of families, social networks, neighborhoods, and communities of interest. Parents also have a past. They come from families, in which they grew up and, like all other children, are influenced by their childhood experiences, including their own parents' approach to their upbringing (Llewellyn, 1997). They also come to being a parent and parenting their own children, like other parents, based on a lifetime of experience in negotiating their place in family and community life. The difference is that for these parents to establish themselves as independent individuals within their society they have to contend with stereotypes about people with intellectual disabilities and with the stigma and social exclusion that typically accompany the label of intellectual disability.

A fundamental theme in this book is that parents with intellectual disabilities and their children continue to carry on with their lives, in their homes and with their extended families, in their neighborhoods and as part of the society and culture in which they live, in spite of stigmatizing attitudes and exclusionary practices. In the literature, however, all too often parents with intellectual disabilities have been studied without due consideration for their present family and social surroundings or those of their earlier life. They are regarded as "standing alone" and held personally and individually responsible for any difficulty that arises, with little attention paid to their familial circumstances and social situations or the broader community and cultural environments of their lives. The stigmatized views about people with intellectual disability, that they are childlike or childish and dependent on others, become sharply focused when adults with intellectual disabilities become parents. Too frequently it is asked how this woman or this man could provide good enough parenting when they themselves require support from others to live as an adult in the community. This view reveals a commonly held stereotype that people with intellectual disabilities are eternal children and unlikely to become adults and therefore are not capable of taking on adult roles like parenting. This incorrect and pessimistic view has led to many barriers for people with intellectual disabilities as parents.

## Insider and Outsider Perspectives

The stereotypical understanding about people with intellectual disabilities makes it hard for others to imagine they could be parents. This also assumes that parenting is a task entirely dependent on the abilities of only one individual, ignoring the important contributions to child rearing in our societies that come from other parents, extended family, community members, public personnel such as teachers, and institutions like preschools and schools. Another stereotypical view of people with intellectual disabilities as passive recipients of care depersonalizes them and negates any understanding of their contribution as active agents in their own lives and the lives of their children and other family members.

For too long, most studies about parents with intellectual disabilities were conducted from an "outsider" perspective. Only occasionally did researchers try to record and describe the essence of parents' lives from the perspective of the parents themselves. One example of an "insider" view is Taylor's (1995, 2000) long-term study of the everyday life of a family he calls the Duke family. Gaining insights into social phenomena through understanding the insider perspective is increasingly accepted in the disability field (Bogdan & Taylor, 1976; Gustavsson, 2000; Walmsley & Johnson, 2003). The chapters in this book take account of parents with intellectual disabilities as social beings, as both actors in their families and communities, and as "acted upon" by the services and systems in their society. In many instances, this understanding comes from studies in which parents with intellectual disabilities are the central narrators on their own lives.

## Learning about Parenting

No child comes with an instructional manual to guide the parents in how to successfully raise them. There are many different ways in which all parents learn about child rearing. One way is from being parented oneself and we all learn about parenting to a greater or lesser extent during our own upbringing. Parents with intellectual disabilities, like most other new parents, may also turn to their own parents and other family members for advice and support, especially when their children are young. Parents can attend parenting classes and there are news-stand magazines devoted entirely to parenting topics and the challenges that parents face, with suggested solutions to overcome these. In addition there are increasingly popular television programs on managing children's behaviors, many of which can be daunting for all parents.

In the research literature much attention has focused on overcoming the perceived inadequacy of parents with intellectual disabilities and the effects of parent education and training programs on their parenting skills (Feldman, 1994; Tymchuk & Andron, 1992; Wade, Llewellyn, & Matthews, 2008). The findings from the studies on parent education and training have unanimously concluded that parents with intellectual disabilities greatly benefit from these programs and that they can learn to take care of their children successfully (Booth & Booth, 1993; Espe-Sherwindt & Kerlin, 1990; Llewellyn, McConnell, Honey, Mayes, & Russo, 2003; McGaw & Sturmey, 1994).

Parenting is an activity in which there is constant change. In effect, all parents "learn on the job" and adapt and change as their child develops and their needs change. In other words, not only does the child grow and develop in the context of the family, but so does the parent. The chapters in this book place particular attention on how parents develop, and how their parenting changes and grows over time.

## Gender and Parenting

Parenting involves adults and children, and of course, men and women. Too often in the research literature and in the popular press, the term parents acts as a proxy or shorthand for mothers. By referring to parents when writing about families, authors ignore the gender differences between mothers and fathers. Gender studies, as well as family studies, have demonstrated the different roles of mothers and fathers within families, in particular when it comes to household work and child care, as well as responsibilities outside the home (e.g., Coltrane, 1989; Connell, 2009; DeVault, 1991). Not only does the term "parents" ignore these gender differences, but in focusing mostly on mothers and calling them parents, this hides the fact that the mother is the one most often responsible for the routine care of home and children. Also, in ignoring gender, the father's role becomes invisible and is not recognized.

Writings about families and disability have the same shortcomings when it comes to gender as the general family literature. This has been demonstrated in disability studies where there is a call for more attention to gender in relation to disability (Kristiansen & Traustadóttir, 2004; Thomas, 1999). Writings about disability, gender, and family life have mostly focused on disabled women's lives, including attention to mothers with intellectual disabilities (Mayes, Llewellyn, & McConnell, 2006; Traustadóttir & Johnson, 2000; Wates & Jade, 1999). Much less attention has been paid to disabled men, and fathers with intellectual disabilities have been almost entirely overlooked in research, in the literature, and in health and social care practice (for an exception, see Sigurjónsdóttir, 2004). In this book we have attempted to include a gender perspective and explore the lives and experiences of fathers, as well as mothers. However, we do recognize that both in this book, and generally speaking, mothers continue to attract greater attention when child rearing is the topic of interest in societies around the world.

## On Terminology

There is no consensus on terminology about disability. Countries use different concepts to refer to the parents who are the focus of this book. Even in countries where English is the majority language, the terminology is diverse and politically contested (Eayrs, Ellis, & Jones, 1993). In the United Kingdom "learning difficulties" or "learning disabilities" are the preferred terms, while in the United States of America terms such as "developmental disabilities" and "mental retardation" have often been used. Recently, however, leading disability associations in the USA have taken up the term "intellectual disability," which is the term most commonly used in Australia and New Zealand. Terminology in other languages is equally varied and complicated and often difficult to translate to English. The term "intellectual disability" is most commonly recognized and used by international associations and organizations.

There are also debates and disagreement about ways to talk about disabled people. Those who follow a social understanding of disability usually say "disabled people," thereby shifting the focus away from the individual to the experiences of oppression by disabling barriers and environments. Those arguing this view point out that "people with disabilities" implies that disability is inherent to the individual, rather than locating its cause in social arrangements (Morris, 1993; Oliver & Barnes, 1998). Others prefer "people with disabilities," which is also often referred to as "people first" language. This term is favored by most people with intellectual disabilities who argue that they want to be called "people first," and not to be addressed first by their impairment (Clement, 2003). In doing this they also want to assert their common humanity, which has often been cast into doubt.

This book is based on a social understanding of disability. Despite that, we have chosen to use the term "people with intellectual disabilities." Intellectual disability is the term most commonly recognized internationally and therefore seemed logical for an international volume. Also, in using the term "parents with intellectual disabilities" we honor the wishes of the parents we have come to know through our many years of advocacy, research, and friendship.

## The Organization of the Book

This multi-authored book aims to link theory and research to practice through providing a clear set of principles to inform good practice and an evidence-based approach to supporting parents with intellectual disabilities. Each chapter provides a brief historical overview of the development of ideas and literature pertinent to the chapter's topic. Building on this, the current state of knowledge is represented by the most up-to-date research evidence drawing on the chapter author's own work and the work of his or her colleagues. The chapters conclude with principles drawn from the research to inform practice. The book is divided into two parts.

Part I, *Family and Community Life*, is largely based on the perspectives of parents and focuses on the everyday lives of parents with intellectual disabilities and their children. In this section the attention is on understanding parents as actors in their families and communities, and their interactions with systems and services.

Part I begins with a chapter titled "Becoming a Mother – Becoming a Father" by Rachel Mayes and Hanna Björg Sigurjónsdóttir. Drawing on findings from studies in Australia and Iceland, this chapter describes the experience of becoming a mother or a father for people with intellectual disabilities and how they negotiate these new roles. The authors illuminate the similarities and differences in experience for men and women. They also challenge service providers and policy makers to recognize that fathers and mothers may be poorly supported by services that do not consider their unique and gendered experiences.

Chapter 2, "Looking Back on Their Own Upbringing" by Gwynnyth Llewellyn and David McConnell, is about parents' own childhood experiences and how, when people become parents, they look to the past to think about the future. Although there has been little research into the childhood experience of parents with intellectual disabilities, a common assumption is that this must be negative. The authors reveal, however, that mothers with intellectual disabilities experience varied upbringing, with at least half the mothers in a community sample experiencing plenty of love, affection, safety, and security. Practitioners need to keep an open mind about parents' childhood experiences, endeavoring to understand each parent's perspective on his or her own upbringing.

In Chapter 3, "Family Within a Family," Hanna Björg Sigurjónsdóttir and Rannveig Traustadóttir argue that, just like in other families, children of parents with intellectual disabilities are raised within their extended families and with the assistance of various professionals and programs in their home communities. The authors warn against the tendency to ignore this larger context and regard parents with intellectual disabilities as isolated individuals who have the sole responsibility of raising their children. To provide an in-depth view of families headed by parents with intellectual disabilities, and the importance of their extended family networks, the authors present stories of three Icelandic families whom they have followed over an extended period.

Chapter 4 offers insights into the lives of children of parents with intellectual disabilities from a study in which the children are the central narrators of their own stories. This chapter, "Children and Their Life Experiences" by Jytte Faureholm, is based on interview research with 23 Danish children of parents with intellectual disabilities beginning in 1994 when they were middle school aged and ending in 2004 when they were young adults. From their perspective, the young people's greatest disadvantage came from the stigma that they experienced as children due to their mother being labeled with intellectual disability. By young adulthood, however, most were leading successful lives, due in no small part to their own determination and assisted by the educational and vocational opportunities that were finally made available to them as adolescents.

Chapter 5, by Gwynnyth Llewellyn and Marie Gustavsson, is titled "Understanding Community in the Lives of Parents with Intellectual Disabilities." The authors argue, from a study with a small group of Australian parents with intellectual disabilities, that the meaning of community participation must take into account that parents with intellectual disabilities are active agents in their own lives in their communities. It is they who capitalize on their physical presence and their belonging to the valued position of parent in society, opening up for themselves opportunities for social inclusion and connectedness.

In Chapter 6, "Citizenship and Community Participation," Brigit Mirfin-Veitch analyzes data from a New Zealand study to show how important active citizenship, social networks, and community participation prior to becoming a parent are for greater parenting success. The "take home" message from the findings of this study is the critical importance of educators ensuring that learning and development in the area of citizenship and participation occur for young people with intellectual disabilities as they do for their non-disabled peers. The author argues that although young adults with intellectual disabilities may need support to understand their citizens' rights and how to exercise those rights, it is essential that they approach parenthood well informed and able to advocate for themselves and their families.

Part I concludes with Chapter 7 by Rannveig Traustadóttir and Hanna Björg Sigurjónsdóttir in which they explore the strategies that parents use in their encounters with services and professionals they fear will remove their children. This chapter, titled "Parenting and Resistance: Strategies in Dealing with Services and Professionals," draws on the authors' long-term involvement with parents and argues that, instead of interpreting some of the actions of parents as a part of their intellectual impairment, these behaviors may be better understood as resistance against oppressive conditions and services that exercise power and control over the lives of parents and their children.

While Part I explores the lives of parents with intellectual disabilities and their children and mostly from the parents' standpoint, in Part II we turn to the systems and services that play such a large role in the lives of families headed by parents with intellectual disabilities. The title for Part II – *Human Services Enabling and Disabling Parents with Intellectual Disabilities* – captures the essence of the chapters in this section. Human services can support parents to parent successfully and their children to lead happy and productive lives. At the same time, human services can be discouragingly disabling and oppressive, and can raise more barriers and present more challenges to parents with intellectual disabilities than the act of parenting itself.

In Part II the contributors explore the various aspects of the human service system that have an impact on parents' lives. The contributions begin with a chapter on parent education, which is currently the most well-documented area of human service delivery for parenting and parents with intellectual disabilities.

Chapter 8, "Parent Education Programs for Parents with Intellectual Disabilities" by Maurice Feldman from Canada, offers a practical guide to the implementation of behavioral and self-directed instructional approaches to teaching parenting skills. There is robust evidence that these approaches are the most effective in parent education programs for parents with intellectual disabilities. The chapter begins with a scholarly review of the development of these programs, elucidates the principles and practices that are known to be effective, and then describes in some detail how to implement efficacious parent education programs.

Chapter 9, "Supported Decision Making for Women and Mothers with Intellectual Disabilities" by Sue McGaw and Sue Candy from the United Kingdom, presents an analysis of the many barriers that confront women and mothers with intellectual disabilities when they are making decisions about everyday and important events in their lives. The authors offer detailed ideas about how to support women and mothers with intellectual disabilities to make informed decisions at the critical life stage of deciding to become a mother and about their active participation in the child protection process if the care and protection authorities become involved in their lives and the lives of their children and family.

Chapter 10, "Turning Policy into Practice" by Beth Tarleton, is based on a study of existing services for parents with intellectual disabilities in the United Kingdom. The aim of this research was to identify examples of positive practices in supporting parents. The study found that although there are positive practices, these are rare and parents were more likely to encounter negative assumptions by professionals who had little knowledge and experiences of working with people with intellectual disabilities. The chapter concludes by suggesting the changes needed in order to bridge this gap between forward-looking policy and current practice.

David McConnell and Hanna Björg Sigurjónsdóttir are the authors of Chapter 11, "Caught in the Child Protection Net." In this chapter they draw on the available research about child protection processes and practices that involve parents with intellectual disabilities to conclude that these are false presumptions so often made about parents with intellectual disabilities, the authors provide ten points vital to promoting natural justice for parents with intellectual disabilities and their children.

Chapter 12, "Turning Rights into Realities in Québec, Canada" by Marjorie Aunos, Laura Pacheco, and Katherine Moxness, presents the story of how a group of committed researcher-practitioners have worked to close the gap between the right for parents with intellectual disabilities to receive appropriate and timely assistance and current service provision in Québec. The authors argue that a multi-agency and many-faceted approach is needed to effectively support parents with intellectual disabilities and their children. The cross-agency initiative described in this chapter involves the development and monitoring of policy and practice standards, the provision of ongoing professional development and networking, continuing to conduct research on topics of local and immediate importance to the parents, and applying the findings to the further development of good practice in the region.

Chapter 13, "Supporting Mothers' Community Participation" by David Mc-Connell and Gwynnyth Llewellyn, offers an evidence-based group approach to strengthening the participation of mothers with intellectual disabilities in their communities and broadening their social networks. The authors argue the importance of building on theory and research in adult pedagogy to successfully engage mothers with their peers in confronting the barriers that prevent them from realizing their personal goals. The findings from the implementation of this approach attest to its success in providing an appropriate learning context that enables mothers to work together to initiate and trial their own solutions in a facilitated supportive environment.

Part II concludes with Chapter 14 by Linda Ward and Beth Tarleton entitled "Advocacy for Change: 'The Final Tool in the Toolbox?'" The authors begin by reminding the reader that UN and European human rights conventions as well as national policies in the United Kingdom state the right to family life for parents with intellectual disabilities and their children. Despite this, parents continue to be at high risk of losing custody of their children. In order to keep their children and bring them up successfully, parents with intellectual disabilities need support, including advocacy support. Ward and Tarleton argue that independent advocacy is an important tool to support parents in their encounters with child protection services, in court proceedings, and to improve professional awareness of what needs to be done to improve their chances of keeping custody of their children.

The book finishes with the Conclusion: "Taking Stock and Looking to the Future." This offers the opportunity to reflect on the research knowledge, current policies and practices, and remaining stereotypes and false assumptions about parents with intellectual disabilities, all of which have been described in this book.

This concluding chapter includes a position statement on parents and parenting with intellectual disabilities endorsed by the International Association for the Scientific Study of Intellectual Disabilities (IASSID) in 2008. This statement brought together members of the IASSID Special Interest Research Group (SIRG) on Parents and Parenting with Intellectual Disabilities from around the world and colleagues interested in this topic, primarily, however, from middle- and high-income countries. The aim of the statement was to present a robust review of the scholarly literature and to draw conclusions from that literature about the current context of the living conditions of parents with intellectual disabilities in high-income countries while recognizing the absence of readily available information on parents living in low-income countries, particularly in the African continent, in South-East Asia, and in countries such as the Baltic states, Eastern European countries, and the former Soviet Union. The position statement also sets out to look to the future and as such is a fitting conclusion to this book.

## Conclusion

This book brings together a scholarly, cross-disciplinary, and multi-national approach to exploring and understanding the lives of parents with intellectual disabilities, their children, and the systems and services that they encounter. It provides an authoritative text on the research and scholarly literature on the topic of parents and parenting with intellectual disabilities. It contains many ideas, some of which are explicit and some of which readers will no doubt initiate, for taking research endeavors forward to create the next generation of research on this topic. The research presented in this book, including the principles for practice accompanying each chapter, provides an evidence-based compendium to guide good practice for novice and experienced practitioners alike. Although regrettably few countries have formulated policy documents and good practice guidance, those that do exist are an inspiration to others and provide an important example of promising directions in creating new futures for parents with intellectual disabilities and their children. Taken as a whole, we sincerely trust this book will help pave the way for equality and justice in the lives of families headed by parents with intellectual disabilities.

As the readers of this book will discover, there is consensus in the research literature that parents with intellectual disabilities can successfully raise their children if they are provided with appropriate supports. This same literature shows that – despite this well-documented evidence of success if given suitable support – services for families headed by parents with intellectual disabilities continue to be few and far between, limited, fragmented, or unreliable. The UN Convention on the Rights of Persons with Disabilities clearly states the right to family life and the elimination of discrimination against disabled people regarding marriage, family life, and parenthood. If this promise is to be fulfilled, we need new ways of approaching and understanding families headed by parents with intellectual disabilities in order to ensure they enjoy the same rights and respect as other families.

## References

Bogdan, R., & Taylor, S. (1976). The judged, not the judges: An insider's view of mental retardation. *American Psychologist, 31*(1), 47–52.

Booth, T., & Booth, W. (1993). Parenting with learning difficulties: Lessons for practitioners. *British Journal of Social Work, 23*(5), 459–480.

Booth, T., Booth, W., & McConnell, D. (2005a). The prevalence and outcomes of care proceedings involving parents with learning difficulties in the family courts. *Journal of Applied Research in Intellectual Disabilities, 18*(1), 7–17.

Booth, T., Booth, W., & McConnell, D. (2005b). Care proceedings and parents with learning difficulties: Comparative prevalence and outcomes in an English and Australian court sample. *Child and Family Social Work, 10*(4), 353–360.

Brandon, M. (1957). The intellectual and social status of children of mental defectives. *Journal of Mental Science, 103*(433), 710–724.

Clement, T. (2003). *Ethnography of people first anytown: A description, analysis and interpretation of an organizational culture.* Unpublished doctoral dissertation, Open University, Milton Keynes.

Coltrane, S. (1989). Household labour and the routine production of gender. *Social Problems, 36*(5), 473–490.

Connell, R. (2009). *Gender in world perspective* ( 2nd ed.). Cambridge: Polity Press.

Danish Ministry of Social Affairs. (1996). *Parenting with intellectual disability.* Copenhagen: Author.

Department of Health/Department for Education and Skills. (2007). *Good practice guidance on working with parents with a learning disability.* London: Author.

DeVault, M. L. (1991). *Feeding the family: The social organization of caring as gendered work.* Chicago: University of Chicago Press.

Eayrs, C. B., Ellis, N., & Jones, R. S. P. (1993). Which label? An investigation into the effects of terminology on public perceptions of and attitudes towards people with learning difficulties. *Disability, Handicap and Society, 8*(2), 111–117.

Edgerton, R. B. (2001). The hidden majority of individuals with mental retardation and developmental disabilities. In A. J. Tymchuk, C. K. Lakin, & R. Luckasson (Eds.), *The forgotten generation: The status and challenges of adults with mild cognitive limitations* (pp. 3–19). Baltimore: Paul H. Brookes.

Espe-Sherwindt, M., & Kerlin, S. (1990). Early intervention with parents with mental retardation: Do we empower or impair? *Infants and Young Children, 2*(4), 21–28.

Feldman, M. A. (1994). Parenting education for parents with intellectual disabilities: A review of outcome studies. *Research in Developmental Disabilities, 15*(4), 299–332.

Gillberg, C., & Geijer-Karlsson, M. (1983). Children born to mentally retarded women: A 1–21-year follow-up study of 41 cases. *Psychological Medicine, 13*(4), 891–894.

Gustavsson, A. (2000). *Inifrån utanforskapet* [Insider's perspective on being an outsider]. Lund: Studentlitteratur.

Kristiansen, K., & Traustadóttir, R. (Eds.) (2004). *Gender and disability research in the Nordic countries.* Lund: Studentlitteratur.

Llewellyn, G. (1997). Parents with intellectual disabilities learning to parent: The role of experience and informal learning. *International Journal of Disability, Development and Education, 44*(3), 243–261.

Llewellyn, G., McConnell, D., Honey, A., Mayes, R., & Russo, D. (2003). Promoting health and home safety for children of parents with intellectual disability: A randomized controlled trial. *Research in Developmental Disabilities, 24*(6), 405–431.

Mayes, R., Llewellyn, G., & McConnell, D. (2006). Misconceptions: The experience of pregnancy for women with intellectual disabilities. *Scandinavian Journal of Disability Research, 8*(2–3), 120–131.

McConnell, D., Llewellyn, G., & Ferronato, L. (2002). Disability and decision making in Australian Care Proceedings. *International Journal of Law, Policy and the Family, 16*(2), 270–299.

McGaw, S., & Sturmey, P. (1994). Assessing parents with learning disabilities: The parental skills model. *Child Abuse Review, 3*(1), 36–51.

Mickelson, P. (1947). The feeble-minded parent: A study of 90 family cases. *American Journal of Mental Deficiency, 51*(4), 644–653.

Morris, J. (1993). *Independent lives? Community care and disabled people.* Basingstoke: Macmillan.

Oliver, M., & Barnes, C. (1998). *Disabled people and social policy: From exclusion to inclusion.* London: Longman.

Sigurjónsdóttir, H. B. (2004). Intellectually limited fathers, their families and formal support services. In K. Kristiansen & R. Traustadóttir (Eds.), *Gender and disability research in the Nordic countries* (pp. 239–254). Lund: Studentlitteratur.

Taylor, C. G., Norman, D., Murphy, J., Jellinek, M., Quinn, D., Poitrast, F., & Goshko, M. (1991). Diagnosed intellectual and emotional impairment among parents who seriously mistreat their children: Prevalence, type, and outcome in a court sample. *Child Abuse and Neglect, 15*(4), 389–401.

Taylor, S. J. (1995). "Children's Division is coming to taka pictures": Family life and parenting in a family with disabilities. In S. J. Taylor, R. Bogdan, & Z. M. Lutfiyya (Eds.), *The variety of community experiences: Qualitative studies of family and community life* (pp. 23–45). Baltimore: Paul H. Brookes.

Taylor, S. J. (2000). "You are not a retard, you're just wise": Disability, social identity, and family networks. *Journal of Contemporary Ethnography, 29*(1), 58–92.

Thomas, C. (1999). *Female forms: Experiencing and understanding disability.* Buckingham: Open University Press.

Traustadóttir, R., & Johnson, K. (Eds.) (2000). *Women with intellectual disabilities: Finding a place in the world.* London: Jessica Kingsley.

Tymchuk, A., & Andron, L. (1992). Project parenting: Child interactional training with mothers who are mentally handicapped. *Mental Handicap Research, 5*(1), 4–32.

United Nations. (1993). *The standard rules on the equalization of opportunities for persons with disabilities.* New York: Author.

United Nations. (2006). *Convention on the rights of persons with disabilities.* New York: Author.

Wade, C., Llewellyn, G., & Matthews, J. (2008). Review of parent training interventions for parents with intellectual disability. *Journal of Applied Research in Intellectual Disabilities, 21*(4), 351–366.

Walmsley, J., & Johnson, K. (2003). *Inclusive research with people with learning disabilities: Past, present and futures.* London: Jessica Kingsley.

Wates, M., & Jade, R. (Eds.) (1999). *Bigger than the sky: Disabled women on parenting.* London: Women's Press.

# PART I

# FAMILY AND COMMUNITY LIFE

# 1

# Becoming a Mother – Becoming a Father

*Rachel Mayes and Hanna Björg Sigurjónsdóttir*

## Introduction

Research into parenting by people with intellectual disabilities consistently refers to parents and parenting. However, the overwhelming majority of studies are about mothers. Fathers with intellectual disabilities are largely ignored and when the discussion is about parents, the particularities of mothers with intellectual disabilities are glossed over. Although "mother" and "father" are gendered terms (Bergum, 1989), there is a lack of critical examination of the role of gender within these families.

We believe that a focus on gender is important for three reasons. The first is because "mother" and "father" are not the same as each other. Becoming a mother is something only women do. Becoming a father is something for men only. In always describing parents with intellectual disabilities without reference to gender, researchers have ignored the fact that the experiences of men and women might be very different.

Historically, men and women with intellectual disabilities have been treated quite differently. The practice of involuntary sterilization, while not exclusively focused on women with intellectual disabilities, was aimed at them (Brady & Grover, 1997). In those societies practicing sterilization it was thought that women had to be prevented from reproducing or society risked the eroding of national intelligence (Pfeiffer, 1994; Radford, 1994; Walmsley, 2000). Almost nothing is known, however, about how these policies affected men with intellectual disabilities.

*Parents with Intellectual Disabilities: Past, Present and Futures*  Edited by Gwynnyth Llewellyn, Rannveig Traustadóttir, David McConnell, and Hanna Björg Sigurjónsdóttir  © 2010 John Wiley & Sons, Ltd

Second, the genderless orientation of the literature means that the experiences of women as mothers have been absorbed in a discussion of parents and parenting, while the experiences of men with intellectual disabilities as fathers have been largely ignored. A search of a regularly updated database of empirical literature identified 445 publications about some aspect of parenting by people with intellectual disabilities (www.healthystart.net.au). Only two of these titles specifically referred to fathers with intellectual disabilities. 67 (15%) referred to mothers alone, while the remainder referred to parents. The majority of empirical studies in the literature include only women participants. Feldman (1994) conducted a meta-analysis of the efficacy of parenting programs for parents with intellectual disabilities. In this analysis, 190 parents were included across 20 studies. In this sample of 190 parents, there were only two fathers; the sample of parents was almost exclusively mothers. In the 20 studies, 18 were about mothers only despite the titles referring to parents. In an updated meta-analysis published in 2008, there is little to suggest that the situation has changed in the intervening 15 years (Wade, Llewellyn, & Matthews, 2008).

A number of researchers have reported that people with intellectual disabilities typically face opposition when they decide to become parents. Such opposition usually occurs when pregnancy is announced (e.g., Booth & Booth, 1992, 1995; Llewellyn & McConnell, 2005; Mayes, Llewellyn, & McConnell, 2006; Pixa-Kettner, 1998; Traustadóttir & Sigurjónsdóttir, 1998). Because the majority of studies are about women, it appears that such opposition is largely aimed at the pregnant woman and not the expectant father. However, the very limited evidence we have about men with intellectual disabilities suggests that they may also face negative reactions when they have children (Llewellyn, 1994; Sigurjónsdóttir, 2004). There is much more work to be done to understand the experiences of men with intellectual disabilities and how these are similar to, or different from, the lived experiences of women with intellectual disabilities.

The third reason a focus on gender is important is that research on families headed by parents with intellectual disabilities informs policy and practice in the field of social services, child protection, and disability services. Traustadóttir and Kristiansen (2004) noted that "Gender is one of the most important yet often unacknowledged dimensions influencing and shaping services and supports for disabled people" (p. 1). A gender-insensitive approach masks potential differences, and so cannot take into consideration the possibly quite different support needs of mothers and fathers who have intellectual disabilities.

A few studies have considered the needs of men and women separately in the context of providing support services to parents with intellectual disabilities. The earliest study, conducted by Mattinson in 1970, examined 32 marriages of people with intellectual disabilities who had been discharged from an institution. She concluded that for 25 of these marriages the relationship was affectionate and largely supportive even in the few where there was considerable stress. Couples were considered to be better off married than single. The remaining marriages were characterized by one partner's heavy reliance on the other. No marriage was deemed predominantly unsatisfactory.

In Australia, Llewellyn (1995) demonstrated the importance of the parent partnership in managing everyday parenting and the central role of the father as a source of support to the mother. Additionally, in Britain, Booth and Booth (2002) found that the majority of male partners played a supportive role in the family. These two studies indicate that fathers are often the primary support to the mother, which highlights the importance of including both parents when providing formal support to these families. In practice, however, this rarely happens. A small study conducted by O'Hara and Martin (2003) demonstrated that family support was not regarded necessary where the father had an intellectual disability unless the mother also had an intellectual disability so "little was offered to help these men to understand the situation or the psychosocial implication of fatherhood" (O'Hara & Martin, 2003, p. 21). Recent research from Iceland reveals that formal family support is typically directed at the mother and child (Sigurjónsdóttir, 2004). The findings indicate that if fathers are not included and embraced as part of the family unit, both fathers and the practitioners can become resentful.

Even fewer studies have taken a gendered perspective in examining the roles and identities of mothers and fathers with intellectual disabilities. Mayes, Llewellyn, and McConnell (2008, in press) examined the experience of pregnancy for women with intellectual disabilities. Their work highlighted that contrary to the asexual stereotypes often used to describe women with intellectual disabilities, these women have similar desires to other women such as wanting to become a mother.

The purpose of this chapter is to examine the experiences of becoming a parent for people with intellectual disabilities and how they negotiate this new role. Our aim is to consider the place of gender in these experiences and particularly to determine the implications of a gendered perspective for policy makers and service providers.

## The Studies

This chapter is based on the findings of two doctoral studies: one from Australia (Mayes, 2005) and the other from Iceland (Sigurjónsdóttir, 2005). Both studies focused on the lived experience of parents with intellectual disabilities during pregnancy and following the birth of the baby. A relatively small number of studies have examined parenting experiences from the parents' own perspectives (e.g., Booth & Booth, 1994; Llewellyn, 1994). The studies we describe in this chapter are the only two we are aware of that deliberately sought parents' experiences prior to the birth of their children. The studies employed qualitative methods and data were collected through both in-depth interviews and participant observation (Emerson, Fretz, & Shaw, 1995; Kvale, 1996; Taylor & Bogdan, 1998).

The Australian study was a phenomenological enquiry into the meaning of becoming a mother for women with intellectual disabilities. This study was conducted over a three-year period from 2002 to 2005. Seventeen women with intellectual disabilities were interviewed on multiple occasions throughout their pregnancies to understand the pregnancy experience and what becoming a mother meant to them.

The Icelandic study on family support services and parents with intellectual disabilities was conducted over a five-year period from 2000 to 2005. This ethnography and narrative inquiry examined how the health and social services systems respond to the diverse needs of these families from the time of pregnancy. The participants were eight families headed by parents with intellectual disabilities and all their support personnel, a total of 75 people. Special emphasis was placed on understanding the fathers' role within the family and the gendered aspect of support (Sigurjónsdóttir, 2004). Below we describe the findings from both studies, paying particular attention to experiences that are gender related.

## Finding Out We're Having a Baby

Only one-quarter of both the Australian and Icelandic families had planned the pregnancy prior to discovering they were expecting a child. Physical signs such as missed periods, tender breasts, or feeling nauseous signaled to the women in both studies that perhaps a baby was on the way. The women told their partners of their suspicions. A visit to the doctor or a home pregnancy test confirmed the pregnancy. Most families, even those who had not planned to have a baby, or who had not planned to have a baby at this time, were delighted with the news.

While the parents-to-be in both studies were excited about the pregnancy, other people around them were not. Extended family members suggested abortion and/or adoption because they were worried about the parents' ability to take care of a child. This discussion was initially aimed more at the mothers than the fathers. One mother described her family's comments as abusive. Her family told her that because of her disability she should not be having a child. They believed her child would be better off cared for by someone else. Another mother sought her partner's strong support after comments from her mother that she would not be able to cope with another child.

In the Icelandic study suggestions about abortion came from the mothers' side of the family, with one exception. The reason most of the fathers' families did not suggest abortion was possibly due to the fact that abortion has to do with the woman's body. Most families, however, did suggest their sons and daughters-in-law give up the child for adoption. When the expectant parents refused to do so, families emphasized that the couple should seek support from social services. In two instances the families of the fathers contacted social services to express their doubts about the expectant parents' abilities. In one case the father's parents notified the expectant couple to child protection authorities. This was in spite of the fact that the parents already had a social worker and good family support organized. To its credit, the child protection agency decided not to interfere.

Disapproval of the pregnancy went beyond what people said to the expectant parents. The actions of families in response to the news illustrated their poor expectations of the couple. One Icelandic expectant mother was pregnant at the same time as her brother's wife. Her family went to a great deal of trouble knitting baby clothes and preparing for the arrival of her nephew or niece. No one in the family knitted clothes for her baby, or anticipated the arrival of her child. This hurt her deeply as it indicated to her that her baby was not as welcome in the family as her brother's baby.

Whether planned or unplanned, discovering a pregnancy leads to intense emotional reactions, ranging from delight to distress to fear. For the Australian women with intellectual disabilities, acknowledging their pregnancies meant the discovery that life was now very different. Their bodies were now working to preserve the life of the unborn child. These bodily actions continued despite the expectant mothers' physical symptoms such as nausea and discomfort, and were unaffected by her emotional reactions or the reactions of her partner and others around her. In this situation of heightened emotional response, the expectant mothers had to make decisions about their pregnancies.

The fathers-to-be in Iceland also experienced heightened emotional responses; however, they had to try harder to ensure that they were consulted on any decisions about the pregnancy. They did not want to be excluded. One Icelandic expectant mother decided to have an abortion. Her mother and her support worker agreed with her decision. Her partner, Halli, was not aware of this as the three women kept him out of the discussion and the decision was made without consulting him. When Halli learned of his partner's intention, he was devastated both because he was looking forward to the birth of this child and because he was a member of a religious group that holds life to be sacred. Halli asked his partner not to go through with the abortion, but her mind was made up. The night before the operation was scheduled Halli showed her an educational DVD about abortion that he had rented from the National Library. The next morning the couple turned up at the hospital to inform them that they had changed their mind and had decided to keep the baby.

The expectant parents in both countries took into account many factors in making decisions about the baby. This decision making was not straightforward. There were financial considerations to think about. There was also the question of whether the baby would be healthy or have a disability. For two Australian women their pregnancies were discovered too late for an abortion to be legally available, despite their requests for one. Importantly, the experiences of the Australian women with intellectual disabilities show that any decision revolves around a baby who is now living inside her. Women with intellectual disabilities do not respond to a hypothetical pregnancy; there is no longer a choice about whether or not to have "a child" in the abstract. The women with intellectual disabilities knew that they must respond to *this* particular baby, their own child.

## Doing the Work of Becoming a Mother

For the expectant mothers the work of becoming a mother centered on their pregnant bodies. Once the decision-making phase was over, the women delighted in their bodies and in their unborn babies, whose physical presence first became more outwardly obvious to them and then to other people. No longer were their pregnant bodies just a swath of symptoms such as morning sickness that had to be endured. Each woman began to consider quite differently the baby she carried. She was not only pregnant; she was going to have *her* baby. After recognizing and accepting the pregnancy, each woman now began to accept the baby as her very own. Rowan, a mother in the Australian study, described how, early in her first pregnancy, she wanted to have an abortion. However, she changed her mind:

> it's also exciting because you sort of see yourself, like another part of yourself . . . because . . . you think, "I have got another little me growing inside me and I wanna see how that turns out." . . . I decided I would have the baby.

Women described the joy and excitement of feeling the baby move inside them, and imagining life with the baby once it was born. Sandelowski and Black (1994) have shown that expectant mothers are involved with their unborn baby in a concrete, personalized way. Bailey (1999) has described women's changing experience of their own bodies and their sense of self as their unborn child became more and more outwardly apparent. For the Australian women with intellectual disabilities, the boundaries between the self as an individual and the self as a mother became blurred, as people commented upon, patted, and prodded the expectant mother's body. Merrilyn, an Australian mother pregnant with her fourth baby, said:

> It's always better towards the end, because it seems real. You know that it's real. This one's different too, when it kicks and moves I think, oh wow, it's a real baby. And you can actually kind of picture it. I can picture myself as a mother again.

As expectant mothers, the women with intellectual disabilities in both studies were acutely aware of the risk that other people would intervene in their lives. As suggested by Llewellyn (1994), negative reactions to their pregnancy signaled that others had little confidence in their abilities to parent. They were also aware that there were people in their lives who had the power to report them to the child protection authorities, who in turn could remove their children. Some mothers had already had child protection authorities involved in their parenting. One of the Australian mothers, Brianna, had a child protection worker visit her within a few days after she brought her first son home. Brianna felt sure that it was her mother who had contacted them, as she was distrustful of Brianna's ability to provide proper care for her infant son.

In response to the risk of losing their soon-to-be-born baby, the expectant mothers in Australia actively arranged their support networks in a strategic way to ensure that the new addition to their family would remain in their care. They sought the support of those people in their immediate and existing network on whom they felt they could rely: those closest to them at the time of their pregnancies. For some women this included their supportive partner, particularly if he was the father of their unborn child. In this well-considered and planned way the expectant mothers secured the support of those they believed would honor their role as mother of their child and excluded those they believed would try to "take over" (Mayes et al., 2008).

## Doing the Work of Becoming a Father

The men in the Icelandic study were proud of their new role and wanted to do everything they could to prepare for the arrival of their babies. Antenatal care and antenatal classes were important for these expectant fathers to confirm their new status both to themselves and to others, and as an avenue to receive information and to provide support to their partners. All of the fathers went with their partners to antenatal services and read the information booklets provided as well as questioning the midwives about pregnancy, birth, and infant care. Although the fathers were very eager to learn, they found that many people had reservations about them in the beginning. One of the midwives, who had been asked by the family social worker not to include the father, said:

> Initially I had doubts about him but these disappeared as time passed. He was always good to work with. Anna usually didn't ask much so I usually had to tell her but he asked a lot of questions. He wanted to know and be well prepared . . . it was enough for her just to be pregnant.

The midwife was impressed with the father and found his questions "both appropriate and relevant, never asking the same question twice." For the Icelandic fathers this close involvement with antenatal care and classes made the pregnancy more real. The Icelandic fathers saw their babies via an ultrasound scan and enjoyed showing the photos of their future offspring to others. This was in direct contrast to the experience of the Australian mothers-to-be for whom antenatal care and classes did not constitute such public recognition of their pregnancy or act as a rite of passage.

When the contractions started the fathers regarded it as their role to call for help and to take their partners to the hospital. Afterward they rang friends and family to proudly announce the arrival of the new family member. All of the fathers were present at the birth except two, who had to wait outside as their partners had unplanned, emergency caesareans. When their partners were taken to the recovery ward, these fathers were allowed to see their babies. One of them said:

> She didn't see the baby at this stage but I did, I saw him. That made me happy seeing such a little child that I had never, I mean, I had seen small children but I had never held them or fed them so it was all first time for me.

The fathers visited their partners every day at visiting hours eager to learn how to take care of their babies.

Like the Australian mothers, the Icelandic fathers knew that most people viewed their fatherhood and family life negatively and they were well aware of the danger that they might lose custody of their children. For one father, his first child had been removed from his care. The partners of two other fathers had also lost custody of their previous children. The risk of child removal is very real. Iceland is a small country with a population of only 300,000. All the fathers knew or had heard about parents with intellectual disabilities whose children had been taken into care.

Most of the fathers were expecting their first child and had no experience in caring for children or role models to follow. Some had doubts about their own parenting ability, but all wanted to learn to take good care of their babies and do everything in their power to ensure they would keep the baby. In response to this very real risk of losing custody of their new baby, the expectant fathers strategically negotiated and secured the support of those beyond their immediate family and friends. They worked to establish a support network consisting of people they knew and trusted, and who were regarded credible enough for "the system." For example, some fathers found a well-respected, non-disabled advocate who would accompany them and their families to child protection meetings as most of the families were notified to child protection authorities at the time of pregnancy. Two fathers created a public presence by telling their story in the media, three volunteered as participants in Sigurjónsdóttir's study, and two hired a lawyer.

Prior to the birth of their babies, therefore, the expectant mothers in the Australian study and the Icelandic fathers-to-be set about gaining support to make sure they would be able to keep their babies. Many of the Icelandic fathers also negotiated support for the family with professionals from generic services. When the baby arrived, however, the support from these services did not turn out to be quite as they had intended. Although the infant nurses and midwives provided support to the father of the new baby as well as to the mother, the support workers from social services and child protection focused mainly on the mother and baby. These social service practitioners tended to ignore the father, who felt left out as all the conversations and instructions were directed almost entirely to the mother. Support workers clearly regarded the mother as having the main responsibility of caring for the baby.

One father described how a psychologist accompanied by a social worker came to his home and told him that the results of a psychological test revealed that he could never take care of a child. When the father asked why this was the case, the psychologist did not answer his question. Instead, he made the father repeat aloud after him, in front of other people present, "I can never take care of a child." The psychologist then said that the father had to understand that "In this house it is your wife who is in charge of both the child and the home. You will have to do what she tells you to do." The father found this extremely hurtful and wondered what kind of marriage it was where one partner had no say in the family or the relationship. He commented:

> For our family life to be normal I need to be the man of the house. I need to feel respected and I cannot accept this.

The Icelandic fathers, all of whom wanted to be good partners and fathers, saw it as their role and duty to protect and speak up for their families. Wanting to do well, they asked staff at the maternity unit and support workers from social services and child protection lots of questions both to confirm they were doing things correctly and to clarify when they received mixed and inconsistent messages from support staff. As a direct result of this help-seeking behavior, many of the fathers were labeled non-compliant and difficult to work with (Sigurjónsdóttir, 2004).

## Discussion

The two studies described in this chapter are the first to our knowledge to explore the experiences of women and men with intellectual disabilities during the pregnancy period and the transition to motherhood and fatherhood. This work highlights the importance of the gendered perspective. The men and women with intellectual disabilities were engaged in becoming parents; however, they were developing fundamentally different identities. This notion has long been recognized by researchers engaged in gender studies (e.g., Oakley, 1979, 1980), but it has been under-explored by disability scholars. Men and women view and experience pregnancy and the postpartum very differently, and as a result their support needs may be quite different.

There are three key points which we wish to draw from the experiences of the women in Australia and the men in Iceland. Gender underpins these points. The first point is about culture and social policy. It is important to recognize that these studies come from opposite sides of the globe. Cultural differences and in particular the social policies of each country account for some differences in the mothers' and fathers' experiences. The second point is that all the expectant mothers in Australia and the Icelandic expectant fathers were engaged in negotiating support for their families; however, they did so in a gendered way. The third point demonstrates a key difference in the expectations held by partners for the father's role compared with the practitioner perspective on the place of fathers in caring for the new baby.

## Culture and policy

Social policies regarding child bearing and parenting vary considerably between Iceland and Australia. In Iceland fathers have a legislative entitlement to a minimum of three months independent paid parental leave (Ministry of Social Affairs, 2000). In Australia, although maternity leave is quite widespread, there is not a similar broad entitlement for fathers, although there are plans for such a scheme in the near future. Only mothers and fathers in the workforce currently have access to parental leave schemes sponsored by their employer (Productivity Commission, 2009).

Another example of cultural and policy variation between the two countries is found in the provision of antenatal care. The rate of infant death and prenatal mortality in Iceland is one of the lowest in the world (United Nations Development Program, 2008). This is believed to be due to a strong cultural tradition for women to attend antenatal care from the time they are 12 weeks pregnant. Fathers-to-be are encouraged to be full participants from the beginning of pregnancy and employers are sympathetic to fathers attending antenatal care with their partners. Antenatal classes form an integral part of this care and are designed for mothers and fathers. Although antenatal classes are optional, the majority of expectant parents attend and pay only a low fee to participate.

In Australia there are no comprehensive national guidelines regarding antenatal care, although this is recommended from the time a woman is 12 weeks pregnant (Hunt & Lumley, 2002). Antenatal classes are voluntary. Class sizes, program content, and access to classes vary widely, even within one geographical area. In some locations, particularly those where there is a greater concentration of disadvantaged families, antenatal classes are poorly attended (Sydney South West Area Health Service, 2008).

It is difficult to determine whether the participation in antenatal classes so highly regarded by the Icelandic fathers-to-be and less so by the Australian mothers-to-be is influenced more by cultural mores, social policy, or gender. The Icelandic men valued antenatal care and classes responding to the cultural tradition or "norm" that expectant parents, including fathers, engage in these activities. Similarly, the women in Australia also followed cultural norms that place less emphasis on antenatal classes. A major point is that in both countries, the men and women with intellectual disabilities acted within their own country's cultural expectations for expectant parents.

## Seeking support

Expectant mothers and fathers with intellectual disabilities reacted to the real or perceived risk of losing custody of their children. How they did this varied considerably. Australian mothers were concerned with garnering support from those closest to them. They wanted to ensure that there were others who would be engaged in caring for their child while still respecting their central role as the child's mother. Icelandic fathers, on the other hand, acted to harness support for their parenting beyond their immediate family and friends, engaging the assistance of formal support services and advocates.

Llewellyn and McConnell (2002) conceptualized the support networks of mothers with intellectual disabilities as a series of concentric circles. In the innermost circle are those people to whom mothers feel closest: those without whom they could not imagine life. In the next circle are those people who are still very important but not as close as those in the inmost circle, with the outer layer typically being practitioners and health and social service agencies (Llewellyn & McConnell, 2002). In line with their findings, the expectant Australian mothers and Icelandic fathers operated across these circles in securing support for their families to counter the risk of losing custody of their soon-to-be-born child. Gender, however, determined the focus of the expectant parents' efforts to gain support. Mothers turned to their immediate support network in the innermost circle. Fathers approached and secured the support of advocates and practitioners in the more distant or outer circle of support. The target of support seeking was gender related; the purpose of the strategies was unanimous in ensuring the support needed to care for the new arrival.

## Contrasting expectations

That the Icelandic fathers were so involved with service agencies is highly significant given that the support workers from these agencies did not expect fathers to be involved in the pregnancy or the early care of the child and therefore largely ignored their needs. The key exception to this was the midwives at the antenatal care and antenatal classes. The midwives' recognition of the father's role and importance in both the pregnancy and birth made each father feel welcomed and that his questions were appreciated. Fathers believed that they had an important part to play in the family and the upbringing of their children, and the midwives' support of this strengthened their confidence in their fathering role.

After the babies were born, however, the Icelandic social services system did not expect the fathers to be involved in the "mothering business." Support workers recognized that mothers needed support with the caring and upbringing of their children but did not extend the same recognition to fathers, leaving the fathers feeling sidelined by professionals. In complete contrast, the partners of the Icelandic fathers, as new mothers, turned to their partners for support and wanted them to share responsibility in the care of their newborn child.

The support expectations of the Icelandic mothers with intellectual disabilities and the support workers are therefore quite different. The responses of the mothers are more aligned with contemporary societal expectations for fathers without disabilities in western cultures. This has the potential to cause problems in the working relationship between parents and support workers and in the parents' relationship. The failure of support services to recognize and support the involvement of fathers with intellectual disabilities in the raising of their children sends a conflicting message to fathers about what their role should be. Practitioners and policy makers need to consider the differences between the experiences of men and women who are becoming fathers and mothers, and in the roles they are trying to achieve. Public policies that encourage and support the involvement of fathers also need to be embraced by those providing support services to non-traditional families.

## Gendered experience

Disability studies have only recently begun to consider issues of gender (Traustadóttir, 2006). Yet, as the two studies demonstrate, the experiences of men and women with intellectual disabilities becoming fathers and mothers are gendered. This gendered perspective presents a more nuanced understanding of parenthood for people with intellectual disabilities than that which is currently described in the literature. Continuing to subsume mothers and fathers under the term parents and failing to acknowledge the fundamental differences between becoming a mother and becoming a father will continue to negate the unique perspectives of women and men as they take on their parenting role.

Consideration of disability is also relatively new to gender studies. Studies of women becoming mothers have been criticized by feminist scholars with disabilities, such as Asch and Fine (1988), for failing to acknowledge their unique experiences of pregnancy and becoming a mother. As they note, it is unacceptable to assume that having a disability eclipses all other social experiences or to view all social experience through the lens of disability. The voices of women with intellectual disabilities have been largely absent from the debate on mothering (Mayes et al., 2006; Mayes et al., in press). Even less attention has been paid to the voices of men with intellectual disabilities in discussions of fatherhood.

## Principles for Practice

The overwhelming focus of practitioners and researchers to date has been on parenting, although in reality this has meant mothers. We strongly recommend that both policy and practice place emphasis on mothers and fathers separately as well as jointly to make visible the gendered nature of parenting. Three practice principles follow from this. First, practitioners must take the time to understand the father's point of view, to value their strengths and abilities, and to support their contribution to their families. This requires practitioners to develop an effective co-working relationship with the father built on recognition of the important role that fathers play in the family. Second, depending on cultural mores and social norms, this may also include recognizing that the father regards himself as the head of his household. He may also be the parent whose role it is to negotiate support services for his family. Finally, practitioners must also recognize that for mothers, mothering also includes their partner or in the absence of a partner, another person with significant responsibility in the upbringing of their children.

The time has come for practitioners and policy makers who support mothers and fathers with intellectual disabilities to consider the influence of gender on each parent's role. Mother and father roles are not the same. The mother identity is not the same as the father identity. Women and men experience parenthood differently and, as a result, their support needs are quite different. Treating their support needs as identical or neglecting the needs of one parent makes the transition to parenthood more difficult for women and men with intellectual disabilities as individuals, as a couple, and for the whole family.

## References

Asch, A., & Fine, M. (1988). Beyond pedestals. In M. Fine & A. Asch (Eds.), *Women with disabilities: Essays in psychology, culture and politics.* Philadelphia: Temple University Press.

Bailey, L. (1999). Refracted selves? A study of changes in self-identity in the transition to motherhood. *Sociology, 33*(2), 335–352.

Bergum, V. (1989). *Woman to mother: A transformation.* Massachusetts: Bergin & Garvey.

Booth, T., & Booth, W. (1992). An ordinary family life. *Community Care, 912,* 15–17.

Booth, T., & Booth, W. (1994). *Parenting under pressure: Mothers and fathers with intellectual disabilities.* Buckingham: Open University Press.

Booth, T., & Booth, W. (1995). Unto us a child is born: The trials and rewards of parenthood for people with learning difficulties. *Australia and New Zealand Journal of Developmental Disabilities, 20*(1), 25–39.

Booth, T., & Booth, W. (2002). Men in the lives of mothers with intellectual disabilities. *Journal of Applied Research in Intellectual Disabilities, 15*(3), 187–199.

Brady, S. M., & Grover, S. (1997). *The sterilisation of girls and young women in Australia: A legal, medical and social context.* Sydney: Human Rights and Equal Opportunity Commission.

Emerson, R., Fretz, R., & Shaw, L. (1995). *Writing ethnographic fieldnotes.* Chicago: University of Chicago Press.

Feldman, M. A. (1994). Parenting education for parents with intellectual disabilities: A review of outcome studies. *Research in Developmental Disabilities, 15*(4), 299–332.

Hunt, J. M., & Lumley, J. (2002). Are recommendations about routine antenatal care in Australia consistent and evidence based? *Medical Journal of Australia, 176*(6), 255–259.

Kvale, S. (1996). *Interviews: An introduction to qualitative research interviewing.* Thousand Oaks, CA: Sage.

Llewellyn, G. (1994). *Intellectual disability and parenting: A shared experience.* Unpublished doctoral dissertation, University of Sydney, Sydney.

Llewellyn, G. (1995). Relationships and social support: Views of parents with mental retardation/intellectual disability. *Mental Retardation, 33*(6), 349–363.

Llewellyn, G., & McConnell, D. (2002). Mothers with learning difficulties and their support networks. *Journal of Intellectual Disability Research, 46*(1), 17–34.

Llewellyn, G., & McConnell, D. (2005). "You have to prove yourself all the time": People with learning disabilities as parents. In G. Grant, P. Goward, P. Ramcharan, & M. Richardson (Eds.), *Learning disability: A life cycle approach to valuing people* (pp. 441–467). Buckingham: Open University Press.

Llewellyn, G., McConnell, D., Cant, R., & Westbrook, M. (1999). Support networks of mothers with an intellectual disability: An exploratory study. *Journal of Intellectual and Developmental Disability, 24*(1), 7–26.

Mattinson, J. (1970). *Marriage and mental handicap.* London: Duckworth.

Mayes, R. (2005). *Becoming a mother: The experiences of women with intellectual disabilities.* Unpublished doctoral dissertation, University of Sydney, Sydney.

Mayes, R., Llewellyn, G., & McConnell, D. (2006). Misconception: The experience of pregnancy for women with intellectual disabilities. *Scandinavian Journal of Disability Research, 8*(2&3), 120–131.

Mayes, R., Llewellyn, G., & McConnell, D. (2008). Active negotiation: Mothers with intellectual disabilities creating their social support networks. *Journal of Applied Research in Intellectual Disabilities, 21*(4), 341–350.

Mayes, R., Llewellyn, G., & McConnell, D. (in press). "That's who I choose to be": The mother identity for women with intellectual disabilities. *Women's Studies International Forum.*

Ministry of Social Affairs. (2000). *Act on maternity/paternity leave and parental leave No. 95/2000 with subsequent amendments.* Retrieved June 10, 2009, from http://eng.felagsmalaraduneyti.is/legislation/nr/3697.

Oakley, A. (1979). *Becoming a mother.* Oxford: Martin Robertson.

Oakley, A. (1980). *Women confined: Towards a sociology of childbirth.* Oxford: Marin Robertson.

O'Hara, J., & Martin, H. (2003). Parents with learning disabilities: A study of gender and cultural perspectives in East London. *British Journal of Learning Disabilities, 31*(1), 18–24.

Pfeiffer, D. (1994). Eugenics and disability discrimination. *Disability and Society, 9*(4), 481–499.

Pixa-Kettner, U. (1998). Parents with intellectual disability in Germany: Results of a nation-wide study. *Journal of Applied Research in Intellectual Disabilities, 11*(4), 355–364.

Productivity Commission. (2009). *Paid parental leave: Support for parents with newborn children.* Report no. 47, Canberra.

Radford, J. P. (1994). Intellectual disability and the heritage of modernity. In M. Rioux & M. Bach (Eds.), *Disability is not measles: Research paradigms in disability* (pp. 9–27). Toronto: Roeher Institute.

Sandelowski, M., & Black, B. P. (1994). The epistemology of expectant parenthood. *Western Journal of Nursing Research, 16*(6), 601–622.

Sigurjónsdóttir, H. B. (2004). Intellectually limited fathers, their families and the formal support services. In K. Kristiansen & R. Traustadóttir (Eds.), *Gender and disability: Research in the Nordic countries* (pp. 239–254). Lund: Studentlitteratur.

Sigurjónsdóttir, H. B. (2005). *Family support services and parents with learning difficulties.* Unpublished doctoral dissertation, University of Sheffield, Sheffield.

Sydney South West Area Health Service. (2008). *Draft Sydney South West Area Health Service Maternity Services Plan 2008–2012.* Sydney: Author.

Taylor, S., & Bogdan, R. (1998). *Introduction to qualitative research methods: A guidebook and resource* ( 3rd ed.). New York: John Wiley & Sons.

Traustadóttir, R. (2006). Disability and gender: Introduction to the special issue. *Scandinavian Journal of Disability Research, 8*(2&3), 81–84.

Traustadóttir, R., & Kristiansen, K. (2004). Introducing gender and disability. In K. Kristiansen & R. Traustadóttir (Eds.), *Gender and disability research in the Nordic countries* (pp. 31–48). Lund: Studentlitteratur.

Traustadóttir, R., & Sigurjónsdóttir, H. B. (1998). *Umdeildar fjölskyldur: Seinfærir/roskaheftir foreldrar og börn eirra* [Contested families: Parents with intellectual impairments and their children]. Reykjavik: Social Science Research Institute, University of Iceland.

United Nations Development Program. (2008). *2007/2008 Human Development Report.* New York. Retrieved June 10, 2009, from http://hdrstats.undp.org/en/countries/data_sheets/cty_ds_ISL.html.

Wade, C., Llewellyn, G., & Matthews, J. (2008). Review of parent training interventions for parents with intellectual disability. *Journal of Applied Research in Intellectual Disabilities, 21*(4), 351–366.

Walmsley, J. (2000). Women and the Mental Deficiency Act of 1913: Citizenship, sexuality and regulation. *British Journal of Learning Disabilities, 28*(2), 65–70.

# 2

# Looking Back on Their Own Upbringing

*Gwynnyth Llewellyn and David McConnell*

## Introduction

When people become parents they often look back on their own childhood experiences. They reflect on the past to find direction for the future. They think about their lives as children, and the way they were parented when they were growing up. Some parents look back and decide that they want to be just like their own parents. Others want to break with the past, and create a different life for themselves and their children.

Understanding the childhood experiences of any parent is an important part of understanding how and why parents act and behave as they do with their own children. There is good evidence in the general parenting literature that the attitudes, beliefs, and parenting practices of the family of origin are a strong influence on the parenting practices of the next generation (e.g., Goodnow & Collins, 1990). This appears to be almost a commonsense observation and many people, on becoming parents, find themselves saying and doing things that their own parents had done, even if they had previously said "I am not going to be like my mother or father"! Scholars studying parents and parenting, however, caution against relying too heavily on understanding parental actions by reference to their mother or father's parenting behaviors given the multi-layered influences on parenting, including the wider family, societal processes, changing cultural beliefs and attitudes, and, of course, changes over time in parenting "fashions" (Goodnow & Collins, 1990; Harkness & Super, 1996).

*Parents with Intellectual Disabilities: Past, Present and Futures*   Edited by Gwynnyth Llewellyn, Rannveig Traustadóttir, David McConnell, and Hanna Björg Sigurjónsdóttir   © 2010 John Wiley & Sons, Ltd

We know very little about how parents with intellectual disabilities experience their own upbringing. The available research is very limited, with no study that we are aware of focusing exclusively on this topic. Up until the 1980s most of the research in the field was conducted in high-income countries and involved parents with intellectual disabilities who grew up in institutions or were admitted to institutions as young people, often in the case of young women when they were deemed to be "wayward and out of control." The dehumanizing conditions in the institutions in these countries have been well documented and it is reasonable to assume that children growing up in institutional care would have very few opportunities to experience substituted parental love and nurturing. Today, however, in high- and middle-income countries most children and young people with intellectual disabilities grow up in their own family, with relatives, or in substitute family care. As a result, parents with intellectual disabilities today are much more likely to have spent their childhood in a family environment.

What do we know about their upbringing? How do parents with intellectual disabilities appraise their parents and their own childhoods? The aim of this chapter is to bring together information from studies both past and present that have made mention of parents' upbringing, and then to present findings from one of our own studies in which we specifically asked mothers with intellectual limitations about their own mothers and how they remembered their childhood.

## Documented Childhoods

### Institutional childhoods

Early research studies on parenting with intellectual disabilities drew attention to the likely detrimental effect of institutional childhoods experienced by many children and young people with intellectual disabilities. For example, writing in the United States of America in the late 1980s, Gath (1988) noted that the parents with intellectual disabilities discussed in the literature

> are very unlikely to have had experiences in childhood that offered any model of good-enough parenting. Those who were brought up in institutions would have had no experience of family life at all, and those who were admitted later, usually in adolescence, had often experienced very poor upbringing and bad relationships before their mild degree of learning difficulties provided the rationale for institutionalization. (p. 741)

Gath's view of the effect of poor upbringing is supported by the work of Quinton and his colleagues in the United Kingdom (Dowdney, Skuse, Rutter, Quinton, & Mrazek, 1985; Quinton, Rutter, & Liddle, 1984). Their empirical studies demonstrated that when women raised as girls in an institution are compared with a general population group, the former show an increased rate of severe parenting difficulties in later life. A proportion of the institutionalized women in these studies had been admitted as "wayward" girls with borderline intellectual disability. However, as Quinton et al. (1984) demonstrated, it was not inevitable that these women experienced difficulties when they became mothers, noting that "the support of a non-deviant spouse and good living conditions in adult life provided a powerful protective effect" (p. 107).

Although deinstitutionalization gained momentum in the latter half of the 20th century, a significant number of people were "released" back into the community prior to 1950. Many of these adults with intellectual disabilities went on to marry and become parents, and have been the subject of research studies. Of the nine studies of parenting after deinstitutionalization from 1947 through to 1983 reviewed by Llewellyn (1990), six studies report that the majority of the over 300 parents provided affection and care, and met the health, hygiene, and clothing needs of their children, with a smaller number of couples in each study unable to provide satisfactory parenting to the extent that as Mattinson (1970) observed, "the standard of care fell below the threshold of community tolerance" (p. 107). In the remaining three studies reviewed, the findings were less positive with each study identifying a larger proportion of the children requiring alternative care.

The difficulties experienced by parents with intellectual disabilities who were institutionalized are not applicable to parents with intellectual disabilities who grew up with their family in the local community. It is relatively easy to study previously institutionalized parents with intellectual disabilities as they are, in a sense, a captive audience. It is somewhat more challenging to conduct research with parents who live in the community and who are not known to the service system. Not surprisingly, most of what we know about the influence of childhood experiences of parenting on present-day parenting by parents with intellectual disabilities comes from studies of people with intellectual disabilities who have been institutionalized, as mentioned briefly above, or who, as parents, become clients of the service system.

## Family-based childhoods

What do we know about the childhood experiences of parents with intellectual disabilities who grew up with their family in the local community? There is little research evidence, however based on the experiences of parents with intellectual disabilities that we have come to know since the mid-1990s, and, on a few insights from past research, it appears that their childhood experiences are quite diverse. Many parents with intellectual disabilities who grew up with their family describe happy, if not entirely carefree, childhoods (McConnell & Llewellyn, 2005). Their own parents, remembered as being "there for them" when they were children, continue to be supportive now that they are adults and parents themselves (McConnell & Llewellyn, 2002; Traustadóttir & Sigurjónsdóttir, 2008). Typically, those parents who remember their childhood positively seek to emulate their own parents and carry out parenting in a similar manner (Llewellyn, 1997), and many turn first to their own parents and to other family members, valuing their guidance and advice above that offered by others (Booth & Booth, 1995; Llewellyn, 1997). In contrast to these happy childhood experiences, other parents with intellectual disabilities who also grew up in their own families describe difficult childhoods in which they were neglected or abused (McConnell & Llewellyn, 2005).

## Neglect or abuse in childhood

There is little epidemiological data available on the proportion of parents with intellectual disabilities who were neglected or abused as children. Most studies have been conducted with parents with intellectual disabilities who are clients of the service system. The findings from these studies must, of course, be treated with caution as sampling of parents with intellectual disabilities from clinical populations potentially introduces a bias. In an early study, Madsen (1979) reported that 75% of her parenting class sample had grown up in institutional care with "little knowledge of family life education or social skills," and for those who grew up with their families in the community, at least 50% "have parents who were either abusive or had neglected them" (p. 195).

More recently, McGaw, Shaw, and Beckley (2007) found that 79.6% of their sample of 49 parents with intellectual disabilities (30 females, 19 males) attending their special parenting service reported abuse or neglect of some form during their childhood on the self-report Childhood Trauma Questionnaire (Bernstein & Fink, 1998), with 55.1% citing multiple abuse/neglect categories. Emotional abuse was the most recurring category; severe to extreme abuse/neglect was the most prevalent trauma reported. This is a high proportion and gives rise for concern, particularly as other studies indicate that childhood abuse and mother's age when she first gave birth are the strongest predictors of depression and adjustment/anxiety symptoms among mothers with intellectual disabilities, suggesting childhood experiences linger into adulthood (Ehlers-Flint, 2002; Tymchuk, 1993, 1994). In their discussion of two families whose children had been placed in foster care due to abuse and neglect, Greene, Norman, Searle, Daniels, and Lubeck (1995) place considerable emphasis on the family of origin. In the first instance, a 22-year-old mother had been physically and sexually abused by her biological parents until she was two years old, when their parental rights were terminated. In the second instance, the mother with intellectual disabilities had been physically and sexually abused by her stepfather. Morton (2000) describes a mother with intellectual disability with a history of childhood abuse which, against her own strongly felt wishes, finds expression in her own parenting behaviors, resulting in her losing custody of her young daughter. However, evidence of inter-generational difficulties from case studies such as that of Greene et al. (1995) and Morton (2000), and in larger and more recent samples such as that described in detail in Cleaver and Nicholson (2007) from the United Kingdom, may not be applicable to parents with intellectual disabilities who grow up in their own families and who are not clients of the service system.

That said, parents with intellectual disabilities across many countries experience negative community attitudes no matter where they spent their childhoods, and often (although not always) family members question their capacity to raise their children successfully (Booth & Booth, 1995; Mayes, Llewellyn, & McConnell, 2006; Tucker & Johnson, 1989). Negativity about parenting by people with intellectual disabilities reflects stereotypical, pejorative attitudes that are widely spread (Brown, 1996; Reinders, 2008; Traustadóttir & Johnson, 2000; Willems, de Vries, Isarin, & Reinders, 2007). It is difficult to estimate the effect of stigmatizing attitudes on the parenting practices of parents with intellectual disabilities, particularly when these may start as early as the discovery of pregnancy. As Booth and Booth (1995) noted, in most families pregnancy is a happy event, while for parents with intellectual disabilities pregnancy is often viewed by others as a mistake never to be repeated rather than an event to be celebrated. Over a decade later, Mayes, Llewellyn, and McConnell (2006) reported that women with intellectual disabilities were continuing to encounter significant opposition to becoming mothers, including being pressured by some if not all family members to have an abortion.

## Childhood experiences and parenting practice

It would not be surprising if a poor home life as a child and/or being institutionalized and/or being neglected or abused while growing up, coupled with negative reactions to becoming pregnant and bearing children, affected how parents with intellectual disabilities rear their children. Alternatively, growing up happily in childhood and as a young adult with one's family who provides support in the early days of parenting is much more likely to result in positive parenting practices. Gustavsson (1997) presented an evocative picture of the potential positive impact of past family experience when he described how a young man with intellectual disabilities and his older sister, also with intellectual disabilities, face the world with confidence and a strong belief in being accepted in society based on strong feelings of mutual experience with their parents, both of whom were also slow learners. Sigurjónsdóttir and Traustadóttir (2000) documented the experiences of women with intellectual disabilities who had become mothers across three generations and demonstrated individual family differences in how girls followed their mothers' parenting practices over these generations. Llewellyn (1997) highlighted the critical importance of informal and family experiences for parents with intellectual disabilities in their quest to be the best parents they could possibly be. In this study, those whose childhoods had been unhappy were determined not to do what their parents had done before them. Parents who had experienced happy childhoods, on the other hand, were very keen to provide similar enjoyable experiences for their children. These studies, although not specifically investigating the influence of childhood on later parenting, all point to the need to better understand the relationship between parents' past experiences and their current parenting practice.

## A Study of Motherhood and Childhood Experiences

To date, the almost exclusive sampling of parents with intellectual disabilities from clinical populations potentially introduces a bias to the findings. Perhaps there is something about their upbringing that predisposes these parents to intervention by the service system. We know that some parents with intellectual disabilities are raising their children with little or no intervention from social care agencies. How do these parents remember their upbringing? We recently completed a study of pregnancy and birth outcomes for mothers with intellectual disabilities. The mothers came from a universal service, an antenatal clinic in their local community, and so we were able to obtain a community sample rather than a clinical sample. This provided the opportunity to involve these women, first as expectant mothers, and then in the first six months of motherhood, in talking with us about their own mothers and their memories of their childhoods. Below we describe this study and the findings in relation to looking back on their own upbringing.

The broad aim of the larger prospective cohort study undertaken in New South Wales, Australia[1] was to understand the factors influencing pregnancy experiences and birth outcomes for women with intellectual disabilities. Over a five-month period, all pregnant women attending their first appointment at two public hospital antenatal clinics in South Western Sydney were invited to participate in the study. Within the recruited 878 women, 33 (3.8%) were identified as having intellectual disability and 24 (2.7%) as women with self-reported learning difficulties. Details of the research design and findings on pregnancy and birth outcomes and prepartum distress in women with intellectual disabilities are published in McConnell, Mayes, and Llewellyn (2008a) and McConnell, Mayes, and Llewellyn (2008b), respectively.

One component of the research design was a sequence of three interviews. Of the 57 women identified with learning difficulties or intellectual disabilities, 25 completed the entire sequence of interviews. The first interview was conducted

[1] Supported by the Health Foundation Sydney South West. Human Ethics Approval, University of Sydney Ref. No. 2926.

as close as possible to the first antenatal appointment (usually early in the second trimester). This interview explored women's thoughts and feelings regarding being pregnant and becoming a mother. The second interview was conducted in the third trimester and incorporated standard measures of depression, anxiety and stress, and support and conflict in interpersonal relationships. The measures were administered by a health professional experienced in working with women with intellectual disabilities. The pregnant women were assisted with reading and understanding test items when this was necessary. The third interview was conducted three to six months after the birth of their baby and explored aspects of mothers' social support, adjustment to life with a new baby, and thoughts about their own mothers and families of origin experiences.

To talk with mothers about their own mothers and their childhood experiences in these third interviews we incorporated questions from the *Parental Bonding Instrument* (PBI) (Parker, Tupling, & Brown, 1979). Details about this self-report instrument can be obtained from Parker, Tupling, and Brown (1979) and Parker (1990). There are 25 items, which are derived from a two-factor "care" and "protection" model of parenting. The care items indicate mother care, at one end characterized by affection, emotional warmth, empathy, and closeness, and at the other by emotional coldness, indifference, and neglect. The protection items at one end suggest mothers allowing independence and autonomy and, at the other, control, overprotection, intrusion, excessive contact, infantilization, and prevention of independent behavior. We introduced the items by asking mothers the following question: "Think(ing) about your Mum when you were a child, let's say up to 16 years old. If I read out a few statements about how some mums are, can you tell me how much it sounds like your Mum?" Mothers respond to each item on a four-point scale: very like, moderately like, moderately unlike, or very unlike.

In these interviews we also asked each mother "to talk a little more about when you were a child," to talk about their childhood and early adolescent experiences, and to share with us their memories of everyday life in their family or where they grew up. We used some probe questions here if needed. These were: When you were a child (around 5 to 12 years or thereabouts), what would you do if you got upset emotionally? What would you do if you got physically hurt, fell and cut yourself, bumped your head, or something like that? How was discipline handled in your family? Were you ever threatened in any way by your parents that they would leave you, or send you away? Were people affectionate in your family with hugs and kisses? Why do you think your parents were the way they were when you were a child? A seventh question dealt with "bad things that might have happened when you were a child such as physical or sexual abuse," with mothers being told, "please don't feel like you have to answer this question, it is a sensitive one."

We found using the PBI items was a useful entrée to our interview discussions with the mothers about their childhood experiences, some of which were painful and very sensitive. From the interview transcripts we were able to identify several themes in the descriptions that the mothers provided about their childhood experiences, and their thoughts about their own mother's actions and behaviors, and how this has influenced and continues to influence the ways in which they parent their own children.

## Thinking back to my own childhood

The mothers came from a community sample and so perhaps it is not surprising that their memories of their childhoods spanned loving and caring family homes to homes where some, although relatively fewer, were left to fend for themselves. 13 of our 25 mothers were within the high care range on the PBI. This means that their childhoods were characterized by affection, emotional warmth, empathy, and closeness. Each of these in their own way reported that their own mothers were "there for them"; however, there were quite marked differences in how this was experienced. We identified three sub-groups.

For the first sub-group of mothers among those who experienced high care, the unifying characteristic was their memory of a strong mother. Their daughters, now mothers themselves, wanted to be good mothers as their mothers had been to them. All wanted to follow their mother's example in teaching the "right thing" to their children. They wanted to follow in their mother's footsteps and parent their children as they had been parented. This meant being kind and loving and not disciplining their children harshly, either not smacking or hitting at all but rather talking to their children to explain right or wrong, or using hitting and smacking as a warning rather than to scare or frighten. All wanted to be fun as their mothers had been, and to be someone to whom their children could talk as they had been able to talk to their own mothers. Most felt their mothers had been there for them when others, for example, teased or made fun of them. Mothers were also remembered as standing up for their daughters at school and helping them, when they could, with their lessons. Fathers were discussed very little, perhaps because of the strong identity of the mother.

The second sub-group of mothers who experienced high care was defined by the many good memories they shared of growing up in their own family. For these mothers, their own mothers had always been there for their children; these children, now as mothers with intellectual disabilities sharing their memories with us, aspired to be like their own mothers – kind and caring and there for their own children no matter what, spending as much time as possible being mothers. Fathers were remembered by the mothers within this grouping, however, more for their absence rather than their presence, physically absent because of work or emotionally absent and rather distant from the everyday action of mothers and children and family life. Having closely involved grandparents, particularly where mothers were working away from the home for part or all of the working week, added to the strong feelings of being cared for. If there was a downside, mothers in this grouping in comparison to the first group-ing described their own mothers as too strict. Sometimes their strict approach was only about some things, at other times about everything, and especially so as daughters began to "spread their wings" and wanted to go out, be with their friends, and move away from family-based activities to activities outside the home.

The third sub-group of mothers who experienced high care (as scored on the PBI scale) reported quite different childhoods. The mothers in this grouping can perhaps best be described as those who spoke about childhoods quite fraught with difficulties and their desire and commitment to create a different type of family for their own children. These mothers talked about how their own mothers had experienced abuse or neglect or very poor circumstances with no opportunities for education. They were sympathetic to their mother's own childhood difficulties, using this understanding to explain some of their mother's behaviors, over-strict (in some cases) or in others under-protective, at the same time as firmly stating, "I will be different myself." One mother, for example, talked about a very strict and physically demanding childhood, which she explained as understandable given that "parents were different then"; another talked about her mother as "never being there," and involved in alcohol and drugs, explaining this as part of her family's cultural environment and that having her mother's sweater in which she wrapped herself brought her mother's love to her; yet another talked about her mother's depression and the difficulties that caused, but noting that she could always rely on her, even when her mother was hospitalized for quite long periods. None of the mothers in this grouping felt uncared for despite the difficult childhoods they had experienced, as had their own mothers before them. As each of the examples above demonstrates, despite exceptional circumstances where, as a child, the mother may have had to fend for herself and develop independence at an early age, all felt cared for and loved by their mothers. On the downside, however, several of these mothers talked openly about sexual and physical abuse in their middle childhood years. So perhaps not surprisingly, a characteristic common to these mothers was being there to protect their children, particularly their daughters. Comments such as "I'll protect her with all my life, and if anyone ever touches her I'll kill them" were quite frequent.

The remaining 12 mothers in our study experienced low care (as scored on the PBI scale). The stand-out characteristic for mothers experiencing low care was an absent mother during their childhood. They universally described their own mothers as not being there for their children. In some cases mothers were physically absent because they left home, leaving their children in the care of fathers or grandmothers. In others, the child, now the mother with intellectual disability, had been sent to live with other members of the family, although none had been in foster or institutional care. Mothers were also absent due to being drug dependent and unaware of their children's needs, or absent by suffering from mental health problems with extreme mood swings, or "absent" from protecting their daughters from abuse at the hands of family members including fathers, close family friends, or, in one instance, casual acquaintances. Physical, sexual, and/or emotional abuse of the children was characteristic of this group, although rarely was this known about outside the family home. These mothers strongly felt the absence of adults in their lives who could ensure their safety and look after their interests. There was no one to whom they could turn. Child protection services were rarely involved, and even if they had been, were remembered as of little help to them as children. For one mother, the involvement of child protection services only made matters worse from her perspective as it resulted in her becoming the mother to her siblings when her own mother was denied access to the home and the children after welfare intervention.

The greater proportion of the mothers who reported low care had also experienced strict control as children. For some this was driven by their parents' strong religious beliefs; for others it was driven by parents who demanded much by way of physical labor from their children. Strict control by parents characteristically resulted in shouting, fighting, and hitting being a regular part of family life. The mothers in this group remembered many ways they had learned as children to try to avoid the inevitable punishments that would follow even seemingly minor misdemeanors. Characteristically, mothers with intellectual disabilities in this group had left home early, sometimes on falling pregnant, other times through involvement with or marriage to an older man.

The childhood memories of the remaining two mothers who experienced low care were quite similar in many ways to the mothers described above. Typically, their mother was a dominant but absent figure in their lives with a physically absent or abusive father or father figure. Similarly too, these two mothers had escaped their childhood by developing a relationship with an older man or becoming pregnant and leaving home. Characteristically low protection dominates the stories of these two mothers. One of the mothers spoke of this when she said of her own mother, "She didn't care about me. I looked after my brother and myself." For this mother, being a loving and caring mother is dedicating oneself 100% to the care of the children. This also means never drinking and always being there so that there is no opportunity for adults to take advantage of her children, physically or sexually, as had happened to her. Her experience of being mothered was fraught with resentment and anger and she is committed to being different from her mother in every single way.

## Thinking about how to be the best mother I can be

An important first point from our findings is that mothers with intellectual disabilities experience various parenting practices in their own childhoods, yet all were committed to being the best mother they could be. It would be simplistic and inaccurate to regard the childhood experiences of mothers with intellectual disabilities as primarily negative – regrettably, a too frequent conclusion founded in the negative stereotypes that continue to surround people with intellectual disabilities and particularly when they become parents.

We found that just over half of the mothers from this community sample experienced high care in their family of origin and particularly from their own mother. These mothers recalled mainly positive childhoods in which they experienced love and affection, support for their own needs, concern for their welfare, and opportunities to develop their own identity. Those who experienced positive childhoods wanted to be a good mother very much like their own mother had been and to follow in her footsteps in bringing up their children. Some mothers, however, felt their own mothers had been over-strict. This may be a result of concern held by many parents about the vulnerability of young girls with intellectual disabilities, particularly those who are out and about in the community, a concern well founded in the alarmingly high proportion of women with intellectual disabilities who are mistreated or abused, physically or sexually (Chenoweth, 1993). Overall, the childhood experiences remembered by all these mothers even when parents were regarded as too strict would fit comfortably within notions of good or good-enough parenting as understood by public authorities responsible for children's welfare and safety (Lindsey, 1994; Thorpe, 1994).

An almost equal number of mothers in this study, 12 in total, experienced low care as children. The mothers who had experienced low care as children typically had been abused or neglected, although rarely by strangers. Their perspectives were strongly influenced by their feelings of not being protected, either by their mother, by other members of their family, or by the care and protection services that were frequently involved in their lives. Not surprisingly, mothers in this group were highly motivated to provide a more nurturing, supportive, and protective environment for their own children than the one that they had experienced. These mothers' experiences suggest an absence of good-enough parenting, either from their own mothers or from other family members, leaving them vulnerable and in need of care and protection. Indeed, in nearly all instances, the public authority responsible for children's welfare and safety had been involved at least once and sometimes over many years with their families. This had not, however, from the mothers' point of view, provided them with the safety and security they desired and that, according to mandated legislative requirements, they deserved.

Parenting is a complex activity influenced by the beliefs, attitudes, and goals of parents and the immediate and more distant societal and cultural influences surrounding parents and their children. An important component of parents' attitudes and beliefs about parenting, particularly as first-time parents, derives from their own experiences as children. Our interviews with the mothers reported here represent a first step in understanding in a more systematic way childhood experiences as they pertain to present-day parenting. In this chapter we have brought together with our findings the limited material available to assist in explaining how the childhoods of parents with intellectual disabilities might indeed be influencing them as parents.

The high proportion of mothers who had experienced abuse as children is similar to that documented in other Australian studies of women with intellectual disabilities (e.g., Chenoweth, 1993) and in British studies (e.g., McCarthy, 1999; McGaw et al., 2007). Understanding how this experience influences mothers in appropriately preparing and protecting their daughters needs to be determined urgently. The mothers in our study typically had young, preschool-age children. How mothers with intellectual disabilities of older children and adolescents can be assisted to ensure their daughters are safe, particularly from family members and those close to the family, needs to be investigated given that most of the abuse reported by these mothers occurred when they themselves were in middle childhood.

## Conclusion

There is good evidence in the general parenting literature that parent, child, family environment, and contextual characteristics such as social support and socioeconomic status influence parenting, child well-being, and intervention outcomes (Belsky et al., 2006). Up until now, there has been less emphasis in the literature on parents and parenting with intellectual disabilities on family environment and contextual characteristics which may influence parenting practices. This study has begun the exploration of one of the historic and familial factors relevant to parenting practices and child maltreatment. The findings demonstrate that understanding the mothers' retrospective accounts of their childhood can uncover parenting practices in their families of origin. We suggest that these may offer a protective effect on their current parenting practices.

## Principles for Practice

There are two primary principles for practice we want to draw from our study.

The first principle for practice to be derived from our findings is the critical importance of understanding parenting by people with intellectual disabilities within a family, social, and community context. Too often, the parenting practices of people with intellectual disability have been viewed through a "disability lens" in which whatever is seen is "blamed" on or explained by the parent's intellectual disability. One important aspect of parenting is the beliefs, values, and attitudes that each parent brings to the child-raising endeavor. Practitioners need to explore, with each parent, their perspective on parenting and their memories of their own parented experience when they were a child. The PBI used in this study complemented by the seven semi-structured interview questions provides one way of seeking empirical data to understand each parent's childhood background.

The second principle for practice is to remain open to the possibility of multiple influences on parents' current parenting practices. As Belsky and many others have described, parenting is a complex, multi-dimensional activity influenced by multiple intra- and inter-personal factors, as well as societal, community, and cultural environments (Belsky, 1984). The relationship is not straightforward between one's own experiences of being parented and one's behavior, attitudes, and beliefs as a parent. It is too simplistic to assume that those parented well as children will automatically parent well themselves. Similarly, it is false to assume that those who experienced very poor parenting will, by default, become poor parents. Research in the area of resilience demonstrates a complex relationship between adversity, risk exposure, and protective factors (Luthar, 2003). An urgent question for researchers is to understand the relationship between adversity and protective factors in childhood for young people with intellectual disabilities so that we can better understand how the experiences of being parented that they bring to parenting affect their parenting practices.

For now, practitioners need to keep an open mind, taking into account the previous and current circumstances of the lives of parents with intellectual disabilities, understanding each parent as an individual within her own family origin and her current family situation, along with the community and societal context, to be able to help each parent, as one of the mothers in this study said, "to be the best parent I can possibly be."

# References

Belsky, J. (1984). The determinants of parenting: A process model. *Child Development*, 55(1), 83–96.

Belsky, J., Melhuish, E., Barnes, J., Leyland, A. H., Romaniuk, H., & the NESS Research Team. (2006). Effects of Sure Start local programs on children and families: Early findings from a quasi-experimental, cross-sectional study. *British Medical Journal*, 332(7556), 1476–1578.

Bernstein, D. P., & Fink, L. (1998). *Childhood Trauma Questionnaire*. San Antonio, TX: Psychological Corporation.

Booth, T., & Booth, W. (1995). Unto us a child is born: The trials and rewards of parenthood for people with learning difficulties. *Australia and New Zealand Journal of Developmental Disabilities*, 20(1), 25–39.

Brown, H. (1996). Ordinary women: Issues for women with learning disabilities. *British Journal of Learning Disabilities*, 24(2), 47–51.

Chenoweth, L. (1993). Invisible acts: Violence against women with disabilities. *Australian Disability Review, 2*, 22–28.

Cleaver, H., & Nicholson, D. (2007). *Parental learning disability and children's needs. Family experiences and effective practice.* London: Jessica Kingsley.

Dowdney, L., Skuse, D., Rutter, M., Quinton, D., & Mrazek, D. (1985). The nature and qualities of parenting provided by women raised in institutions. *Journal of Child Psychology and Psychiatry, 26*(4), 599–625.

Ehlers-Flint, M. L. (2002). Parenting perceptions and social supports of mothers with cognitive disabilities. *Sexuality and Disability, 20*(1), 29–51.

Gath, A. (1988). Mentally handicapped people as parents: Is mental retardation a bar to parenting? *Journal of Child Psychology and Psychiatry, 29*(6), 739–744.

Goodnow, J., & Collins, W. (1990). *Development according to parents: The nature, sources and consequences of parents' ideas.* London: Erlbaum.

Greene, B. F., Norman, K. R., Searle, M. S., Daniels, M., & Lubeck, R. C. (1995). Child abuse and neglect by parents with disabilities: A tale of two families. *Journal of Applied Behavior Analysis, 28*(4), 417–434.

Gustavsson, A. (1997). Integration, stigma and autonomy: Bright and dark sides of the subculture of integration. In A. Gustavsson & E. Zakrzewska-Manterys (Eds.), *Social definitions of disability* (pp. 190–208). Warsaw: Wydawnictwo "Zak."

Harkness, S., & Super, C. (1996). *Parents' cultural belief systems: Their origins, expressions, and consequences.* New York: Guilford.

Lindsey, D. (1994). *The welfare of children.* New York: Oxford University Press.

Llewellyn, G. (1990). Parents with an intellectual disability: Perspectives from the literature. *Australia and New Zealand Journal of Developmental Disabilities, 16*(4), 369–380.

Llewellyn, G. (1997). Parents with intellectual disability learning to parent: The role of informal learning and experience. *International Journal of Disability, Development and Education, 44*(3), 243–261.

Luthar, S. S. (Ed.). (2003). *Resilience and vulnerability: Adaptation in the context of childhood adversity.* New York: Cambridge University Press.

Madsen, M. K. (1979). Parenting classes for the mentally retarded. *Mental Retardation, 17*(4), 195–196.

Mattinson, J. (1970). *Marriage and mental handicap.* London: Duckworth.

Mayes, R., Llewellyn, G., & McConnell, D. (2006). Misconception: The experience of pregnancy for women with intellectual disabilities. *Scandinavian Journal of Disability Research, 8*(2&3), 120–131.

McCarthy, M. (1999). *Sexuality and women with learning disabilities.* London: Jessica Kingsley.

McConnell, D., & Llewellyn, G. (2002). Stereotypes, parents with intellectual disability and child protection. *Journal of Social Welfare and Family Law, 24*(3), 1–21.

McConnell, D., & Llewellyn, G. (2005). Social inequality, "the deviant parent" and child protection practice. *Australian Journal of Social Issues, 40*(4), 553–566.

McConnell, D., Mayes, R., & Llewellyn, G. (2008a). Women with intellectual disability at risk of adverse pregnancy and birth outcomes. *Journal of Intellectual Disability Research, 52*(6), 529–535.

McConnell, D., Mayes, R., & Llewellyn, G. (2008b). Pre-partum distress in women with intellectual disabilities. *Journal of Intellectual and Developmental Disability, 33*(2), 177–183.

McGaw, S., Shaw, T., & Beckley, K. (2007). Prevalence of psychopathology across a service population of parents with intellectual disabilities and their children. *Journal of Policy and Practice in Intellectual Disabilities*, *4*(1), 11–22.

Morton, M. (2000). Unhappy families: Violence in the lives of girls and women. In R. Traustadóttir & K. Johnson (Eds.), *Women with intellectual disabilities: Finding a place in the world* (pp. 63–68). London: Jessica Kingsley.

Parker, G. (1990). The Parental Bonding Instrument: A decade of research. *Social Psychiatry and Psychiatric Epidemiology*, *25*(6), 281–282.

Parker, G., Tupling, H., & Brown, L. B. (1979). A parental bonding instrument. *British Journal of Medical Psychology*, *52*(1), 1–10.

Quinton, D., Rutter, M., & Liddle, C. (1984). Institutional rearing, parenting difficulties, and marital support. *Psychological Medicine*, *14*(1), 107–124.

Reinders, H. S. (2008). Persons with disabilities as parents: What is the problem? *Journal of Applied Research in Intellectual Disabilities*, *21*(4), 308–314.

Sigurjónsdóttir, H. B., & Traustadóttir, R. (2000). Motherhood, family and community life. In R. Traustadóttir & K. Johnson (Eds.), *Women with intellectual disabilities: Finding a place in the world* (pp. 253–270). London: Jessica Kingsley.

Thorpe, D. (1994). *Evaluating child protection*. Buckingham: Open University Press.

Traustadóttir, R., & Johnson, K. (Eds.). (2000). *Women with intellectual disabilities: Finding a place in the world*. London: Jessica Kingsley.

Traustadóttir, R., & Sigurjónsdóttir, H. B. (2008). The "mother" behind the mother: Three generations of mothers with intellectual disabilities and their support networks. *Journal of Applied Research in Intellectual Disability*, *21*(4), 331–340.

Tucker, M. B., & Johnson, O. (1989). Competence promoting versus competence inhibiting social support for mentally retarded mothers. *Human Organization*, *48*(2), 95–107.

Tymchuk, A. J. (1993). Symptoms of psychopathology in mothers with mental handicap. *Mental Handicap Research*, *6*(1), 19–35.

Tymchuk, A. J. (1994). Depression symptomatology in mothers with mild intellectual disability: An exploratory study. *Australia and New Zealand Journal of Developmental Disabilities*, *19*(2), 111–119.

Willems, D. L., de Vries, J.-N., Isarin, J., & Reinders, J. S. (2007). Parenting by persons with intellectual disability: An explorative study in the Netherlands. *Journal of Intellectual Disability Research*, *51*(7), 537–544.

# 3

# Family Within a Family

## Hanna Björg Sigurjónsdóttir and Rannveig Traustadóttir

## Introduction

The birth of a baby is a happy event, not just for the parents but also for other members of the extended family, and especially for the grandparents and siblings. When a new baby is born, family and friends come to visit bringing gifts and to celebrate the newest family member. A new child also means the roles within the family change; daughters and sons become mothers and fathers, brothers and sisters become aunts and uncles, mothers and fathers become grandparents, and if the new parents already have children, they become big brothers and big sisters. New roles bring new responsibilities, which different family members take on with varying degree of success. Extended families come together around a new baby, who often brings families closer together, especially mothers and daughters.

We are acutely aware of the significance of a new baby in families. Both of us have recently become grandmothers, Hanna Björg for the first time, and Rannveig has had her third granddaughter. Like other grandparents, both of us love our little grandchildren. We want to be involved in their lives, spend time with them, and provide the support we can for our daughters and grandchildren. Family relations, however, are complex and although we want to be involved in the lives of our daughters, we also want to respect their ways of raising their children and their independence and privacy. New parents can be sensitive to interference from others, and grandmothers are not always sure how much assistance is enough and when to let the new parents figure things out by themselves.

*Parents with Intellectual Disabilities: Past, Present and Futures*   Edited by Gwynnyth Llewellyn, Rannveig Traustadóttir, David McConnell, and Hanna Björg Sigurjónsdóttir   © 2010 John Wiley & Sons, Ltd

Most countries have established an extensive network of programs to support the successful upbringing of children and to ensure their health and safety. Among these are prenatal care, health care for newborn babies, preschools, schools, summer camps, music schools for children, sports programs, and other leisure activities. Although the degree to which families and communities support the upbringing of children varies, parents are clearly not the only caretakers. Instead, children are raised within the network of extended family and with assistance from institutions and initiatives society has established to ensure the development and well-being of children and youth.

Despite the common knowledge described above, when it comes to parents with intellectual disabilities, there is a tendency to ignore the larger context and regard the parents as isolated individuals who have the sole responsibility of raising their children. The stereotypical and pathological view of people with intellectual disabilities as incompetent has resulted in 40–60% of children being removed from their care (Booth & Booth, 1994; McConnell, Llewellyn, & Ferronato, 2002). In fact, parents with intellectual disabilities are the group of parents at most risk of losing custody of their children and the discriminatory practices they often encounter in child protection proceedings have been documented extensively (e.g., McConnell & Llewellyn, 2000). We believe that one of the main reasons for this high level of child removal is the misconception that parents with intellectual disabilities are isolated individuals who raise their children without the same assistance as other parents. Professionals seem to disregard their extended family and community network and instead appear to operate on the assumption that the welfare of the children is solely dependent on the parents' abilities and skills.

In this chapter we want to draw attention to the fact that, just like in other families, children of parents with intellectual disabilities are raised within their extended families and with the assistance of various institutions and programs in their home communities. We begin with a review of some of the research that has focused on parenting with intellectual disabilities and highlight what we can learn from this literature about parenting in context. This is followed by a description of our own research with parents with intellectual disabilities and their children. From this research we have selected the stories of three families. We have written the stories in collaboration with the families with the aim to provide an insider view of the experiences of parents with intellectual disabilities in raising children within an extended family network.

## Parenting in Context – Learning from the Research Literature

The research literature on parents with intellectual disabilities has been steadily growing over the past decades. Early on, research in this area focused mostly on the perceived inadequacy of parents, the risk to their children, and the effects of parent education and training programs (Feldman, 1994; Tymchuk & Andron, 1992). More recently the attention has been shifted to the support provided to parents with intellectual disabilities by family members, neighbors, friends, and formal support services. Examples of this research can be found in many countries, such as Booth and Booth's (1994, 1998) research projects in Britain which focused on families headed by parents with intellectual disabilities and their adult children. In Australia, Llewellyn, McConnell, and colleagues have carried out various studies with large numbers of families examining their support networks (Llewellyn, 1995, 1997; Llewellyn & McConnell, 2002; Llewellyn, McConnell, Cant, & Westbrook, 1999; Mayes, Llewellyn, & Mc-Connell, 2008). Our own research in Iceland has examined the social support networks of families headed by parents with intellectual disabilities and the role of extended family members and formal services in the upbringing of children (Sigurjónsdóttir, 2005; Sigurjónsdóttir & Traustadóttir, 2001; Traustadóttir & Sigurjónsdóttir, 2008). These and numerous other studies demonstrate that parents with intellectual disabilities, like all other parents, need assistance and services to ensure the health, well-being, and development of their children. Furthermore, substantial research and clinical data have documented that, with appropriate supports, parents with intellectual disabilities can successfully raise their children (see, e.g., Ehlers-Flint, 2002; Espe-Sherwindt & Kerlin, 1990; Guinea, 2001; McGaw & Sturmey, 1994; Stenfert-Kroese, Hussein, Clifford, & Ahmed, 2002; Tarleton, Ward, & Howarth, 2006; Tucker & Johnson, 1989; Tymchuk, 1992).

Parents with intellectual disabilities have an impairment that can bring obstacles to their parenting. This means that, for this group of parents, good and appropriate support from family and community programs is extremely important. However, it is also important to point out that research indicates that when parents with intellectual disabilities encounter difficulties in raising their children, it is not necessarily the impairment that is the primary reason. Instead, studies from different parts of the world indicate that stress factors that are not related to the intellectual disability seem to create more difficulties (Booth & Booth, 1998; Pixa-Kettner, 1999; Taylor, 1995, 2000). Research also suggests that intelligence is not a good indicator of parental success. Many other issues are equally important, such as poverty, unemployment, and history of abuse (Hoffman & Mandeville, 1998; Tymchuk & Andron, 1990).

The research literature demonstrates that parents with intellectual disabilities are best supported by members of their extended family (Booth & Booth, 1993; Ehlers-Flint, 2002; Guinea, 2001; Llewellyn & McConnell, 2002; Llewellyn et al., 1999; McGaw, 1998; Traustadóttir & Sigurjónsdóttir, 2008). Mothers with intellectual disabilities feel closest to and most comfortable receiving assistance from family members who are their usual and primary source of support. When needing advice or help, mothers prefer seeking assistance from their family members rather than from formal support services (Llewellyn & McConnell, 2002). Help from family members is particularly welcomed when it increases the parents' confidence in their parenting role and is consistent with the parents' own values and ideas (Llewellyn, 1995). It is also particularly important for mothers of newborn babies that the practical assistance they receive acknowledges and affirms their central role as the mother of the baby (Mayes et al., 2008). Some researchers have found that support provided by extended family members is not always regarded as helpful by parents, who sometimes feel it is more of a constraint than a resource (Llewellyn et al., 1999; Tucker & Johnson, 1989).

Although family members are frequently the most important source of support for parents with intellectual disabilities, it is important to acknowledge that some parents with intellectual disabilities have little or no contact with extended family. Studies have found that the amount of support from family varies and some parents may not receive any help from their families (Andron & Tymchuk, 1987; Llewellyn, 1995; Llewellyn & McConnell, 2002; Zetlin, Weisner, & Gallimore, 1985).

We can sum up this literature by saying that it demonstrates how important it is to consider parenting in context rather than regarding parents as isolated individuals. Parents with intellectual disabilities, like other parents, raise their children within the network of their extended family and rely on support services, school programs, health services, and other community programs aimed at supporting families with young children. In their families, like in other families, parenting is a shared responsibility and many people take part in raising the children. Stereotypical assumptions about the incompetence of people with intellectual disabilities as parents are not grounded in the research literature, which, on the contrary, shows that when provided with appropriate support from family and community, parents with intellectual disabilities can successfully raise their children.

## Research with Parents

Our knowledge of the lives of parents with intellectual disabilities and their children derives from long-term involvement with them through research and advocacy. Since 1994 we have carried out various research projects with parents with intellectual disabilities and their children. Our methods have been qualitative (Taylor & Bogdan, 1998), involving spending time with families during participant observations and carrying out individual and focus group interviews with parents, their adult children, extended family members, and professionals (Emerson, Fretz, & Shaw, 1995; Kvale, 1996). Many of these projects have been collaborative and called for the active participation of parents themselves (Walmsley & Johnson, 2004). Our relationship with the parents has been long term and many of those we met during our first studies in the 1990s are still involved in our projects. The same is true for many of the parents we have met since then. The parents' involvement has developed and changed and some of them now act as consultants and collaborators rather than informants.

In the autumn of 2002 some of the parents established a parent group with Hanna Björg's help. Since then, she and they have met every other week over the winter months. The group is a self-advocacy group for parents where they share information and support each other in the parenting role. The group also advocates for the rights of people with intellectual disabilities to have children and establish families and educates others about parenting with intellectual disabilities. The education is particularly directed toward professionals and service providers.

Due to this long-term involvement, we have taken part in many events in the lives of the parents and their families. We have been invited to children's and adults' birthdays, to weddings, christenings, confirmations, and funerals, and we have witnessed children being born, entering preschool and school, and children being removed from their parents' care. Families have moved, parents have divorced – and found new partners. Through the years we have also observed changes in extended family networks and relations, and in the services and supports provided by the service system.

To provide an in-depth view of parents with intellectual disabilities, their children, and their family context, we present stories of three families whom we have known since our first studies in the 1990s. These families have given us permission to tell their stories and they have collaborated in putting them together. Their names have been changed to protect their privacy.

## Parenting in Context – Three Stories of a Family within a Family

Iceland is a small country with a population of about 300,000 people. Family ties are strong and most people live close to their extended families. Until the middle of the 20th century it was common for three generations to live together, and, in most families, the extended family still takes an active part in supporting its children and grandchildren. The stories of the three families headed by parents with intellectual disabilities presented below reflect that, although these families may need extra support to raise their children, they have many things in common with other young people in Iceland who are becoming parents and starting families with the support of their extended families.

### Birna

We first met Birna Njálsdóttir in 1996. She was in her late 20s, a single mother of three children who lived in her parents' household with her children. When she was in her early 20s, Birna met the father of two of her children and they lived together for five years in a flat they purchased with the assistance of a social housing scheme. Birna was a full-time homemaker and her partner worked outside the home. This was before she had her children, and although she enjoyed living independently with her partner and running her own home, she was concerned about his abusive drinking and the violence against her that frequently occurred when he was drunk. When she was pregnant with her first child she left her partner and moved back into her parents' home where she raised her daughter with the support of her parents. The father of her child showed little interest in being involved and was mostly absent. Two years later, as the result of a casual relationship, Birna had a second child. Later Birna reestablished the relationship with her former partner, the father of her first child, and became pregnant. The relationship did not last long, mostly because of Birna's fear of abuse.

Birna lived with her three children in her parents' household for a decade. Her existence revolved around the children, who were the most precious things in her life. The fathers have not been involved in the children's lives and have provided no support in raising them. It is Birna's extended family, and primarily her mother, who have assisted her in raising her children. Both Birna and her mother were full-time homemakers and shared the work around the house. Birna's mother also took an active part in raising the children.

Birna and her mother have refused to accept support from the service system. The reason is a series of negative experiences with professionals and services. One of these incidents was related to the State Diagnostic Center to which one of Birna's daughters was referred. The professionals at the Diagnostic Center concluded that the little girl was "slightly behind in her development" and needed extra assistance in some areas. The Center assigned a social worker to Birna's case to assist her with filling out forms and other practical things. Birna liked the social worker and trusted her completely. She was therefore shocked when she received a letter from the child protection services signed by a child protection officer who turned out to be Birna's social worker. Birna and her family felt betrayed by the social worker. This incident led to other negative interactions with the service system, which increased the family's fear of the system that they regard as unreliable, unpredictable, and hostile. The system had the power to remove the children, which Birna and her family feared above all else, so they decided it would be best to stay clear of the system and out of view as much as possible.

Birna also found it difficult to interact with the staff at her oldest daughter's preschool, whom she feels were prejudiced against her. At the outset she was on good terms with them and felt like they treated her and her daughter well. Birna was open and honest with the preschool staff and told them she had attended a special school as a child. After the preschool staff learned about this they started treating Birna differently and in a negative way. Birna and her mother, who often picked the little girl up from preschool and attended meetings with Birna, both felt humiliated and talked down to by the staff. As a result they stopped sending the little girl to this preschool.

The negative interactions between Birna and her family on the one hand and the service system on the other led to a deep distrust of professionals. Birna lived in constant fear that she might lose her children. She felt threatened by a system that did not trust her or her mother to take care of the children. As a result Birna did not dare to live on her own and she did not want to accept any services. She was defensive and felt she had little control of her own life. She seldom left the house because she was scared that "something might happen at home while I'm away." Prior to Birna's conflict with service professionals she occasionally went out on weekends. After the conflicts started, she stopped going out and said she did not want to give the professionals any reason whatsoever to remove her children.

Fear of the system and service professionals brought Birna and her extended family closer together. They have had to rely on each other and were determined not to have anything to do with the services. For many years Birna was pleased with this arrangement and grateful to be able to live in her parents' home. She is close to her mother and felt welcomed and protected living with her parents. Although she was content and felt safe, she wished she could live more independently with her children.

As time went by Birna's desire to establish herself as an independent adult grew stronger. She wanted to live on her own, keep her own home, set her own rules, buy her own groceries, and be independent from her parents. But she was too afraid of the service system to live on her own. She feared that if she moved away from her parents' home she would lose the custody of her children. A couple of years ago she met a good man and fell in love with him. The two of them rented an apartment in the same neighborhood where Birna's parents live. Birna feels that this new relationship provides her with similar protection to that she enjoyed in her parents' home. Birna is still close to her parents, who continue to provide her and her children with assistance and support but in different ways than before.

## Fjóla and Ingvar

At the time Fjóla and Ingvar realized they were expecting a baby they were both abusing alcohol and were having financial difficulties. When their extended families learned about the pregnancy they became worried about the welfare of the baby and about Fjóla and Ingvar's abilities to raise a child. It was Ingvar's mother who contacted social services, informed them about the young couple's situation and lifestyle, and asked social services to provide the support and services Fjóla and Ingvar needed in order to be able to take on the role of parents.

Fjóla and Ingvar were in their 20s; they did not take life too seriously and loved to hang out, drink, and have fun. However, they did express a strong desire to keep their baby. Both the social worker and members of their extended families made it clear to the couple that in order to keep custody of the baby, they would have to stop drinking, settle down, strictly follow the social worker's advice, and accept the support they were offered. Fjóla and Ingvar did not like this interference at all but decided to comply as they believed it was their only hope of keeping their child.

One week before the baby was born Fjóla and Ingvar moved into a training flat where they received support and training in childcare for six months. During this time their extended families kept in frequent contact and visited them and their baby son. At the end of the six-month period Fjóla and Ingvar moved with their son into their own home, an apartment provided through social services. When they moved, their social worker organized support in collaboration with Fjóla, Ingvar, and their families. Everyone agreed that it would be best if the assistance came from family members. However, the social worker believed that the help the young couple needed was so extensive that it was above and beyond what was reasonable to expect the extended family to take on. Thus, she suggested that Ingvar's mother and sister be hired by the social service office as support persons to provide Fjóla and Ingvar with intensive in-home support and assistance with various practical matters.

When Fjóla and Ingvar moved into their new home with their 6-month-old son, the support arrangements were in place. Ingvar's mother and sister took turns in assisting them. They visited the family daily, helped with childcare, and provided practical help with the finances so that Fjóla and Ingvar could gradually pay off the debts they had accumulated during their drinking days. Ingvar's sister or his mother also went with them every week to do grocery shopping in low-budget supermarkets. In addition to this support from extended family members, the social worker organized what she called "neighbor support." A woman was hired to live in the apartment building where Fjóla and Ingvar lived. She did not receive a salary. Her compensation was to live rent-free in her apartment on the floor below Fjóla and Ingvar. Her role was to be there for the family as a good neighbor, assist them if and when needed, and to keep an eye on them and inform social services if anything "went wrong," as it was phrased.

Fjóla and Ingvar were pleased with this arrangement. They liked the fact that their neighbor was there for them to call on if needed, but that she never interfered. They were also pleased that their extended family was supporting them. Although sometimes tired of having people around, Fjóla says it was "better than having strangers." There was no one they trusted better than their family members to take care of their son, and Fjóla said "it was good for the boy to get to know his family."

Five years after they had their first child, Fjóla and Ingvar had a second son. They still had the same social worker and the same neighbor support, and Ingvar's family assisted them when needed just like before. By the time their younger son started in preschool at the age of two years, the family moved to another neighborhood.

In 2009, the brothers were 9 and 14 years old. Fjóla and Ingvar keep in close contact with their extended families and still accompany Ingvar's sister every week to the grocery store.

Fjóla and Ingvar are very proud of their two sons and want them to have a good upbringing. They no longer need the intensive support they received when their sons were young, but they still have the same social worker who organized the supports that made it possible for them to keep and raise their two sons. Today their relationship with their extended families is primarily characterized by companionship and mutual support, rather than their being solely on the receiving end. Fjóla and Ingvar sometimes ask for practical help or advice, but they also support their parents who are becoming elderly. They also babysit the children of Ingvar's sister, who has children of a similar age as Fjóla and Ingvar's sons, and the children often sleep over in each other's homes on weekends.

When Fjóla and Ingvar first came into contact with the social welfare services due to Fjóla's first pregnancy, many people were pessimistic about the prospect of their being able to get their act together and raise a child. They had multiple problems and a lifestyle incompatible with parenting a child. With the help of extended family and an understanding and supportive social worker, they managed to turn their lives around and become successful parents of two beautiful boys. Fjóla and Ingvar's strong desire to keep their first baby was their incentive to change their lives and gave them the strength to learn and adapt as their sons have developed.

## Halldóra

Halldóra Gunnarsdóttir and Kristján Jónsson were in their late 20s when we first met them in 1998. At that time they had a four-year-old son, Gunnar. Kristján worked in a factory and Halldóra stayed at home taking care of their son.

When she told her mother about the pregnancy, her mother wanted Halldóra to have an abortion. Halldóra has epilepsy and some complicated health issues. Her mother was concerned about possible negative effects of the pregnancy on Halldóra's health. She also worried that Halldóra would not be able to take care of a child. Although this had not been a planned pregnancy, Halldóra refused to have an abortion. She wanted to have her baby. When it became clear that Halldóra was determined to have her child, her mother contacted the local disability services office, informed them Halldóra was expecting a baby, and asked for all the assistance that was rightfully hers. The worker, who had never supported parents with intellectual disabilities, contacted the antenatal services and the local social services. Together these agencies, in cooperation with Halldóra's mother, created a network of support to enable Halldóra and Kristján to take care of the baby. When Halldóra became pregnant she and Kristján lived in a flat owned by disability services, which also provided them with in-home support twice a month. When Gunnar was one year old Halldóra and her parents bought a house with an attached apartment where Halldóra, Kristján, and Gunnar lived. This meant that Halldóra was close to her mother, who was her main source of support and assisted her in taking care of Gunnar.

In addition to receiving assistance from her mother, Halldóra had support workers from disability services, and when Gunnar was a baby she was visited every day by a community nurse who advised Halldóra about nutrition and how to take care of the baby. Halldóra was pleased with the support she and her family received. She liked most of her support workers and described some of them as friends. In particular she liked the fact that her aunt was one of the workers. It made Halldóra feel more secure to have someone who was close to her, who understood her, and whom she could trust. The support was most intensive at the beginning when Gunnar was a baby, but it was gradually reduced. By the time Gunnar started in preschool at the age of three, the formal support to take care of him was terminated. Disability services believed that Halldóra was quite capable of raising her son with assistance from her mother and other family members. From then on Halldóra only received in-home support from disability services.

When Gunnar was four years old, Halldóra and Kristján divorced. Kristján moved out and Halldóra and her son continued living in the apartment in her parents' house. Halldóra liked her living arrangements, which allowed her to live independently and still be close to her parents. The closeness, however, had both positive and negative sides. The positive and most important thing according to Halldóra was the security of being close to her mother. Although she had received extensive, well-coordinated, and successful support from many service agencies, Halldóra had a deep-seated fear of professionals and the system. Despite the good services and positive attitudes of the professionals she and her family had encountered, Halldóra was convinced that her mother "ensures that Gunnar will not be taken away from me," as she phrased it.

The downside of being so close to her parents was that Halldóra felt her mother interfered too much in Gunnar's upbringing and bossed her around with regard to personal affairs like finances. Things were made even worse when Halldóra's mother was hired by social services to provide Halldóra with personal support. Halldóra said it was very hurtful for her to watch her mother fill out the form about what they had been doing and how many hours they had spent together.

As Gunnar grew older it became increasingly difficult for Halldóra to live so close to her parents. She said: "It became somehow impossible for me to separate my home from theirs." Her feelings became more and more ambivalent and she started to regard her mother as intrusive, overprotective, and overpowering.

What Halldóra initially saw as help became interference with finances, child upbringing, and personal affairs far beyond what she wished for. In an attempt to keep her privacy, Halldóra put a sign on the door between the two apartments saying: "Please Knock Before Entering!" Her father respected this but her mother never did. This irritated Halldóra, who wanted nothing more than to live independently on her own, but she worried that moving away from her parents might result in her losing her son. Halldóra clearly remembers the day when she made the decision to move out:

> I was making us ready and had put his best clothes on the bed. My mom walked into the room and said "these pants match the other pullover better" and then Gunnar asked me "should I do as she says or as you say?" That was it. The next day I went to the social services office and asked them for help so we could live independently.

At the social services office Halldóra met two of her former support workers and asked for their help. They offered to organize a meeting with Halldóra, her parents, and people from social services. Initially Halldóra felt that she was not taken seriously. She said the meeting was difficult, her mother did not want her to move out, and did not feel she had in any way been intrusive with regard to Halldóra and her son. The professionals who attended the meeting knew Halldóra's mother and hesitated in going against her will. When Halldóra did not give in and insisted she wanted to move, the others decided to respect her wish. As it turned out, it was Halldóra's mother who helped her to find the apartment that Halldóra bought and moved into.

At this time, in June 2009, Halldóra and her son, who was now 14 years old, had lived in their new flat for four years. During these years Halldóra often felt the need to fight both her mother, "who still knows best," and the professionals who want to make decisions on her behalf about what type of support she should get. Halldóra dislikes it very much when others try to control her and she therefore avoids seeking help. Although she cares deeply for her parents, whom she meets frequently, she avoids asking them for any kind of assistance. When she needs some advice or someone to talk to she turns to the aunt who used to support her when Gunnar was younger. The aunt is the person Halldóra trusts most because she never tries to control her. At this point in her life it is most important for Halldóra to lead an independent family life with her son.

## Conclusion

Raising children involves a concerted effort by parents, extended family members, and community services and programs where the family usually plays the most important part. In this chapter we have considered the importance of the family network for parents with intellectual disabilities and their children. The stories of the three families reflect that parents with intellectual disabilities believe that to retain custody of their children, they consider it essential to have support and protection from extended family members. They believe that without such help it would be difficult, even impossible, for them to keep their children. This led the parents to stay very close to their extended families and they depended on their assistance. At the same time, it was important for the mothers with intellectual disabilities to be acknowledged as the main caregiver and a central person in their child's life. The three stories also draw attention to the gendered aspects of family life. In the three families, family life is profoundly gendered. The fathers, if present, work outside the home and the women, most often mothers and grandmothers, continue to carry the major responsibility for childcare and housework.

In writing this chapter we have drawn on our long-term involvement with parents with intellectual disabilities and their families. We also drew on our own experiences of family life. In reflecting on our own families, we recognize many of the same joys and dilemmas of family life, and our status as new grandmothers has confirmed for us the importance of extended family networks.


## Principles for Practice

There are some important lessons we can draw from this chapter.

- The first and most important lesson is to understand families headed by parents with intellectual disabilities in the context of their extended family and the community where they live.
- When providing support to parents with intellectual disabilities and their children, it is essential that these services build on and strengthen the support given by the extended family.
- Supports and services for parents with intellectual disabilities and their children should be planned and carried out in collaboration with the parents and their extended families.
- Service providers and professionals need to acknowledge and respect the mothers as the main carers in their child's life.
- In supporting parents, it is important to respect their need to lead independent lives and assist them to establish and run their own homes.
- It is important to provide parents with intellectual disabilities with the supports that take their particular situation into consideration. At the same time we encourage people to acknowledge the similarities of families headed by parents with intellectual disabilities and other families.

# References

Andron, L., & Tymchuk, A. (1987). Parents who are mentally retarded. In A. Craft (Ed.), *Mental handicap and sexuality: Issues and perspectives* (pp. 238–262). Tunbridge Wells: D. J. Costello.

Booth, T., & Booth, W. (1993). Parenting with learning difficulties: Lessons for practitioners. *British Journal of Social Work, 23*(5), 459–480.

Booth, T., & Booth, W. (1994). *Parenting under pressure: Mothers and fathers with learning difficulties.* Buckingham: Open University Press.

Booth, T., & Booth, W. (1998). *Growing up with parents who have learning difficulties.* London: Routledge.

Ehlers-Flint, M. (2002). Parenting perceptions and social supports of mothers with cognitive disabilities. *Sexuality and Disability, 20*(1), 29–51.

Emerson, R. M., Fretz, R. I., & Shaw, L. L. (1995). *Writing ethnographic fieldnotes.* Chicago: University of Chicago Press.

Espe-Sherwindt, M., & Kerlin, S. (1990). Early intervention with parents with mental retardation: Do we empower or impair? *Infants and Young Children, 2*(4), 21–28.

Feldman, M. A. (1994). Parenting education for parents with intellectual disabilities: A review of outcome studies. *Research in Developmental Disabilities, 15*(4), 299–332.

Guinea, S. M. (2001). Parents with a learning disability and their view on support received: A preliminary study. *Journal of Intellectual Disabilities, 5*(1), 43–56.

Hoffman, C., & Mandeville, H. (1998). Welfare reform and parents with disabilities. *Impact, 11*(1), 20–21.

Kvale, S. (1996). *InterViews: An introduction to qualitative research interviewing.* London: Sage.

Llewellyn, G. (1995). Relationships and social support: Views of parents with mental retardation/intellectual disability. *Mental Retardation, 33*(6), 349–363.

Llewellyn, G. (1997). Parents with intellectual disabilities learning to parent: The role of experience and informal learning. *International Journal of Disability, Development and Education, 44* (3), 243–261.

Llewellyn, G., & McConnell, D. (2002). Mothers with learning difficulties and their support networks. *Journal of Intellectual Disability Research, 46*(1), 17–34.

Llewellyn, G., McConnell, D., Cant, R., & Westbrook, M. (1999). Support network of mothers with intellectual disability: An exploratory study. *Journal of Intellectual and Developmental Disability, 24*(1), 7–26.

Mayes, R., Llewellyn, G., & McConnell, D. (2008). Active negotiation: Mothers with intellectual disabilities creating their social support networks. *Journal of Applied Research in Intellectual Disabilities, 21*(4), 341–350.

McConnell, D., & Llewellyn, G. (2000). Disability and discrimination in statutory child protection proceedings. *Disability and Society, 15*(6), 883–895.

McConnell, D., Llewellyn, G., & Ferronato, L. (2002). Disability and decision making in Australian care proceedings. *International Journal of Law, Policy and the Family, 16*(2), 270–299.

McGaw, S. (1998). Working with parents who happen to have intellectual disabilities. In E. Emerson, C. Hatton, J. Bromley, & A. Caine (Eds.), *Clinical psychology and people with intellectual disabilities* (pp. 193–209). Chichester: Wiley & Sons.

McGaw, S., & Sturmey, P. (1994). Assessing parents with learning disabilities: The parental skills model. *Child Abuse Review*, 3(1), 36–51.

Pixa-Kettner, U. (1999). Follow-up study on parenting with intellectual disability in Germany. *Journal of Intellectual and Developmental Disability*, 24(1), 75–93.

Sigurjónsdóttir, H. B. (2005). *Family support services and parents with learning difficulties.* Unpublished doctoral dissertation, University of Sheffield, Sheffield.

Sigurjónsdóttir, H. B., & Traustadóttir, R. (2001). *Ósýnilegar fjölskyldur: Seinfærar/ þroskaheftar mæður og börn þeirra* [Invisible families: Mothers with intellectual limitations and their children]. Reykjavík: University of Iceland Press.

Stenfert-Kroese, S. B., Hussein, H., Clifford, C., & Ahmed, N. (2002). Social support networks and psychological well-being of mothers with intellectual disabilities. *Journal of Applied Research in Intellectual Disabilities*, 15(4), 324–340.

Tarleton, B., Ward, L., & Howarth, J. (2006). *Finding the right support? A review of issues and positive practice in supporting parents with learning difficulties and their children.* London: Baring Foundation.

Taylor, S. J. (1995). " Children's division is coming to take pictures": Family life and parenting in a family with disabilities. In S. J. Taylor, R. Bogdan, & Z. M. Lutfiyya (Eds.), *The variety of community experience: Qualitative studies of family and community life* (pp. 23–45). Baltimore: Paul H. Brookes.

Taylor, S. J. (2000). "You are not a retard, you're just wise": Disability, social identity, and family networks. *Journal of Contemporary Ethnography*, 29(1), 58–92.

Taylor, S., & Bogdan, R. (1998). *Introduction to qualitative research methods: A guidebook and resource.* New York: John Wiley & Sons.

Traustadóttir, R., & Sigurjónsdóttir, H. B. (2008). The "mother" behind the mother: Three generations of mothers with intellectual disabilities and their family support networks. *Journal of Applied Research in Intellectual Disability*, 21(4), 331–340.

Tucker, B., & Johnson, O. (1989). Competence promoting versus competence inhibiting social support for mentally retarded mothers. *Human Organization*, 48(2), 95–107.

Tymchuk, A. (1992). Predicting adequacy of parenting by people with mental retardation. *Child Abuse and Neglect*, 16(2), 165–178.

Tymchuk, A., & Andron, L. (1990). Mothers with mental retardation who do or do not abuse or neglect their children. *Child Abuse and Neglect*, 14(3), 313–323.

Tymchuk, A., & Andron, L. (1992). Project parenting: Child interactional training with mothers who are mentally handicapped. *Mental Handicap Research*, 5(1), 4–32.

Walmsley, J., & Johnson, K. (2004). *Inclusive research with people with learning disabilities: Past, present and futures.* London: Jessica Kingsley.

Zetlin, A., Weisner, T., & Gallimore, R. (1985). Diversity, shared functioning, and the role of benefactors: A study of parenting by retarded persons. In S. K. Thurman (Ed.), *Children of handicapped parents: Research and clinical perspectives* (pp. 69–95). New York: Academic Press.

# 4

# Children and Their Life Experiences

*Jytte Faureholm*

## Introduction

This chapter addresses the experiences of children of parents with intellectual disabilities. It is based on interview research with 23 children who were followed over a period of 10 years, beginning in 1994 when they were 8–12 years of age and ending in 2004 when they were young adults aged 18–22 years. This study was a part of the author's doctoral research (Faureholm, 2007).

Children who grow up with a mother or a father with intellectual disability have been neglected by researchers, even though, for more than 75 years, these children have been considered at risk, with limited opportunities to establish an independent and valued adult life. Contrary to this common view, the majority of the young people in this study have carved out an existence for themselves as independent, responsible, and competent citizens. Despite a childhood and youth characterized by exclusion, discrimination, and stigma due to their mother's impairment and their family's status in society, they manage quite well as young adults.

The study focused on the children's own descriptions and views of growing up and becoming young adults. The study asked the following questions:

- What is the relationship like between mother and child in families where the mother has intellectual disability?
- In what way does the mother's impairment influence the child's life outside the home, at school, during leisure activities, in the local community, and so on?
- Which resources do the children benefit from as they grow up?

*Parents with Intellectual Disabilities: Past, Present and Futures* Edited by Gwynnyth Llewellyn, Rannveig Traustadóttir, David McConnell, and Hanna Björg Sigurjónsdóttir © 2010 John Wiley & Sons, Ltd

## Research About Children of Parents with Intellectual Disabilities

At present, we have only limited knowledge about adult children raised by parents with intellectual disabilities (Booth & Booth, 1996, 1998; Dowdney & Skuse, 1993). Researchers at both national and international levels have shown little interest in children of parents with intellectual disabilities compared with children of other parents who have difficulties raising their children due to alcohol or drug abuse, or parents who are mentally ill (Perkins, Holburn, Deaux, Flory, & Vietze, 2002).

To date, some 30 studies have been published worldwide about children of mothers with intellectual disabilities. Most have concentrated on the zero to three year age group (Booth & Booth, 1996, 1998; Feldman & Walton-Allen, 1997). Only a few of these studies have attempted to document how these children develop emotionally and socially during childhood and youth, yet many conclude that the majority of the children will face serious problems. They are presumed to grow into less competent adults and it is assumed that they will need public support to mature properly. Most of the studies indicate that children are at risk of intellectual, academic, and behavioral problems. Boys may be affected more than girls, and children with average or above-average intelligence may demonstrate greater social and emotional maladjustment than children with below-average intelligence quotients (Feldman, 2002; Feldman & Walton-Allen, 1997; Gillberg, Geijer-Karlsson, & Rasmussen, 1983; McGaw & Newman, 2005; Rönström, 1983).

In contrast, the main conclusions of a smaller number of studies (Booth & Booth, 1998; Perkins et al., 2002) and the one reported in this chapter (Faureholm, 2007) represent a more optimistic perspective on the children in spite of the often rough and exclusionary reactions with which they have to contend during their childhood and adolescence. For example, using an interaction and relation-oriented model, Perkins et al. (2002) conducted a study of the self-esteem of normally functioning children of mothers with intellectual disabilities. 18 girls and 18 boys aged 9–17 answered questionnaires about the relationship with their mother. These authors found that the child's perception of stigma surrounding the mother and their attachment to their mother was mediated by the warmth of their mother's caregiving style. Positive self-esteem was characteristic of children of mothers with a warm caregiving style.

Unavoidably, children are affected by the fact that their mothers are diagnosed as having intellectual disability and have thus been accorded client status in many societies (Booth & Booth, 1998). Children growing up in a family with a mother (and often a father) with intellectual disability live with the reality that the conditions for their development and socialization inside and outside the family have in many ways been negatively influenced by their mother's impairment. Carol Rambo Ronai, the daughter of a mother with intellectual disability, describes her life situation in the following way: "There is no doubt that my mother's status as a person with mental retardation has been the context from which all the other aspects of my life have emerged" (Ronai, 1997, pp. 430–431).

Research with children of parents with intellectual disabilities does not usually regard the children as active subjects in the collection of the empirical data. The children's own voices, their opinions and experiences from everyday life, are rarely the focus, despite the widespread perspective that the child is an autonomic and competent person to be respected. Although the awareness of children's rights has grown and considering children separately from their family has entered the consciousness of legislators, professionals, parents, and the children themselves, children generally, and in particular children of parents with intellectual disabilities, are too often looked upon as passive participants in research and in family intervention (Andersson, 1998; Newman, 2003; Sandbæk, 2002).

## The Study

The Danish study presented below is an attempt to shed light on the growth and developmental conditions of children brought up by their parents with intellectual disabilities, from the beginning of school age until young adulthood. The investigation is based on the narratives of the children and young people themselves.

The aim of the interview study was to capture the child's perspective of everyday life based on the children's and later the young adults' own description and construction of their reality. By everyday life I refer to what actually took place in their regular daily routines, how they were cared for at home, homework, relationship with friends, and their leisure time – all the things that give life content and meaning (Andersson, 1998).

The study was planned as a longitudinal interview study. The 23 children (11 boys and 12 girls) who took part in the study were followed over a period of 10 years. The children, who came from 20 families, were interviewed twice. The first time was in 1994 when they were 8–12 years old, and then again 10 years later in 2004 by which time they were young adults. Midway through the study, information about the children and their families was also gathered from the families' caseworkers. Of the 23 children, seven (two boys and five girls) were considered to have mild intellectual disability. At the second interview 20 participants (8 men and 11 women), now young adults (18–22 years old), were available to be interviewed.

The interviews with the young adults often developed into conversations where the dialogue and their reflections focused on their upbringing, conditions while growing up, and their speculation about the future. The interviews were tape-recorded, transcribed, and analyzed according to four themes: strain, vulnerability, resistance and resilience, and consequences. These themes are incorporated in this chapter to highlight the participants' childhoods and their growing up conditions. The chapter addresses the following aspects: everyday life within the family, school and friends, support from public authorities, and life as adolescents and young adults. The chapter ends by highlighting some of the major conclusions of this study and presenting some principles for practice that can be learned from the research.

## Everyday life within the family

### Mother is "different"

All 23 children grew up with their parents until they reached school age or thereabouts. Later, and at different points in time, three of the boys and three of the girls were put into more or less permanent foster care outside the home. Most of the children were aware that their mother was "not like most people," and that was the reason she received social welfare benefits. The participants did not know, either as children or as young adults, that their mother had been diagnosed as intellectually disabled and received public assistance for that reason. One of the young people said:

> I didn't really know much until you contacted me now. This is not something you think or talk about very much. My mother once told me that when she was three to four years old, something happened involving a fireplace that she fell into and was unconscious for five minutes – and then she had some problems speaking and such. I didn't think much of it. I just thought, so this is how it is. I have wondered that perhaps there was brain damage. We never discussed it. This is something she told me about 10 years ago. But it isn't something I've thought about . . . It isn't as if this is that bad when you know her.

When the children started school they realized their mother could not help them with their homework. As the teasing started at school, they also became aware that conditions at home were lacking, for example, with poor hygiene. The mother's shortcomings in practical matters at home meant that they were exposed to mockery and derogatory remarks from others. For most of them, their mother's love for them outweighed this humiliation. As one of the boys remarked:

> Mother hasn't been able to help me write – or help me with my homework. She hasn't taught me how to brush my teeth – and mother hasn't told me that one should take a bath now and then. So, this is just something I've had to learn later . . . These were simply oversights. And it's the only thing, I feel, that has made me different.

## "I am very pleased with my mother"

Most of the participants were caring, protective, and loyal toward their family. They were particularly attuned to their mother's and their younger siblings' needs. This warm and close bond with their mother can perhaps be explained by their experience of having a loving mother, as Perkins et al. (2002) found in their study. One of them said: "A mother like mine – she has been very, very loving towards me all the way. And this is a fact. When all is said and done these are the things you remember – so I am very pleased with my mother." Another said: "As far as my mother is concerned, I have never, ever doubted that she loved me. Never, ever. It's always been tenderness, love, and care."

For periods of time, some participants' relations with their mother were characterized by strong ambivalent feelings that swung from love and devotion to anger and irritation, an observation also noted by Pipping (2004) and Ronai (1997). This was most obvious in the interviews when the participants were young adults. It was not until they became teenagers that the children began to wonder openly about their parents and question their upbringing, which in many ways had led to their being mistrusted and excluded, and not part of their peer group. Until then, their home was a haven that had protected them against the hardships of the outside world. The children spent a lot of time at home and this compensated for the families' limited social network. They brought home knowledge and information through what they learned at school and about events in the outside world. Later the young people also functioned as guardians, who defended the home against vandalism and derogatory attacks on the family (see also Pipping, 2004; Ronai, 1997).

The participants rarely spoke negatively about their mothers. They knew they did not have the same kind of upbringing and possibilities as other children and young people, and referred to the social devaluation that they saw as a side-effect of their mother's impairment (Kristiansen, 1993). The families' status as outsiders in the local community meant that as children and later as young people, they were not considered as competent and independent maturing individuals (see Llewellyn & McConnell, 2005; McConnell & Llewellyn, 2000).

## Alternating between being children and adults

Most of the children had many responsibilities at home, and in some areas they acted as adult children or young carers. They made particular contributions, not only with practical matters such as doing the laundry, cleaning house, running errands, and so on, but also with respect to emotional connections within the family.

The study of the young adults revealed significant gender differences with regard to practical work in the home. The girls took on many more household tasks. The traditional gender pattern within the family may be one of the reasons why several of the girls in the study became mothers while still young, dropped out of school, and were dependent on social support. Also, when growing up the girls were noticeably much more concerned about their family than were the boys. Compared with the boys, the girls generally gave an impression of lower self-esteem, poorer health, and had more emotional difficulties in dealing with problems. The girls were also less aware of the difficulties connected to the somewhat unusual conditions within their families. They seldom realized how their mother's impairment affected the family's situation. The girls were more easily content and were less inclined than the boys to take part in activities outside the home.

For a small number of the children, the role as a young carer had serious psychological consequences. For several young people, having to act like a parent led to symbiotic ties to their parents which caused depression at the time when independence from their family should have taken place. For others, the adult role they had taken on earlier than usual had a positive effect, leading to a display of a high level of independence and courage to deal with the world (Fraser, 2003; Gustavsson, 1995, 1997; Rutter & Rutter, 1997).

One of the girls developed a symbiotic relationship with her parents which she is still struggling with as an adult. The girl developed a phobia for school early on. She did not dare leave her parents for fear of their being separated. The father was often very drunk and she frequently had to act as a negotiator between her parents. There was no physical violence between the parents, but the situation was very volatile, "because my mother was mentally ill," she said. At the same time, she believes having to tackle things by herself made her stronger :

> I've become strong (by helping) because I had to manage so many things on my own. It's something about having to deal with different things. I wasn't very old when I had to decide what was best for my younger sister because mother was mentally ill and I couldn't deal with my father's drinking, and that he didn't care about anything. So all the time I have felt I was my parents' mother.

## The relationship with the rest of the family

In the first interviews, most of the children were thrilled about the grandparents with whom they often spent time. There were also cousins, aunts, and uncles, many of whom lived fairly close by. In the interviews when they were young adults, perception of the family network was quite different. For a few of the young men, some members of their extended family network had become their "rescuer" in their everyday life. These family members listened to them, backed them up, and showed understanding of their everyday challenges as well as the lack of insight they received from their parents when they were facing difficulties. These members of the family network stimulated the young men's self-esteem and gave them courage to fight their battles. Within the family network, their own family life was put in perspective. This was important in terms of the young person's self-perception and helped them understand that they had to take charge themselves to carve out an independent existence in the future. One of the young people said: "I can do this and that on my own. It is possible to accomplish things on your own. I can deal with most things on my own. That's enough for me. I always did my homework no matter how hard it was. There was nobody at home to help me so I just had to deal with it."

The family network could, however, also create interruptions and be destructive to the young person's family, especially the children. In some families, drinking was the main issue and the children witnessed drunkenness and fighting at family gatherings. The family network could also be discriminating and exclude the children and their parents. This motivated the children even more to back up their mother. One of the participants said:

> The three of us (mother, father, and son) feel that we get shoved aside from the family a bit, because we didn't take part in any snobbery. So, we've just said, alright – they do their thing and we do our thing. This may be because my mother has some problems. She may become upset about nothing, but she's learned to control it quite well . . . Nowadays, she can cope with just about anything. For my part I can only say that I couldn't care less – for my mum is my mum – and she is the world's best mother. If they can't accept her, then I can't accept them. That's how it is. And I will look after my mum, if that's an issue. I don't care what the rest of them do.

## The community, school, and friends

The children's stories paint a fairly gloomy picture of society's reaction toward their families. Most of the young adults had experienced being excluded from their environment. This exclusion took place on many levels. In the neighborhood some of the families were called names and were attacked verbally or physically. The children often witnessed cruel incidents and there were many instances when they had to defend their family against vandalism.

Almost all the children received some degree of special education. This often took place outside their regular classroom. For the children, it felt humiliating to be removed from their usual classroom, and it felt degrading not to be able to learn the academic subjects at the same pace as the rest of their classmates. When the young people looked back on their time at school, they particularly remembered the special education classes. Many of them emphasized that they themselves put in an extra effort to prevent their younger siblings from suffering the same fate – that is, getting special education.

> My little sister is doing very well. "You must remember to do your homework." This is what I say when we talk on the telephone. At school she's fine. She doesn't get special education – and if there is any hint of that I go and get involved. It can

be frightening. They talk to you as if you were a small child. You get material from the small children. That was irritating. The positive side was that they helped with the lessons.

The children who had the worst experiences were those who throughout most of their school career received mainly special education. They were subject to hostile remarks and animosity on the way to and from school and in their neighborhood. As young adults, they reported that this had had lasting psychological effects.

Booth and Booth (1998) noted that children of parents with intellectual disabilities were likely to be automatically excluded from the regular school system and routed to special education arrangements, and hence labeled as intellectually disabled. This was exactly the experience of the young people involved in the study described in this chapter. As young adults, most of the participants recalled teasing and mobbing within and outside school. For some of them this took the form of systematic persecution that lasted several years. Harassment, crude remarks, and physical attacks occurred everywhere, at school and in their neighborhood. During childhood, many of them were excluded from their peer group and therefore isolated from having friends during their childhood. The children's self-esteem suffered many serious blows. The shame and anger at being turned away and ostracized had "branded" them. They described the time at school as a socially degrading period of their life. They were classified as deviant, under-achievers, and inferior compared to other children.

## A turning point

11 of the 23 children had attended "after-school" (in Danish *efterskole*). The after-school is a specific Danish school program offered to young people aged 14–18 years. It is a residential school with the primary aim of providing general education with a focus on the whole person and emphasizing the personal development of the students. The after-school has the same academic requirements as elementary school. Going to the after-school was a turning point for the young people in this study. They spoke highly of their stay there and maintained that it helped them to gain significant strength and faith that they had the resources and competence to use for a better future. Two of the young people said:

> To go to an after-school is like a new start. There are new teachers and new persons there. And the teachers don't know you – like the other teachers did. So you can start by showing what you really can do. This has helped a lot. Now I can both read and spell. There you have the solidarity that's missing elsewhere. I would therefore advise anyone to go to after-school.

> The past years have been very good. Since I left elementary school and went to the after-school, everything has changed. This has been really good. I've had the chance to show that I manage alright – if I just do things the right way.

These quotes clearly show that the stay at the after-school has been very important for these 11 young people and their personal and vocational development. Most importantly, at this school they experienced, perhaps for the first time, that they were not stupid but could learn to read, write, and do math. Several also discovered they managed well in the academic subjects and got good grades. The appreciative and supportive environment of the after-school offered the young people education and a social forum that gave them a chance to rehearse the skills that they had been trying to grasp for many years.

At the after-school, the young people experienced a new life, resurgence after earlier defeats, and the chance to develop permanent social and personal relationships with their peers. Their motivation to continue studying or find work was also boosted. The stay at the after-school transformed their excluded identity as outsiders to an inclusive youth identity, where they were integrated in a community of their peers.

## Support from public authorities

All the families in the study received government social welfare benefits and supports. The mother's pension contributed to the families' basic needs with regard to the household economy and housing. Official assistance also came in the form of a family caseworker who visited the family regularly and a nurse who also came by on a regular basis. Many of the children had an extra support person at preschool and later received help with homework. Several of the children spent holidays and weekends with support families. Six children were placed into foster homes or into an institution. The social system also covered the cost of the children's one or two years' stay at the after-school in their teenage years.

Almost all the families were provided with stable, continuous, and comprehensive support throughout most of their children's upbringing. Still, this support did not have the desired effect, demonstrated by the number of children placed in foster care. This finding supports that from another Danish study by Skov (2003), which showed that 45% of children of parents with intellectual disabilities in Denmark were placed out of the home (see also Booth, Booth, & McConnell, 2005; McConnell & Llewellyn, 2000).

Many of the participants felt like they lived with a degree of insecurity because they received no explanation as to why their family was so attached to and dependent on the official authorities. The silence surrounding the mother's diagnosis as intellectually disabled created a mystery around their lives and prevented them from understanding why the rest of their family network and their community considered them different.

Most of the young people claimed they were invisible to support workers who regularly came to their homes. Many did not receive the help that they felt was necessary in their everyday lives. The young people said the focus of these visits was almost solely on their parents, their mother's impairment, and the difficulties it brought. Most of them, therefore, blamed society for a lack of awareness of their often difficult situation, not least outside the home and the exclusion they experienced.

The young people also pointed out that the support workers treated the family in humiliating and belittling ways. They said that, at times, they advised their parents to decline help from the social system at home, because of the discriminatory treatment of their family, especially of their parents. It was, therefore, not uncommon for support workers to be replaced because of these critical reactions from these children and young people. According to Danish law, all children must be involved in any social casework affecting their lives. Yet the young people in this study stressed that neither their parents nor they themselves were sufficiently included when the authorities made decisions about the circumstances in their homes. The children who were removed from the home and brought up in foster care felt especially betrayed. One of the young men, whose sole anchor in life today is his mother, revealed:

> It hasn't always been easy – it should be obvious, to move so often. I think I've lived in 15 different places – I don't have the exact count – there have been so many places. It's been very stressful to have to get used to so many people all the time – and I really have had problems in that respect. I haven't been able to get used to anyone. I didn't know where I was when I woke up in the morning . . . I've given up on getting attached to anyone – it's a tendency I have developed.

About one-third of the young adults said they were satisfied with the support they had at home. These young people typically had back-up from many sources, from one or more individuals in their family network, and from support workers from the public authorities. Support workers who still visited this particular group of young people had conversations with them, and included all the family members when the service system made decisions about their lives. This way of providing support was highlighted by the young people because it emphasized empowering practice where support workers respected, valued, and enhanced the parents' and the children's competence (see Tucker & Johnson, 1989; Espe-Sherwindt & Crable, 1993; Espe-Sherwindt & Kerlin, 1990; Llewellyn & McConnell, 2005).

## Life as adolescents and young adults

From the time the children were around 15 years old, more than half of them became independent young people, just like others their age. They also strove to obtain a positive self-image. More than half the young people managed to face the challenges that were a part of their everyday life. As young adults, most gave an impression of individual strength and vision for the future with regard to education, work, sweethearts, and an independent existence. Despite the difficulties surrounding their childhood, which made them outsiders and psychologically vulnerable, most of the young adults had managed to mobilize strength and competencies to overcome difficulties that might otherwise have trapped them in an ongoing hopeless existence.

## Resilience

The young people's resilience manifested itself in the following ways. They had worked hard to create an independent existence, tried to overcome mobbing and humiliating reactions from their surroundings, taken the initiative to look for work or get an education, and they were active members of different social networks including family, friends, and colleagues. In this context, resilience should not be considered the opposite of life without risks and difficulties. Although the young people demonstrated empowered lives, partly through their own strength and partly through support from their social network and official agencies, they had also at times been through difficulties, oppression, and tragic circumstances that had caused them unhappiness.

The young people who have managed best in life showed during their teenage years that they were tough, robust, bold, brave, and provocative. The majority of the young adults were satisfied with their life situation. In their opinion, they benefited from the following (see also Werner, 1993):

- they learned how to tackle the situation at home;
- they grabbed opportunities when they saw the benefit in improving their everyday situation;
- they received positive support from their family network;
- they demonstrated social competency;
- they were independent in their activities;
- they used their resources;
- they received positive attention as youngsters from their closest caregiver;
- they received support from a teacher and/or persons from the service system.

The following quote illustrates the young people's struggle to manage in everyday life:

When I started elementary school, I had some problems . . . I was behind – I wasn't as good as the others. But then I battled my way upward and ended among those in the middle. And this is where I've stayed and I've been satisfied with that. The day I stood there at my graduation, I was extra happy. It was a great victory for me!

Again and again, the young people mentioned that the first time they were acknowledged as being on the same level as others their age was when they were at the after-school. Here the seed of toughness and resilience that characterized their actual, everyday lives could flourish and grow. Anger and contempt toward the system were relatively strongly rooted in the majority of these young adults. They missed having "regular" parents, and they had experienced condescension, resentment, and lack of appreciation by all their family members. According to Honneth (2003, 2006), this emotional reaction can set the scene for developing resilience. From this point of view, the contempt that developed as a result of the negative treatment these young people had received may have created the foundation for their resilient reactions because this humiliating treatment clashed with their sense of justice, which is "connected to respect for one's own worth, honor or integrity" (Honneth, 2003, p. 37).

## Conclusion

The study confirms that children of parents with intellectual disabilities are at increased risk of facing a variety of difficulties while growing up. This is partly because of the parents' lack of insight and competence with regard to upbringing and care, and partly because the environment treats all the family members with disrespect and scorn. The mother's impairment leads to labeling that stigmatizes the entire family and affects the social conditions of the children. Most of the children were excluded and rejected by other children at school and in the neighborhood. The hardships and isolation were most acute for children with severe learning difficulties.

Despite these less than positive childhood experiences, most of the children had managed to overcome the difficult conditions they experienced when growing up by the time they reached young adulthood. The decisive change in their self-esteem was primarily a result of their stay at the after-school. The time spent there was crucial to the development of their identity and boosted their self-confidence and vitality. For the first time, they did not feel stupid and were able to learn reading, writing, and math. Mothers' love for their children, continuing support from individual family members, and respectful, flexible, and empowering support from official agencies were also decisive in enabling these young adults to establish an individual and independent existence.

The study shows that, despite tough odds, the children managed fairly well in life. This research also demonstrates that the children and young people of parents with intellectual disabilities are resourceful and want to use their resources when given the opportunity. They are not victims or passive spectators. They try to cope with the inner (internalized) barriers and the external (social) obstructions that make their life conditions hard (see Gustavsson, 1995, 1997). The majority of these young adults challenge the common view that children of parents with intellectual disabilities are predetermined to share the same social status as their parents. More than half graduated from the nine-year compulsory school with a final exam. None of them was involved in crime, drug abuse, or drinking.

There was a clear difference between the young men and the young women. Most of the young women appeared to be particularly vulnerable. Five of the women were clients of the service system and lived on benefits. At first glance, their future seems to suggest a life with limited chances to progress and a weak social network. Several had not completed their compulsory education. Four had children when they were around 18 years and were single mothers. These children did not spend time regularly with their fathers, most of whom were unemployed and just getting by on social support.

The young men's future, on the other hand, looked bright. "You've got to fight for things – not just give up," said one of them in the last round of interviews. This attitude was common among the young men. Seven of the boys were only children and in the boys' families, contrary to the girls' families, there were no divorces. Furthermore, none of the girls was the only child in the family. This family background may have had an influence on the pronounced gender difference in the children's development and later their development as a young adult.

In families where the parents are identified as intellectually disabled, the general rule in Denmark is to provide continuous and comprehensive support while the children are growing up. These families have good housing, and social welfare benefits provide a decent basis for existence. Yet, the number of children in these families who are placed out of the home is still alarmingly high. According to the children who grow up in these families, it is society's prejudiced view of the family and incompetent support workers that cause the too frequent removal of children from their home (Kollberg & Folkeson, 1996; Traustadóttir & Sigurjónsdóttir, 2008). The young adults in this study proposed that official support should be organized in such a way as to create realistic possibilities for the family to understand and influence decisions about how to meet its need for help. The bottom line is that the family should have a partnership with the authorities so that, together, they can define the most pressing problems that face the family, which should retain the right to propose the form and content of the support it receives. The major conclusion of this study is that even if children of mothers with intellectual disabilities grow up under difficult circumstances, they manage relatively well as adults.

## Principles for Practice

To date, very few programs specifically target the needs of children of parents with intellectual disabilities. It is fair to say that many programs assume that if practitioners work with parents to improve their parenting practices and behaviors, the children's lives will automatically be better. The findings from this study suggest otherwise, primarily because the outcomes of the social conditions and stigmatization affect every facet of their life situation. A first principle for practitioners is to take into account the social and community context in which the children are growing up as well as their home situation. Practitioners will need to identify particular difficulties that the children are facing in their community and society, which, as the study demonstrates, change over time, and ensure that the appropriate support is in place to assist the children.

Disturbingly, in this study the effects of the mother's intellectual impairment, such as being slow at learning, were also attributed to their children. This resulted in others having decreased expectations of the children and their capacity to learn and develop. A second principle is that practitioners must be wary of expecting too little from the children of parents with intellectual disabilities based on stereotypical assumptions about their parent's incompetence. They must be mindful that each child, as an individual, deserves to be understood on his or her own merits and receive services and supports tailored to that child's needs, including regular education opportunities. The findings from this study suggest that two groups of children are most at risk. Girls are more at risk than boys, as are children in families with more than one child. Practitioners need to provide multiple opportunities and specific programs to ensure that, as they grow up, the young women develop positive self-esteem and a maturing sense of their own identity. Understanding the unique needs of each child in families with more than one child is also critically important, and practitioners will need to pay particular attention to gender differences in families with siblings and the different responses and reactions of each child, dependent on his or her personality and position in the family structure.

Of paramount importance for practitioners is the requirement that they work in a collaborative partnership with parents with intellectual disabilities and their children. The young adults in the study described in this chapter appreciated those practitioners who helped them to make the most of their life opportunities. Regrettably, they also identified too many practitioners who rendered them, as children of parents with intellectual disabilities, "invisible" in their own and their families' everyday lives. The third principle therefore is for practitioners to work collaboratively with the children and young people to help them learn resilient and productive ways to engage with a society that is frequently less than welcoming, and too often actively rejecting.

The final principle for practice arising from this study is the requirement for practitioners to actively engage with local communities, policy developers, and public authorities who continue to implement practices that are stigmatizing based on a label of parental intellectual disability. These practices continue to blight the lives of children whose mothers and/or fathers have intellectual disabilities and thus make their lives and the difficulties they face far more challenging than they need be. Practitioners working with parents with intellectual disabilities are perfectly positioned to lead by example, to be good role models, to be informative and empowering, and, by doing so, to enhance the social situation in which children of parents with intellectual disabilities grow into adulthood.

# References

Andersson, G. (1998). Barnintervju som forskningsmetod [The child interview as a research method]. *Nordisk Psykologi, 50*(1), 18–41.

Booth, T., & Booth, W. (1996). Parental competence and parents with learning difficulties. *Child and Family Social Work, 1*(2), 81–86.

Booth, T., & Booth, W. (1998). *Growing up with parents who have learning difficulties.* London: Routledge.

Booth, T., Booth, W., & McConnell, D. (2005). Care proceedings and parents with learning difficulties: Comparative prevalence and outcomes in an English and Australian court sample. *Child and Family Social Work, 10*(4), 353–360.

Dowdney, L., & Skuse, D. (1993). Parenting by adults with mental retardation. *Child Psychology and Psychiatry, 34*(1), 25–47.

Espe-Sherwindt, M., & Crable, S. (1993). Parents with mental retardation: Moving beyond the myths. *Topics in Early Childhood Special Education, 13*(2), 155–175.

Espe-Sherwindt, M., & Kerlin, S. L. (1990). Early intervention with parents with mental retardation: Do we empower or impair? *Infants and Young Children, 2*(4), 21–28.

Faureholm, J. (2007). *Man må jo kæmpe. Børns opvækst i familier med udviklingshæmmede forældre* [You've got to fight: Children growing up in families of parents with intellectual disabilities]. Unpublished doctoral dissertation, Danish University of Education, Copenhagen.

Feldman, M. A. (2002). Children of parents with intellectual disabilities. In R. J. McMahon & R. D. Peters (Eds.), *The effects of parental dysfunction on children* (pp. 205–223). New York: Kluwer.

Feldman, M. A., & Walton-Allen, N. (1997). Effects of maternal mental retardation and poverty on intellectual, academic and behavioral status of school-age children. *American Journal on Mental Retardation, 101*(4), 352–364.

Fraser, M. W. (2003). *Risk and resilience in childhood: An ecological perspective.* Washington, DC: NASW Press.

Gillberg, C., Geijer-Karlsson, M., & Rasmussen, P. (1983). Utvecklingsstörda föräldrar och deras barn [Parents with intellectual disabilities and their children]. Långtidsopföljning av 41 barn vid 1- 21 års alder. *Socialmedicinsk Tidskrift, 4–5,* 260–265.

Gustavsson, A. (1995). Utvecklingsstörningens personliga och sociala betydelser [The personal and social meaning of intellectual disability]. *Socialmedicinsk Tidskrift, 72*(6–7), 245–254.

Gustavsson, A. (1997). *Integrering från den första integreringsgeneration* [Integration and the first integration generation]. Unpublished working paper, Stockholm University.

Honneth, A. (2003). *Behovet for anerkendelse* [Need for recognition]. Copenhagen: Hans Reitzels Forlag.

Honneth, A. (2006). *Kampen om anerkendelse* [Fighting for recognition]. Copenhagen: Hans Reitzels Forlag.

Kollberg, E., & Folkeson, Y. (1996, December). Who's fit to be a parent? Parenthood, mental retardation and psychotherapy. In *Parenting with intellectual disability: Report from the Conference* (pp. 129–138). Snekkersten, Denmark.

Kristiansen, K. (1993). *Normalisering og verdsetning av sosial rolle* [Normalization and social role valorization]. Oslo: Kommuneforlaget.

Llewellyn, G., & McConnell, D. (2005). You have to prove yourself all the time: People with learning disabilities as parents. In G. Grant, P. Goward, & M. Richardson (Eds.), *Learning disability: A life circle approach to valuing people* (pp. 441–467). Buckingham: Open University Press.

McConnell, D., & Llewellyn, G. (2000). Disability and discrimination in statutory child protection proceedings. *Disability and Society, 15*(6), 883–895.

McGaw, S., & Newman, T. (2005). *What works for parents with learning disabilities?* London: Jessica Kingsley.

Newman, T. (2003). *Children of disabled parents: New thinking about families affected by disability and illness.* Lyme Regis: Russell House.

Perkins, T. S., Holburn, S., Deaux, K., Flory, M. J., & Vietze, P. M. (2002). Children of mothers with intellectual disability: Stigma, mother–child relationship and self-esteem. *Journal of Applied Research in Intellectual Disability, 15*(4), 297–313.

Pipping, L. (2004). *Kärlek och stålull. Att växa upp med en utvecklingsstörd mamma* [Love and steel wool: Growing up with intellectual disability]. Stockholm: Gotha Förlag.

Ronai, C. (1997). On loving and hating my mentally retarded mother. *Mental Retardation, 35*(6), 417–432.

Rönström, A. (1983). *Mentally retarded parents and their children: A follow-up study of 17 children with mentally retarded parents.* Stockholm: Children's Ombudsman.

Rutter, M., & Rutter, M. (1997). *Den livslange udvikling – forandring og kontinuitet* [Lifelong development: Continuity and change]. Copenhagen: Hans Reitzels Forlag.

Sandbæk, M. (2002). *Barn og foreldre som sociale aktører i møte med hjelpetjenester* [Children and parents as social actors when meeting the social services]. Oslo: NOVA, Norwegian Social Research.

Skov, A. (2003). *Udviklingshæmmede som forældre – myter og fakta* [People with intellectual disabilities as parents – myths and facts]. *Rapport fra konferencen Familier under pres.* Ringsted: UFC Handicap.

Traustadóttir, R., & Sigurjónsdóttir, H. B. (2008). The "mother" behind the mother: Three generations of mothers and their family support networks. *Journal of Applied Research in Intellectual Disabilities, 21*(4), 331–340.

Tucker, B. M., & Johnson, O. (1989). Competence promoting vsersus competence inhibiting social support for mentally retarded mothers. *Human Organization, 48*(2), 95–107.

Werner, E. E. (1993). Risk, resilience, and recovery: Perspectives from Kauai Longitudinal Study. *Development and Psychopathology, 5,* 503–515.

# 5

# Understanding Community in the Lives of Parents with Intellectual Disabilities

*Gwynnyth Llewellyn and Marie Gustavsson*

## Introduction

Parents are a part of families, social networks, neighborhoods, and communities. Parents with intellectual disabilities live within our communities; they do not exist in isolation. They respond to their circumstances but they are also actors and active agents in their own lives. As for others in the community, their lives are lived in a web of relationships with individuals and social structures, some of which are more intimate, more enduring, and closer to home, others of which are more distant, less frequently encountered, and perhaps more fragmented. Thinking about parents with intellectual disabilities as active contributors to communities as well as recipients of support and services is quite new in the international literature. This chapter sets out to understand community in the lives of parents with intellectual disabilities. To do this we take a "from the ground up" standpoint: that is, from the perspective of parents themselves.

A strong focus of research studies since the end of the 1990s has been on devising programs and support services to assist parents in the often challenging tasks of parenting. Following on from the earlier research tradition of examining the question about whether parents with intellectual disabilities could be or become competent parents, researchers turned their attention to developing parent education programs to change, develop, or modify parents' behaviors. While such programs are successful in teaching parents new skills, their focus is on the individual parent and their child or children. Missing from this equation

*Parents with Intellectual Disabilities: Past, Present and Futures*   Edited by Gwynnyth Llewellyn, Rannveig Traustadóttir, David McConnell, and Hanna Björg Sigurjónsdóttir   © 2010 John Wiley & Sons, Ltd

is an understanding of other influences in parents' lives, broadly grouped as social, contextual, and environmental factors.

In searching for issues which may influence parenting by people with intellectual disabilities, social support is considered a likely contributor to parenting success (Feldman, Varghese, Ramsey, & Rajska, 2002). Tucker and Johnson (1989) coined the phrase "competence promoting and competence inhibiting support" to capture whether the support offered by family members and others to parents with intellectual disabilities was advantageous to their parenting. Support for parents with intellectual disabilities is typically assumed to come from individuals acting alone, for example, a grandmother helping her daughter or a social service practitioner supporting a mother. There are some exceptions, however. For example, Llewellyn, McConnell, Cant, and Westbrook (1999) classified support givers as supportive ties acknowledging that support could come from a dyad such as a brother and sister-in-law acting jointly as a supportive unit. Although studies in this tradition capture the parents' (usually the mothers') perspectives on the support coming from others, the parent's role as an agent in creating and sustaining support relationships is noticeably absent. Recently, and in an innovative turn, Mayes, Llewellyn, and McConnell (in press) used a phenomenological approach to capture mothers' active negotiation in creating and maintaining their support networks during pregnancy and following the birth of their baby.

What is missing from these studies, however, as Lunsky and Neely (2002) point out, is the community dimension of earlier conceptualizations of social support. Researchers in the field of parenting with a disability appeared to have strayed from Cobb's (1976) classic definition that includes the phrase "belongs to a network of communication and mutual obligation" (p. 300), and Sarason's (1974) definition of "the feeling that one is part of a larger, dependable and stable structure" (p. 157). Along with other researchers, we were already aware of the social isolation frequently experienced by mothers with intellectual disabilities and their desire to be more included in their communities (Feldman & Walton-Allen, 1997; Llewellyn, McConnell, & Bye, 1998). Missing from our work was a critical dimension of belonging – connectedness to and participation in the community.

This study is the result of collaboration between researchers from Australia and Sweden who together set out to address this gap. Our overall purpose was to describe and understand the meaning and relevance attributed to being a part of the community by parents with intellectual disabilities. We aimed to investigate community participation by parents with intellectual disabilities and to ascertain the usefulness of an interview guide that could be used by practitioners to assist parents with intellectual disabilities to participate successfully in their communities. Based on our understanding of the interpretive tradition in disability research (see, e.g., Ferguson, Ferguson, & Taylor, 1992), we proposed to achieve these aims by discussing with a small group of parents their experiences of community and the meaning and relevance of these experiences.

## People with intellectual disabilities being part of the community

Historically, *living in* the community rather than in an institutionalized setting was thought to be "good enough" with regard to inclusion of people with intellectual disabilities in the community. Now, *being part* of the community is an important criterion against which community inclusion is judged. Exactly what constitutes being part of the community is not always clear, however. Inclusion in the community could be defined as physical presence and a degree of social participation (Myers, Ager, Kerr, & Myles, 1998). Another definition specifies three essential components: choice and control in where you live, things to do including both productive and leisure activities that are personally meaningful, and relationships with family, friends, and neighbors (McColl et al., 1998).

Inclusion of people with disabilities could be seen as an excellent example of how research and political endeavors become intertwined (e.g., Becker, 1967; Punch, 1994). In the international context, the Standard Rules on the Equal-ization of Opportunities for Persons with Disabilities (United Nations, 1994) promote equal participation for people with disabilities and provide guidelines for nation-states on how to achieve this. The rules refer to the right of being a part of society overall and specifically address access to medical care, reha-bilitation, support services, accessibility (in all spheres of society), education, employment, income maintenance and social security, family life and personal integrity, culture, recreation, and sports and religion. The UN Convention on the Rights of Persons with Disabilities (2006) expands the notion of equal par-ticipation to include "Full and effective participation and inclusion in society" (Article 3, point c).

The ideas behind promoting the participation of people with intellectual disabilities in the community, however, are older than the Standard Rules and the UN Convention. The principle of normalization variously conceptualized by Nirje (1969, 1980) in the Nordic context and Wolfensberger (1972, 1980) in North America expresses the value of community integration or inclusion. As a driving ideology for change since the 1960s, normalization, with its concern for people with intellectual disabilities to be part of socially condoned rhythms of everyday life, also draws upon earlier theories – theories of exclusion – including the labeling theory of deviance of Becker (1963) and on total institutions and stigma of Goffman (1961, 1963), among others.

These theoretical and ideological influences have led to an implicit as-sumption deeply embedded in disability research that people with intellectual disabilities *ipso facto* are not "naturally" a part of the community. In consequence, as Bogdan and Taylor (1987) suggest, disability research has focused on exclusionary practices and outcomes for people with intellectual disabilities rather than attending to instances of community acceptance. This is most clearly demonstrated in the dominant stream of disability service work dedicated to examining, fostering, facilitating, evaluating, and judging the community participation of those on the "outside looking in" (Myers et al., 1998). Locating studies or stories of "positive" community acceptance and belonging is immeasurably more difficult than studies of exclusion and programs to remedy exclusion. Indeed, as Culham and Nind (2003) noted only a few years ago, there is a danger of failing to recognize everyday instances of inclusion in an over-enthusiastic rush to identify exclusionary practices and ways to overcome them.

The notion of community participation and the term "participation" took on a new meaning for people with impairments with the publication of the *International Classification of Functioning, Disability and Health (ICF)* (World Health Organization, 2001). This publication endeavored to understand impairment and potential accompanying disability in a new way by taking into account medical, biopsychosocial, and environmental-cultural influences in the lives of individuals in any given community. Participation, in this international classification, is defined as "involvement in a life situation." Participation restrictions therefore "are problems an individual may experience in involvement in life situations." Involvement, for example, can mean taking part or being included or engaged; being involved in a life situation also brings in the concepts of being included or having access to resources.

The term "community" has suffered a similar unidimensional fate to that of inclusion. As noted by Bess, Fisher, Sonn, and Bishop (2002), the idea of community "evokes images of the small town or close neighborhood. . . . It is an idealization in place and time of feeling a part of a place, with those around knowing and caring about us" (p. 3). However, there are many meanings that can also be attributed to community. To suggest but a few, community can be a political entity (e.g., nation-state or grouping of states such as the Nordic countries) as well as a geographic location (e.g., southern hemisphere, island continent, New Jersey, capital city, and so on); a set of social networks (e.g., kin, work-based, student group) and relationships (e.g., intimate, close, acquaintances); and/or a psychological sense of place or belonging (my hometown, school community, young mothers' playgroup, and so on). There are also communities of interest (religious affiliation, sporting groups, volunteer work) and communities of necessity (strata plan organizations, parents' and friends' associations).

The diverse meanings given to participation (inclusion, integration, and involvement) and the typically loose definition of community (of which there are many) make researching *being part of the community* a challenging endeavor. In this chapter we report on our journey through this minefield as we sought to describe and understand how a small group of parents engaged with and participated in their communities, and the meaning this participation held for them.

## The Study

The theoretical perspective underpinning this qualitative study is phenomenology based on Schutz (1967, 1970) and his portrayal of the life-world as repetition of contacts with people and the meanings given to those contacts. Of particular note is the innermost circle of the life-world known as the most proximal zone of relevance which has greatest immediacy to the individual. In this view, the everyday routines of life provide opportunities for regular contact, and the knowledge and assumptions that individuals bring to these routine contacts help to make sense of their interactions. The question then is how to identify the everyday routines of life experienced by parents with intellectual disabilities. Here we turned to the argument first proposed by O'Donnell and Tharp (1990) and elaborated more fully by Gallimore and colleagues (e.g., Gallimore, Goldenberg, & Weisner, 1993) that the basic unit of analysis in community ought to be the activity setting.

### The focus of the study

Activity settings can be thought of as the architecture of everyday life; these settings construct and support the routines in which we engage as individuals, as family members, as employees, as students, as volunteers, and so on. As Gallimore et al. (1993) argue, activity settings are in part social constructions of the participants and in part "determined" by cultural and social mores. Studying the activity settings and activities, we propose, provides insights into the complex nature of the proactive (social construction) and reactive (response to cultural and social mores) participation that parents with intellectual disabilities experience as they participate in community life.

Having established that activity settings would provide our unit of analysis, we were forced to consider which settings to examine and how these could be investigated. To answer this we returned to the literature on sense of community and on community integration (inclusion) in an attempt to comprehensively elucidate the "compartments" of community life.

From the literature on sense of community we drew on the well-established notion that community can be thought of as *locational* (for example, the geographic location of the neighborhood or suburb in which one lives) or *relational*, where the defining feature is commonality of pursuit (e.g., employment), or issue (e.g., disability advocacy group), or characteristic (e.g., parenting group), or beliefs (e.g., religious affiliation) (Sarason, 1974). From the community inclusion literature we drew on the now often-quoted saying, community is about "something to do, somewhere to live and someone to love" (cited in McColl et al., 1998). We proposed therefore to explore something to do through employment, education, volunteering, and leisure. To explore somewhere to live we decided to study the neighborhood settings in which parents spent their time. Finally, we considered that someone to love would potentially permeate all aspects of everyday life so that questions about people would naturally fall into our five areas of employment, education, volunteering, leisure, and neighborhood. Naming "compartments" of everyday life in this ordinary and rather concrete way we surmised would also facilitate discussions with parents about their participation in the community (a decidedly abstract and, as noted above, poorly defined concept). As a safety net, we added an additional compartment, "Other important aspects of community life," to capture additional settings in which parents met and felt connected with people but that did not fall easily into the five areas already mentioned.

Having decided on the settings, we turned our attention to the questions to be asked about participation in these settings. Using the concept of activity settings as a unit of analysis in community research has been assisted by Gallimore and colleagues (e.g., Gallimore et al., 1993) distinguishing five discrete aspects for consideration as follows: (1) *personnel* present during an activity; (2) salient cultural *values and beliefs*; (3) the operations and *task demands* of the activity itself; (4) the *scripts* for conduct that govern the participant's actions; and (5) the *purposes* or *motives of* the participants. In addition to these five areas we were also interested in two other aspects: satisfaction with participation and the dynamic nature of activity settings. Satisfaction was operationally defined as "what is good and what is not so good about (the activity setting)." Change over time and desired changes were considered by asking "How was it before?" and "Has anything changed?" and "What would you like to change?" respectively.

## The participants

The study was conducted in metropolitan Sydney, Australia, over a six-month period in 2003. Participants in this study were four mothers and one father, all with different life-stories and all with a long-standing connection with the researchers from University of Sydney. This group of parents grew up with their own parents, with the exception of the father, who spent his youth in an institution. They could be compared to the sample in Gustavsson's Swedish study, which he refers to as the first "integration generation" (Gustavsson, 1998).

The first mother has three children aged 11, 10, and 6 years old. Recently separated from her husband, her story is very much that of being a working woman. The next mother's story is one of being the mother of a daughter taken into care and who, at four years of age, is the real motivation for her to keep her life going and to develop as a person. The third mother grew up as part of the "special" system, attending special education classes and, on leaving school, going to a sheltered workshop. Becoming pregnant overturned her structured days and routines of life and drew her mother back in as her closest support and ally. Now her days revolve around her growing son, who is 14 years old, her craftwork at her local church, and her "special" sporting activities. The prime identity for the fourth mother is that of being a wife and mother. At the time of the study she had three boys aged nine, four and two years and was three months pregnant with her fourth child. The father in our study is the recently separated husband of the first mother. Until 17 years of age his only relationships were in an institution, where he was told what to do and who should be his friends. Life from then on, for him, has been about learning to make choices, who to trust, and how to develop his life, and now also his children's lives in their community.

Due to trustful and long relations with the researchers these parents have over the years contributed to research projects on parenthood and disability. They are not only experts on their own lives, they also have valuable skills developed through practice in reflecting on their experiences. Their willingness to share their reflections and ability in doing so provide a unique opportunity to redress in some small way the marginalization of voices from parents with intellectual disabilities. Their experiences living in the community may differ quite substantially from those of other parents who spent their early lives in institutions or currently live under the watchful eye of care and protection services.

## The interviews and informal observations

The data were gathered through two rounds of interviews and informal observations. In the first round, four of the five parents took part in an informal and conversational-style individual interview about their thoughts on community and integration/participation. The parents' views and understandings on these matters along with an analysis of the literature provided the basis for the development of a semi-structured interview guide. The interview guide was then used in another round of interviews with the same four parents and the fifth parent. Interviews with three participants took place in their homes or, in one instance, at the participant's leisure activity, and each lasted around two hours. The interviews with the other two participants were conducted on two separate occasions at their homes and workplace and together lasted around five hours. Each interview was tape-recorded for later transcription and extensive field notes were kept on parents participating in their everyday community activities, wherever possible.

## Understanding the parents' narratives

Our approach to analyzing the data gathered through the informal observations and more structured interviews was first to develop a detailed story for each of the parents, from the tapes and transcripts. These stories portrayed the parents' views of themselves – for example, working woman – and in relation to others – such as wife and mother – and the relative emphasis they placed on, and meaning they gave to, the various things they do or the compartments of their everyday lives.

We chose to analyze the conversational data, our observations, and the stories in three ways. In the first, we utilized the notion of community as locational, for example, as neighborhood and public spaces. In this analysis, we described how parents understood their participation in their immediate geographic community. In the second, we examined the notion of community and compartments of everyday life as relational. Although we realize that each of these compartments of everyday life such as volunteering and work is activity and task driven, our interest was in parents' involvement and participation – their web of relationships – rather than the functions they carried out or their "performance." Our final analytic approach, which built on the other two, focused on the strategies the parents used to connect with other people in their neighborhood and in their communities of interest. In the next section we describe parents' participation in their community in locational terms. We follow this with a section describing the relational aspect of parents' participation. In each section we present examples of the strategies that parents use to connect with their local community and their communities of interest.

### Locational

For the parents in this study, being part of the local community is having a physical presence in public areas such as the street, local parks and shops, cafés, clubs, and restaurants. None of the parents has car transport, so being out and about walking, taking the bus, and waiting at the train station assumes large amounts of time in everyday life. Much of this time is spent in meeting and talking with people in the neighborhood and local community. Although some of this contact is fleeting, it is a regular part of their daily or weekly routines.

Knowing the neighbors or local shopkeepers is an important part of parents feeling at home and comfortable in their local area. One mother socializes with people living in her street. The other parents talked about their neighbors as friendly but not close, which they say is typical in their neighborhood. Children, the parents say, are the best way to make contact with others as it is much easier to talk about children when meeting others in the street, at the park, or sharing playground equipment.

Traveling by bus offers another opportunity for these parents to be part of their communities, with the bus drivers and other passengers getting to know them, their children, and their routines. For one mother, walking around (but not buying) in her local shopping plaza offers her the opportunity to pass the time of day with shopkeepers whom she has come to know since the birth of her son over 14 years ago. One mother works in a town center and during lunch time often "catches up" spontaneously with former workmates or neighbors. Each of the parents preferred to leave shopping to times without the children when they could possibly do so. Then they could, for example, frequent the same café, get to know staff by name, talk to them, and perhaps then count them as a friend.

The activities that parents do with their children such as waiting in the doctor's surgery or in the corridor at the social services agency, or taking the children to swimming or Little Athletics, create a feeling of being a "regular" parent like other families in the community. At these activities, parents talking to other mothers and fathers and sharing stories contributes to their sense of friendship, of participation, and of belonging in their local community. Parents' own local activities also bring them into contact with other adults: Bingo was by far the most popular pastime that was enjoyed by parents attending alone or with friends or acquaintances.

## Relational

The parents in this study felt a relational belonging when they had mean-ingful connections with others over and above the meetings that take place serendipitously as part of living in a local community. The father participating in the study talked about the importance for him of "Reading other people and see(ing) if they respect you and accept you" – something that he believes people with disabilities do extremely well, as he does; something one has to learn when living with a disability. An important part of this respect and acceptance, he believes, is that he is accepted as a parent, as a father to his three children. By identifying as a parent, he felt he belonged together with others who identify in the same way.

Parents in this study had several identities and thus belonged to several communities. All belonged to the community of parents but some also belonged to other communities as an employee or as a volunteer. For all, however, the strongest sense of belonging came from being a parent, which opened up opportunities to belong to the community of parents – a broad church in any local community. Exchanging ideas with other parents at the school gate about coping with children strongly connected these parents with intellectual disabilities with the broader category of parents. Engaging in child-related activities, such as joining other parents in helping with reading at their children's school, connected parents into volunteer and potentially work-related activities, such as working in the school library. For the mother whose daughter was taken into care, being recognized as a parent still remained very important even though her daughter does not live with her. She talked about how at the places where she does voluntary work they frequently ask her about her daughter, which contributed to her feeling of belonging to the wider community of parents.

Parents in this study also experienced a relational sense of belonging from their wider personal connections. Some of the parents gained a sense of belonging from ongoing warm, caring relationships with their family of origin. For others, a sense of belonging with family of origin did not exist because of earlier institutionalization (the participating father) or because of previous or current difficult home lives. Connectedness with friends, sharing interests, activities, having "good talks," making jokes, and also showing appreciation of their jokes offered another level of relational belonging. At yet another level, one mother was keen to continue to meet new people and make new friends and described how she actively pursued this by inviting some acquaintances living nearby to her "hens' party" before her wedding, which has brought them closer together now.

The parents in this study also understood their place in the community as someone who was/is disabled. This was not a straightforward alignment with the label "intellectual disability." They frequently used terms such as slow or having special learning needs. For one mother who hates the idea of disability, everyone is the same, no one has a disability. She said: "To me everyone is normal no matter what they got wrong with them . . . no one is perfect." On the other hand, the father participating in the study said: "we all have disabilities – they take different forms – and everyone does not realize this." For some, there was an understandable pride in "overcoming" their disability, their strong desire to advocate for others with a "label," and their commitment to stand up for themselves. Their greatest pride was in their achievements as a person, as a participating member of the community, and as a parent. For example, two mothers are active volunteers: Volunteering at their child's school or at the local family support services provides a position which contributes to a right to be part of those settings. One mother has now written about her life, an activity that several years earlier she could not have contemplated. Another has recently attained her driver's license, proving to herself and her mother that she could do this against all odds.

Looking to the future, the parents said, there will be challenges but each will provide an opportunity for learning and progress. This sense of I can too, of achievement and purpose, pervaded parents' talk about the future, about how they can influence what happens to them and how they can work toward a desired outcome. These plans for the future are founded in making more contacts, working on oneself, for example in learning to read and write, gaining more skills to get a job, and having more time to use for one's own wishes as the children grow older, all of which, it seems to us, represent the parents belonging to and having a place in their communities.

# Discussion

From the findings of this study, it appears that the routines of everyday life with children provide multiple settings for parents with intellectual disabilities to connect with and participate in their communities. First and foremost this occurs through location, from being out and about in the community, an essential part of life with young children as parents go about the business of shopping, taking their children to school or the local park, and accompanying their children as they pursue leisure activities. This is about "being there" in the local community. Their engagement locally is of necessity and choice. Some of the contacts that occur through being there in the community can be understood in terms of Granovetter's (1983) notion of weak ties. Ringsby-Jansson (2002) has applied Granovetter's concept to the everyday life of people with intellectual disabilities living in group homes. That study showed the importance of acquaintances in semi-public spaces for some of the participants' social life and their well-being. The extent to which parents with intellectual disabilities in this study might be called participators or observers relied in large part on their everyday routines (whether they were at home all day or went out to work) and their life opportunities prior to becoming parents, such as special education and sheltered workshop or special class in the local school and mainstream employment. Parents in the former group not surprisingly had a smaller circle of friends from their school and pre-parenting years; those in the latter group knew more people from school, and from former and current places of employment.

Second, the routines of everyday life with children provide multiple opportunities for parents with intellectual disabilities to relate to diverse groups within their communities. At the simplest level, being a parent gives the person with an intellectual disability the right to belong to the socially valued group *parent*. Much of the activity of parents focuses on their children, which in turn provides many opportunities for persons with intellectual disabilities who are parents to develop relational connections to others in their community. Once part of the group (or often, as we have seen here, of multiple groups), parents with intellectual disabilities associate, as do other group members, through the shared activities of the particular group. For example, watching the children at sporting activities and/or helping out with coaching, washing uniforms, providing snacks, and so on.

Being busy with the everyday routines of families concretizes the part of parents with intellectual disabilities as community participants. These parents are doing normal things as other parents are supposed to do, such as cleaning the house, mowing the lawn, feeding the children, going shopping. Belonging, as we saw in our earlier discussion of involvement, is about a subjective sense of community participation – the sense we might have of "fitting in," "being in the right place," or "feeling right." These parents with intellectual disabilities know the social codes (defined by Gallimore et al., 1993, as the scripts that govern participants' actions). Listening to and telling about life experiences and problems cements their social connectedness and reinforces their sense of belonging. Is their desire to fit in, to be defined as a good parent, a worthwhile employee, or a useful voluntary worker any stronger or different than other parents in the community? We do not know. We do know, however, that the parents in this study want to do the right thing, that is, what other parents do, which is fundamental to a sense of belonging and connectedness. Whether this is more important or qualitatively different because of their intellectual disability is not possible to answer from this study.

Bogdan and Taylor (1987) and Myers et al. (1998) both emphasize, along with many other scholars, that being connected with others and accepted in a community, whether geographic or a community of interest, reflects in no small part the responsiveness of that community to people with disabilities. Edgerton (1993) showed over the course of several studies that many previously institutionalized people with intellectual disabilities sought protection from the lack of responsiveness under a cloak of competence. In this way, they mitigated the likely negative effects of being "discovered" as a person with disability. The experiences of the parents in this study help expand the notions of acceptance and responsiveness to encompass another social process, namely, of belonging as a parent. The underlying notion of (*dis*)ability derived from people first and self-advocacy discourse and epitomized in one-liners such as "nothing about us without us" and "labels are for jars, not people" was in evidence as our parents worked hard to be recognized as competent and not thought of as different.

## Conclusion

In this study we set out to investigate community participation by parents with intellectual disabilities and to ascertain the usefulness of an interview guide for practitioners to assist parents with intellectual disabilities to access their communities successfully. We began this study knowing that parents are a part of families, social networks, neighborhoods, and communities. We thought, however, that while this may be the case for many "ordinary" parents, it may not necessarily be the case for parents with intellectual disabilities, who, like others with intellectual disabilities, may continue to suffer the consequences of institutionalization, marginalization, and lack of acceptance by the community more broadly.

The findings from our study demonstrate that this particular group of parents with intellectual disabilities are indeed living ordinary lives within their communities. We are acutely aware that this may not be the case for all parents with intellectual disabilities; we chose, however, to begin exploring an understanding of community in the lives of parents with intellectual disabilities with parents whom we knew well and who would participate with us, as professional informants and partners, in this endeavor. To reiterate the point made earlier by Culham and Nind (2003), there is a danger of failing to recognize everyday instances of inclusion in an over-enthusiastic rush to identify exclusionary practices and ways to overcome them. In contrast, the parents in this study clearly demonstrate instances of inclusion in everyday community life.

The interview guide that we developed for this study comprised several compartments of everyday life. Naming the things parents do as employment, education, volunteering, leisure, and neighborhood with a safety net compartment for any additional important activities provided an easy and accessible way to discuss with the parents their experiences of community and the meaning these held for them. Using the concept of activity settings as the unit of analysis within each compartment led naturally to asking questions about who was participating, for example, in going shopping, when, how, why, and where, which the parents found easy to answer and provided opportunities for further discussion. The interview guide also proved particularly useful in talking with parents about their community participation in their role as parents, and the participation that occurred as a person living within their local community. The interview guide is available on request from the first author.

This exploratory study, which focused attention on the activity settings and activities of parents' everyday lives, has provided insights into the complex nature of the proactive and reactive participation that parents with intellectual disabilities experience as they participate in community life. Most importantly, from our perspective, it has opened up the possibility, rarely recognized in the now extensive literature on parents with intellectual disabilities, that mothers and fathers with intellectual disabilities are active and self-directed agents in their own lives. The process central to their social belonging and connectedness derives not from others but from their initiatives in capitalizing on their physical presence in their local neighborhood and their belonging to valued positions in society, with that of being parent being at the top of the list.

As a cross-sectional study, the findings represent one point in time in the parents' lives. Talking with and observing parents' participation has thrown light on the processes by which parents build on their physical presence in their neighborhood and public spaces and belong to communities of interest. Much of what we have seen comes from parents taking the initiative. There remains much to be learned about whether connections also occur in incidental ways, by chance, or whether connections may be mediated by others. Understanding parents' belonging through the eyes of others would go some way to a fuller understanding of the circumstances in which making connections occurs and the conditions that facilitate or hinder participation in the community.

## Principles for Practice

A fundamental principle for practitioners working with parents with intellectual disabilities is to understand social and community context in the lives of the parents they serve. As we and others have noted, professionals play a larger-than-life role in the everyday lives of many parents with intellectual disabilities and their families, with some parents identifying only professionals in their support networks (Llewellyn & McConnell, 2002; Tarleton & Ward, 2007). This situation suggests that, for these parents, connectedness to community may be fragile indeed given the limited involvement possible for professionals over time in the lives of their clients. Helping parents build their relationships with the community is therefore an essential part of good practice.

A second principle is the critical importance of including connectedness to community as a goal within the support plans or intervention programs for parents with intellectual disabilities. Several programs are now available to assist practitioners develop appropriate goals, plans, and interventions to help parents with intellectual disabilities meet people, make friends, and get out and about in their community. A supported learning program developed in the United Kingdom is described in Booth and Booth (2003). The Australian Supported Learning Program – Me and My Community – is described in McConnell, Dalziel, Llewellyn, Laidlaw, and Hindmarsh (2008) and is available in a package format with leader's manual and parent workbooks (on request from the first author of this chapter).

A final principle is that, of necessity, practitioners must investigate ways to include parents with intellectual disabilities in their communities that utilize and build on already existing opportunities within the local community. The findings from this study suggest that the most frequently occurring community participation activity for parents with intellectual disabilities is being involved with their children's activities at school, in leisure settings, and in everyday interactions in the streets and parks of the local neighborhood. Practitioners should wisely turn their attention to developing strategies to expand, deepen, and strengthen these naturally occurring opportunities for parents with intellectual disabilities to participate proactively and responsively within their local communities.

## References

Becker, H. (1963). *Outsiders: Studies in the sociology of deviance.* New York: Free Press.

Becker, H. (1967). Whose side are we on? *Social Problems, 14,* 239–247.

Bess, K., Fisher, A., Sonn, C., & Bishop, B. (2002). Psychological sense of community: Theory, research, and application. In A. Fisher, C. Sonn, & B. Bishop (Eds.), *Psychological sense of community: Research, applications, and implications* (pp. 3–22). London: Kluwer Academic.

Bogdan, R., & Taylor, S. (1987). Towards a sociology of acceptance: The other side of the study of deviance. *Social Policy, 18*(2), 34–39.

Booth, T., & Booth, W. (2003). Self-advocacy and supported learning for mothers with learning difficulties. *Journal of Learning Disabilities, 7*(2), 165–193.

Cobb, S. (1976). Social support as a moderator of life stress. *Psychosomatic Medicine, 38*(5), 300–314.

Culham, A., & Nind, M. (2003). A critical analysis of normalization: Clearing the way for inclusion. *Journal of Intellectual and Developmental Disability, 28*(1), 65–78.

Edgerton, R. B. (1993). *The cloak of competence: Revised and updated.* Berkeley: University of California Press.

Feldman, M. A., & Walton-Allen, N. (1997). Effects of maternal mental retardation and poverty on intellectual, academic, and behavioral status of school-age children. *American Journal on Mental Retardation,101*(4), 352–364.

Feldman, M. A., Varghese, J., Ramsey, J., & Rajska, D. (2002). Relationship between social support, stress and mother–child interactions in mothers with intellectual disabilities. *Journal of Applied Research in Intellectual Disabilities, 15*(4), 314–323.

Ferguson, P. M., Ferguson, D. L., & Taylor, S. J. (Eds.). (1992). *Interpreting disability: A qualitative reader.* New York: Teachers College Press.

Gallimore, R., Goldenberg, C. N., & Weisner, T. S. (1993). The social construction and subjective reality of activity settings: Implications for community psychology. *American Journal of Community Psychology, 21*(4), 537–559.

Goffman, E. (1961). *Asylums: Essays on the social situation of mental patients and other inmates.* Garden City, NY: Anchor Books.

Goffman, E. (1963). *Stigma: Notes on the management of spoiled identity.* Englewood Cliffs, NJ: Prentice-Hall.

Granovetter, M. (1983). The strength of weak ties: A network theory revisited. *Sociological Theory, 1,* 201–233.

Gustavsson, A. (1998). *Inifrån utanförskapet: Om att vara annorlunda och delaktig* [Inside the outside perspective]. Stockholm: Johansson & Skyttmo.

Llewellyn, G., & McConnell, D. (2002). Mothers with learning difficulties and their support networks. *Journal of Intellectual Disability Research, 46*(1), 17–34.

Llewellyn, G., McConnell, D., & Bye, R. (1998). Perception of service needs by parents with intellectual disabilities, their significant others, and their service workers. *Research in Developmental Disabilities, 19*(3), 245–260.

Llewellyn, G., McConnell, D., Cant, R., & Westbrook, M. (1999). Support network of mothers with an intellectual disability: An exploratory study. *Journal of Intellectual and Developmental Disability, 24*(1), 7–26.

Lunsky, Y., & Neely, L. (2002). Extra-individual sources of social support as described by adults with mild intellectual disabilities. *Mental Retardation, 40*(4), 269–277.

Mayes, R., Llewellyn, D., & McConnell, D. (in press). "That's who I choose to be": The mother identity for women with intellectual disabilities. *Women's Studies International Forum.*

McColl, M., Carlson, P., Johnston, J., Minnes, P., Shue, K., Davies, D., et al. (1998). The definition of community integration: Perspectives of people with brain injuries. *Brain Injury, 12*(1), 15–30.

McConnell, D., Dalziel, A., Llewellyn, G., Laidlaw, K., & Hindmarsh, G. (2008). Strengthening the social relationships of mothers with learning difficulties. *British Journal of Learning Disabilities, 37*(1), 66–75.

Myers, F., Ager, A., Kerr, P., & Myles, S. (1998). Outside looking in? Studies of the community integration of people with learning disabilities. *Disability and Society*, *13*(3), 389–413.

Nirje, B. (1969). The normalization principle and its human management implications. In R. B. Kugel & W. Wolfensberger (Eds.), *Changing patterns in residential services for the mentally retarded* (pp. 179–195). Washington, DC: President's Committee on Mental Retardation.

Nirje, B. (1980). The normalization principle. In R. J. Flynn & K. E. Nitsch (Eds.), *Normalization, social integration and community services* (pp. 31–50). Baltimore: University Park Press.

O'Donnell, C., & Tharp, R. (1990). Community intervention guided by theoretical development. In A. S. Bellack, M. Hersen, & A. E. Kazdin (Eds.), *International handbook of behavior modification and therapy* (pp. 251–266). New York: Plenum Press.

Punch, M. (1994). Politics and ethics in qualitative research. In N. Denzin & Y. Lincoln (Eds.), *Handbook of qualitative research* (pp. 83–97). Thousand Oaks, CA: Sage.

Ringsby-Jansson, B. (2002). *Vardagslivets arenor – om människor med utvecklingsstörning, deras vardag och sociala liv* [The arenas of everyday life: About the daily and social lives of people with intellectual disabilities]. Göteborg: Institutionen för socialt arbete, Göteborg University.

Sarason, S. B. (1974). *The psychological sense of community: Prospects for a community psychology.* San Francisco: Jossey-Bass.

Schutz, A. (1967). *The phenomenology of the social world.* Evanston, IL: Northwestern University Press.

Schutz, A. (1970). *On phenomenology and social relations: Selected writings* ( H. R. Wagner, Ed.). Chicago: University of Chicago Press.

Tarleton, B., & Ward, L. (2007). Parenting with support: The views and experiences of parents with intellectual disabilities. *Journal of Policy and Practice in Intellectual Disabilities*, *4*(3), 194–202.

Tucker, M. B., & Johnson, O. (1989). Competence promoting versus competence inhibiting social support for mentally retarded mothers. *Human Organization*, *48*(2), 95–107.

United Nations. (1994). *The standard rules on the equalization of opportunities for persons with disabilities.* New York: Author.

United Nations. (2006). *Convention on the rights of persons with disabilities.* New York: Author.

Wolfensberger, W. (1972). *The principle of normalization in human services.* Toronto: National Institute on Mental Retardation.

Wolfensberger, W. (1980). A brief overview of the principle of normalization. In R. J. Flynn & K. E. Nitsch (Eds.), *Normalization, social integration, and community services* (pp. 7–30). Baltimore: University Park Press.

World Health Organization. (2001). *ICF: International classification of functioning, disability and health.* Geneva: Author.

# 6

# Citizenship and Community Participation

*Brigit Mirfin-Veitch*

## Introduction

Caring for and rearing children safely and well is one of the most rewarding and challenging tasks of adulthood, with many personal and societal factors interacting to make this task easier, or to pose enormous barriers to successful parenting. While there has been a necessary research emphasis on the quantity and quality of support parents receive, it is also clear that we may need to look more broadly in order to determine other factors that also have the potential to impact on a person's ability to parent successfully. This chapter is based on a three-year New Zealand-based study which sought the perspectives of parents with intellectual disabilities in order to gain an in-depth understanding of the factors that hindered or helped them in their parenting roles. Through an analysis of study data, the importance of a real and sustained experience of citizenship and community participation for parents with intellectual disabilities was identified. Specifically, findings generated through this study suggested that adults with intellectual disabilities who approached and experienced pregnancy, childbirth, and parenting within a framework of active citizenship and community participation tended to experience greater parenting success. This chapter has the purpose of exploring some of the markers of active citizenship and community engagement, and discusses the parenting outcomes for two different parents who parented in either the presence or absence of commonly defined markers of social inclusion.

*Parents with Intellectual Disabilities: Past, Present and Futures*   Edited by Gwynnyth Llewellyn, Rannveig Traustadóttir, David McConnell, and Hanna Björg Sigurjónsdóttir   © 2010 John Wiley & Sons, Ltd

## Citizenship

For the purposes of this chapter a broad description of citizenship and community participation as it pertains to individuals with intellectual disability is provided with an acknowledgment that both these concepts have their own comprehensive, and often interrelated, literature. Ryan (1997) defined citizenship as being: "about a person's capacity to fully participate in all dimensions of social, political and community life" (p.19).

In Ryan's view, active citizenship refers to a process whereby people are able to participate in decisions that affect their lives, to receive and understand information, and to make decisions that are of their own choosing. That is, active citizenship denotes not just having rights, but also possessing a level of knowledge that facilitates a process whereby a person is able to exercise those rights. Ryan advocates that citizenship for people with intellectual disabilities can only be enhanced by increasing their participation in the community. Furthermore, in exercising their right to participate in both the political and social spheres, changes by which people with intellectual disabilities are more readily accepted as active citizens will eventually occur. As Ryan (1997) notes,

> This process of enhancing citizenship by community participation does not engage people as passive recipients of welfare services but as active citizens engaged in articulating and changing the world in which they live. (p. 19)

## Community participation

While community participation is an important goal for all people with disabilities, it is one that has been difficult to achieve for adults with intellectual disabilities in New Zealand. This difficulty has been experienced despite the presence of government policy that endorses the principle of community participation (Associate Minister of Social Services and Employment, 2001; Minister for Disability Issues, 2001).

The concept of community is highly debated and has been the subject of considerable theoretical discussion (Bray & Gates, 2003). In its broadest sense, community participation is a general concept which views "community" as a geographic space, which includes the ordinary and varied activities of other citizens (Bray & Gates, 2003). In the field of disability research, it has been common for community to be viewed as the opposite of the type of segregation or isolation in institutional facilities that has been experienced by many people with intellectual disabilities. Community has also been described by a number of researchers as comprising three interrelated components – place, people, and a sense of belonging (Walker, 1999). To experience community participation, one must feel a sense of place in one's community, be involved in a variety of social networks, and feel a sense of belonging. Meaningful community participation involves much more than simply living in any given community (Taylor, Bogdan, & Lutfiyya, 1995). In applying this lens, various New Zealand researchers now characterize the social position of people with intellectual disabilities as "strangers" to their community, living in but seldom of this social and political landscape (Milner & Kelly, 2009; O'Brien, 2003).

When we consider the lives of parents with intellectual disabilities, all too often markers of citizenship and community participation are absent from their lives. To really feel part of a community, people with disabilities need to be involved in a variety of social networks, and to feel a sense of connection to where they live. In a recent collaborative study with people with disabilities, Milner and Kelly (2009) identified five qualitative indicators of participatory membership and belonging. For these people with disabilities, participation needed to: be self-chosen; communicate a positive and autobiographical social identity and place; be bound by reciprocally valued social exchange; include participatory expectations; and occur in places of psychological safety.

During the process of learning about the broad and varied life experiences of parents with intellectual disabilities, an interest developed in the impact of the presence or absence of citizenship and community participation on parenting outcomes for parents with intellectual disabilities.

## The Research Study

This chapter is based on research conducted with 19 New Zealand parents with intellectual disabilities. While it is difficult to be specific about exactly how many parents with intellectual disabilities there are, New Zealand parenting prevalence figures suggest that 2.51 families per 1,000 families include one or more parents with intellectual disabilities (Mirfin-Veitch, Bray, Williams, Clarkson, & Belton, 1999). Parenting research has consistently reported a high rate (30–50%) of child removal from parents with intellectual disabilities (Booth & Booth, 2004), and this finding has also been reflected in the New Zealand context (Conder, Mirfin-Veitch, Sanders, & Munford, 2008; Mirfin-Veitch et al., 1999). Against this backdrop, and due to the resulting increase in demand for information, services, and support designed to meet the needs of parents with intellectual disabilities, a three-year qualitative study was conducted.

The broad aim of the research discussed in this chapter was to identify and understand the barriers that prevent policy and support services in New Zealand from adequately meeting the needs of parents with intellectual disabilities. The study was conducted using a longitudinal design that located parents firmly at the center of the research. This approach enabled the research team to understand the history of family and parental development over time, and also supported the development of strong researcher–participant relationships.

The quality of these relationships meant that parents felt comfortable not only sharing current parenting experiences, but also elaborating on their individual life histories. The research team was interested in learning from the parents themselves about the context of their past and present lives, and how the human relationships they had experienced impacted on their current ability to parent. This approach is consistent with Bronfenbrenner's (1979) ecological model of human development and family functioning. Gaining such an in-depth and personal knowledge of the complex issues confronted by parents with intellectual disabilities and the ways in which parents (and others) responded to, and interpreted, these issues was viewed as being best achieved using a qualitative research approach.

Thirteen mothers and six fathers with intellectual disabilities participated in repeated, in-depth qualitative interviews. The researchers were assisted by a semi-structured interview schedule but explored issues at each interview that were motivated by and/or dependent on what was particularly relevant to each parent at the time of interview. Parents were interviewed between one and six times over the course of the study depending on their personal circumstances and when they joined the study. Parents were also asked to nominate a range of formal and informal supporters whom they perceived as providing valuable assistance, and these individuals were also interviewed, usually more than once, during the study period. Most (13) of the parents had already lost custody of their children and, as a consequence, their children lived in out-of-home care. In some cases children had been removed at or soon after birth, while other parents had cared for their children for longer periods including up to five years of age. Interview transcripts were analyzed using a general inductive approach (Thomas, 2006), and one important theme to emerge from an analysis of the parents' transcripts – the presence or absence of citizenship and community participation – provides the focus of this chapter.

As already noted, the quality of the research relationships that we were able to develop throughout the conduct of this study was critical to the overall success of the research. We were aware that many of the parents we were seeking to recruit were likely to have, or to have had, ongoing involvement with statutory care and protection services and the family court system. Indeed, this was the case for almost all of the parents who chose to participate in this study. For many, involvement with New Zealand's statutory care and protection service had commenced during their own childhood. The parents had often experienced a long history of surveillance, intervention, and questioning. The research team carefully considered who to approach and how to talk in an ethically sound and respectful manner. Researchers new to the field often find this quite challenging; we have shared how we addressed methodological and ethical issues in some detail in two recent reports (Munford, Sanders, Mirfin-Veitch, & Conder, 2008a; Munford, Sanders, Mirfin-Veitch, & Conder, 2008b).

# Parents' Stories

This study enabled us to learn from parents with intellectual disabilities over time about their childhood and about their experiences as an adult. We find that one of the most illuminating ways to present the contrast and diversity so frequently apparent in the lives of parents with intellectual disabilities is to tell their individual stories. In order to illustrate the impact of parenting in the presence or the absence of citizenship and community participation, the stories of two different parents are presented.

## Nicky's story

Nicky grew up in a close and loving family. While her parents had separated and then divorced when she was a child, she remained close to both her parents and had a positive relationship with her siblings. She attended her local school and remained a member of her regular class. Her family advocated energetically on her behalf and they expected that the opportunities open to other members of the family as they progressed throughout school would also be available to Nicky. She aspired to get a job, and loved to meet her friends to socialize and talk.

At the time we met Nicky she was in her early 20s and was a full-time, stay-at-home mum to her young daughter. Nicky lived in a rented home with her own mother and two other family members. Her child lived happily within this extended family environment and was clearly attached to Nicky. The seemingly happy scene of family and parenting within which we first made our acquaintance with Nicky was hugely different to the circumstances that prevailed when she found herself to be pregnant.

Nicky's pregnancy occurred as a result of non-consensual sexual intercourse. Nicky knew the father of her baby and had gone on a date that culminated in sex that she did not plan to have. No criminal charges resulted from this encounter. Despite this distressing experience, when she discovered that she was pregnant Nicky immediately told a friend, and then her mother. Her pregnancy was not treated as a disaster but instead Nicky, along with her mother and other extended family members, began a process of thinking critically about how she would like to respond to her pregnancy. All options were explained to Nicky. She was supported to attend her general practitioner, who confirmed her pregnancy, and then a thorough discussion took place over a number of weeks about the options available to her as a young, single woman who now was in the position of having an unplanned pregnancy. Abortion, adoption (including in-family adoption), and keeping the baby herself were all raised, explained to, and considered by Nicky. At the time we first met Nicky, her baby had been born and was living with her. Nicky explained to me why she had not considered abortion or adoption as viable options. Abortion, in her view, equated to killing a baby. This did not fit with her own values and as a consequence she quickly eliminated this as an option. Further illustrating her engagement in the decision-making process around her unplanned pregnancy, Nicky also explained why she considered and rejected inter-family adoption. In Nicky's view, she would have found it too emotionally difficult to see her child parented by extended family members rather than by her. Consequently, for Nicky, the only decision that was ethically and emotionally viable was to raise her own child.

With the full support of her family, Nicky moved forward with her plan to have her child. A support plan was developed that included a midwife, formal support from a nanny directly following the birth, and less intensive support from both a generic family support organization and a disability support service. Despite this comprehensive prior planning, Nicky's family observed intense scrutiny of Nicky at the time of her daughter's birth as hospital staff reacted to the idea of a young woman with intellectual disabilities having a child rather than taking the time to explore Nicky's individual circumstances. Nicky's own mother and other members of the support configuration advocated strongly on her behalf, and fortunately intervention from statutory child protection services was circumvented.

Nicky's decision to give birth to and parent her baby impacted on other members of her family, particularly Nicky's own mother. In order to support her daughter, she was required to make significant changes to her own life. First, the family moved into a new rented home. The home was chosen on the understanding that Nicky would eventually take over the rental of the property and that the rest of the family would move out. This was based on the family's expectation, even prior to the baby's birth, that Nicky would be a competent mother and would not need the close support of her family indefinitely. This attitude illustrated the extent to which Nicky's family believed in her and her ability to do well as a parent. While Nicky was surrounded by support, she was expected to take responsibility for the care of her child and to be at the heart of any decision making. If her family felt she was becoming over-reliant on their support, or if she was perceived as starting to take advantage of the availability of their support, she was reminded of her responsibilities as a parent. At the time of writing, when Nicky's little girl was three years old, Nicky continued to parent her young child with the support of her family, to attend the local family services in her neighborhood, and to make plans for further education and training in order to improve her chances of getting a job in the future.

## Suzanne's story

When we first met, Suzanne was living alone in a large, dilapidated home situated in the outer suburbs of a New Zealand town. Despite the fact that Suzanne's son had not lived with her for a number of years at that time, a mutually loving relationship between mother and child was evident in the proudly displayed photographs, and from the artwork and messages of love from a child to a parent typically displayed in many New Zealand family homes. Suzanne was eager to talk about her son, who had been removed from her care at the age of five. The shock and ongoing grief that this event had caused for Suzanne were palpable, and over two years after her son had been removed from her care, she continued to appear to be confused about why she had lost custody. She also found it difficult to understand why her efforts to have him returned to her care were unsuccessful, despite her extensive efforts to achieve reunification.

From the time of our first meeting Suzanne talked extensively about her family life. She had one sibling with whom she was close but had a strained relationship with her mother and step-siblings. Suzanne said that she was always in a special class at school, and this segregation from her peers was compounded at the beginning of her teenage years. Her mother by this stage had two much younger children, and because she required Suzanne's help with the housework and babysitting, Suzanne was totally withdrawn from school to fulfill these tasks on a daily basis. Suzanne saw the problem between her and her mother as being that "she didn't really want me when I was born, she wanted to get rid of me but my dad stopped that, said no." Suzanne's break from her family became total when she was sexually abused by a family member in her mid-teens, and was raped by another person known to her. After telling a trusted adult, Suzanne was removed from her family home and received formal support from an intellectual disability service. While she appreciated the support she received, Suzanne decided to get her own place and from then on either lived alone or, occasionally for short periods, with a partner. Her pregnancy, when she was about 30 years old, signaled the end of her relationship with the baby's father. Soon after the baby's birth, Suzanne was supported by a much older man whom she saw as having a positive impact on her and her baby's life. Her relationship with this man ended, however, when Suzanne saw some of his associates as potentially creating an unsafe environment for her and her child. Suzanne's parenting had been the subject of attention from statutory child protection services from the time of her child's birth.

Suzanne experienced difficulty in developing and sustaining safe and supportive relationships with men. She was very keen to have a relationship, feel loved, and to have the kind of happy family life that she felt her son deserved. However, what she often described were relationships that were dangerous, both emotionally and physically, abusive of her generous and loving nature, and which led her further away from her goal of parenting her child. The men who came into Suzanne's life were generally perceived by those in formal support roles as having the potential to be harmful to Suzanne's child. Suzanne would eventually choose her desire to be reunited with her child over her need to have a partner and would end these relationships. However, she was never rewarded with her son coming home. Her fear of choosing the wrong people to be part of her life was one of the factors that contributed to an increasingly impoverished informal support network.

Despite Suzanne's ambition to have her child returned to her care, the reality was that her access and rights as a parent gradually eroded over time. At the time of our first meeting, Suzanne parented her child three days per week and had limited support while she did so. Over the three years of the study, however, Suzanne increasingly saw the time she had with her son being reduced and the level of supervision to which she was subject being augmented. Suzanne gradually lost trust in the people who were formally supporting her and believed that they were there to "spy" on her and to report her failings to child protection. She also felt that her efforts to address the issues that she understood contributed to the decision to remove her child from her care went unnoticed and unrewarded. At the conclusion of this research, Suzanne was seeing her child once a week and the visit was supervised. She had almost resigned herself to the fact that it was unlikely that her son would ever be returned to her care.

## Parenting in the Presence and Absence of Citizenship and Community Participation

The key characteristics of community participation have been identified as including: a personal sense of control; support; having control over decisions; taking part in the social life of a community; having a network of personal relationships; being involved in community places and activities; and being free from discrimination and abuse.

Both Nicky and Suzanne had demonstrated citizenship by exercising their individual right to have a child. However, as their individual stories illustrate, there was a vast difference in their parenting experiences. Nicky parented in the presence of an implicit sense of citizenship and explicit experience of community participation. Nicky's story was characterized most significantly by the presence of a loving family. Perhaps more importantly, however, the unconditional love that Nicky received from her family was coupled with an expectation that she had the same rights and the same aspirations as other family members. She was centrally involved in the decisions relating to her own life and was given the necessary information to make the right decisions for her. She was supported in the decisions that she made and difficulties were treated as simply problems to overcome, not as evidence that she could not cope. Nicky's family and support network set up the support to succeed, not to fail, and long-term rather than short-term solutions were implemented, thus demonstrating the commitment to Nicky being a full-time and long-term parent. Also central to Nicky's story was friendship, a regular and typical social life, and involvement in a range of community activities. Nicky did not see the need to access specialist services because her local community services met her needs and she felt comfortable using them. Despite the difficult circumstances surrounding Nicky's pregnancy, she was treated with dignity and respect and remained an active participant in the decisions that were made about her own and her baby's well-being. These all represented a culmination of the real and sustained markers of citizenship and community participation that had characterized Nicky's path to adult life and parenthood.

While Nicky's story provides a positive example of parenting, Suzanne's story represents an experience at the opposite end of the continuum. In contrast to Nicky, Suzanne's experience was characterized by a dysfunctional family life that had begun in early childhood and endured throughout her adult life. Suzanne was not supported by her own family in any way when she had her baby and had only minimal and infrequent contact with a few members of her family. An early assault on her right to active citizenship can be seen in her withdrawal from school, with seemingly no thought to the ongoing impact of this loss of access to education. Suzanne had led a life characterized by neglect and discrimination, and she had experienced serious sexual, physical, and emotional abuse on a regular and ongoing basis. She had little access to education or information that may have contributed to positive decision making, and subsequently she experienced a lack of control over the decisions that had an impact on her right to parent or to develop an ongoing relationship with her child. Suzanne had few personal relationships because of her fear of associating with the "wrong people"; therefore, her social isolation was extreme. Despite a personal ambition to get a job, the closest Suzanne came to achieving this was to attend an adult literacy course that did not result in any employment opportunities. Also absent from Suzanne's life was any real involvement in community activities. Like the social typology of the "stranger" living in but not of her community, Suzanne seemed to see herself as divorced from the social and political life of her community. Her only involvement came in snapshots as individuals involved with her child moved in and out of her life, or in visits to the local park during her increasingly reduced access visits. The markers of active citizenship and community participation were largely absent from Suzanne's life.

## Conclusion

The findings generated through this New Zealand study of parenting have illustrated that the presence or absence of citizenship and community participation impacts significantly on the ability for parents with intellectual disabilities to achieve a "good-enough" standard of parenting. While it is extremely important to address and to resolve parenting difficulties in a formal, immediate, and individualized manner, this research has shown that it is also crucial to consider the wider issues of citizenship and community participation. Unfortunately, many people with an intellectual disability continue to reach adulthood without a strong sense of citizenship or connection to their local community. Social isolation has been consistently identified as a common experience for people with intellectual disabilities, and in the case of parents with intellectual disabilities, this lack of connection to and participation in their local community is likely to have a negative impact on their parenting. An often-used expression in New Zealand is that "it takes a community to raise a child." This message has been used in the context of the promotion of family health and well-being and acknowledges publicly that parents need support to parent successfully. For the parents with intellectual disabilities who participated in this New Zealand study, this assumption has particular relevance. As illustrated by the contrasting stories of Nicky and Suzanne, those parents who recognized and were able to exercise their rights as citizens, and who had strong family and community relationships, were more likely to be seen as successful parents and to retain care and custody of their children. Those parents whose lives had been characterized by exclusion, social isolation, and disconnection from their local community were more often the parents who struggled to reach the standard of good-enough parenting, or who parented under surveillance for long periods.

The issues raised through this chapter represent an attempt to highlight my view that some of the difficulties faced by parents with intellectual disabilities may not be able to be resolved simply by focusing on the immediate and obvious support needs of parents. In order to work toward achieving a context within which parents can achieve ongoing parenting success, efforts must be focused on achieving participation and citizenship within all of the communities with which people with intellectual disabilities interact throughout their life course. Without wider structural and attitudinal change within the social and political activities that bind communities together, discrimination, child removal, and a high degree of surveillance will continue to characterize the parenting efforts of many adults with intellectual disabilities.

It is also critical that future support and service initiatives consider the issues of citizenship and community participation and identify and implement practical ways to ensure that parents do not continue to be marginalized and isolated within their local communities. There are a number of ways in which formal supports and services can encourage and facilitate citizenship and community participation.

## Principles for Practice

Educators must ensure that the education curriculum is accessible to young people with intellectual disabilities so that learning and development in the area of citizenship and participation can occur in the same way they do for their non-disabled peers. Young adults with intellectual disabilities may need support to understand both their rights as citizens and how they can go about exercising those rights. Transition programs are an obvious context within which to include a focus on developing understanding of these areas.

Programs and services designed to support parents should explore the life histories of individual parents in order to understand how these experiences may impact on a person's current parenting abilities. In doing so, a greater responsiveness to families' needs is likely to be achieved.

Citizenship means more than having rights; it is underpinned by the premise that individuals will exercise those rights. The opportunity to develop self-advocacy skills may be a necessary component of support for many parents who may not have gained the skills to self-advocate during their childhood, adolescence, and early adult life. Furthermore, for some parents effective support will include an advocacy component.

It is common for parents with intellectual disabilities to be "in" but not "of" their local community. Parenting in isolation is detrimental to both parents and their children, making it critical that parents are supported to create positive, meaningful, and self-sustaining relationships within these communities. Encouraging and supporting parents to attend and gain acceptance within local groups and typical family activities may lead to a reduction in formal support for some families.

# References

Associate Minister of Social Services and Employment. (2001). *Pathways to inclusion: Improving vocational services for people with disabilities*. Wellington: Department of Labour.

Booth, W., & Booth, T. (2004). A family at risk: Multiple perspectives on parenting and child protection. *British Journal of Learning Disabilities, 32*(1), 9–15.

Bray, A., & Gates, S. (2003). *Community participation for adults with an intellectual disability: Review of the literature prepared for the National Advisory Committee.* Dunedin: Donald Beasley Institute.

Bronfenbrenner, U. (1979). *The ecology of human development.* Cambridge, MA: Harvard University Press.

Conder, J., Mirfin-Veitch, B., Sanders, J., & Munford, R. (2008). "I've got to think of him. . .": Relationships between parents with intellectual disabilities and foster parents. *Developing Practice, 21,* 17–25.

Milner, P., & Kelly, B. (2009). Community participation and inclusion: People with disabilities defining their place. *Disability and Society, 24*(1), 47–62.

Minister for Disability Issues. (2001). *The New Zealand Disability Strategy: Making a world of difference – Whakanui Oranga.* Wellington: Ministry of Health.

Mirfin-Veitch, B., Bray, A., Williams, S., Clarkson, J., & Belton, A. (1999). Supporting parents with intellectual disabilities. *New Zealand Journal of Disability Studies, 6,* 60–74.

Munford, R., Sanders, J., Mirfin-Veitch, B., & Conder, J. (2008a). Ethics and research: Searching for ethical practice in research. *Ethics and Social Welfare*, 2(1), 50–66.

Munford, R., Sanders, J., Mirfin-Veitch, B., & Conder, J. (2008b). Looking inside the bag of tools: Creating research encounters with intellectually disabled parents. *Disability and Society*, 23(4), 337–347.

O'Brien, P. (2003). Envisioning the future without the social alienation of difference. *International Journal of Disability, Development and Education*, 50(1), 17–38.

Ryan, R. (1997). Participatory processes for citizenship for people with intellectual disabilities. *Interaction*, 10(4), 19–23.

Taylor, S. J., Bogdan, R., & Lutfiyya, Z. M. (1995). *The variety of community experience: Qualitative studies of family and community life*. Baltimore: Paul H. Brookes.

Thomas, D. (2006). A general inductive approach for analyzing qualitative evaluation data. *American Journal of Evaluation*, 27(2), 237–246.

Walker, P. (1999). From community presence to a sense of place: Community experiences of adults with developmental disabilities. *Journal of the Association for Persons with Severe Handicap*, 24(1), 23–32.

# 7

# Parenting and Resistance: Strategies in Dealing with Services and Professionals

*Rannveig Traustadóttir and Hanna Björg Sigurjónsdóttir*

## Introduction

People with intellectual disabilities are widely presumed to be incompetent as parents and many studies show that they are at high risk of having their children removed. The research literature reports that between 40 and 60% of parents with intellectual disabilities lose custody of their children (Booth & Booth, 1994; McConnell, Llewellyn, & Ferronato, 2002). As a result, many parents live in fear of the service system and have developed various strategies to try to ensure their children are not removed from their care.

In this chapter we present an analysis of the strategies parents with intellectual disabilities employ in their dealings with a service system they often view as hostile and powerful. The chapter focuses on the ways in which parents resist the stereotypical notion of them as incompetent and their attempts to minimize the risk of losing their children. We base the analysis on our long-term, ongoing involvement with parents with intellectual disabilities, primarily as researchers but also as advocates. Since 1994 we have carried out various research projects with parents with intellectual disabilities and their children (e.g., Sigurjónsdóttir, 2004, 2005; Sigurjónsdóttir & Traustadóttir, 2001; Traustadóttir & Sigurjónsdóttir, 2008). Our methods have required us to spend long periods of time with families headed by parents with intellectual disabilities and many of the projects have been collaborative and called for the active participation of parents (Walmsley & Johnson, 2003). Our relationship with the parents has spanned many years and some of the parents we met during our first studies in the 1990s are still involved in our projects in various ways.

*Parents with Intellectual Disabilities: Past, Present and Futures*   Edited by Gwynnyth Llewellyn, Rannveig Traustadóttir, David McConnell, and Hanna Björg Sigurjónsdóttir   © 2010 John Wiley & Sons, Ltd

We begin the chapter by reflecting on how resistance has been understood and discussed in relation to people with intellectual disabilities in general. We then turn our attention to resistance and parents with intellectual disabilities and outline some of the historical and social contexts of their lives. Following this is our analysis of the various strategies parents use in interacting with services they fear will take away their children. Combating discrimination and resisting institutional regimes and other powerful services are recurring themes in the lives of people with intellectual disabilities. We conclude the chapter by arguing that the strategies used by parents with intellectual disabilities in resisting the power of the services system are a continuation of the struggle for human rights of people with intellectual disabilities.

## Resistance and People with Intellectual Disabilities

The term *resistance* is widely used in many academic fields as well as in social and political action. In the social sciences this concept usually refers to people's attempts to counter the actions or effects of someone or something, withstand such actions, or oppose them. In the field of intellectual disability, resistance has most commonly been used in relation to the institutionalization of people with intellectual disabilities. An increasing number of personal narratives by people who have lived in these institutions describe how these people resisted the dehumanizing and oppressive conditions of institutional life. An example of this is a recent book devoted to examining resistance in this context titled *Exploring Experiences of Advocacy by People with Learning Disabilities: Testimonies of Resistance* (Mitchell et al., 2006). The book consists of collections of personal accounts and academic reflections that explore how people with intellectual disabilities have spoken up for themselves and resisted oppression.

In another volume exploring institutional life and deinstitutionalization from the perspective of people with intellectual disabilities, resistance is one of the major themes in the personal accounts of people with intellectual disabilities (Johnson & Traustadóttir, 2005). This book describes the many different ways people with intellectual disabilities have protested conditions in the institutions; they have spoken up, become angry, hidden, run away, taken their cases to court, fought, exhibited "challenging" or "bad" behaviors, and found support from others.

These two books provide a new perspective on many aspects of the lives of people with intellectual disabilities. Instead of portraying such individuals as passive victims of their surroundings, these personal accounts present them as active agents in shaping their environment and managing their lives. Many describe various methods of resistance, either as individuals or as a group effort, sometimes leading to formalized self-advocacy.

One provocative aspect of these books is their presentation of an alternative way of understanding behavior that is commonly understood as challenging, difficult, bad, or problematic. These books propose we approach such behaviors with a new perspective and interpret them as a form of resistance, thereby defining them in a more positive way as logical responses to oppressive treatment and not as a "defect" of the individual (see, e.g., Dale, 2006; Nind, 2006; O'Brien, 2005; Owen, 2006). A common theme in these accounts is people's struggle to resist powerful services, professionals, and staff that presume they should be in control of the lives of people with intellectual disabilities. In these writings the institutions are characterized as the most oppressive in exercising power and control over all aspects of people's lives. A close look at the lives of people with intellectual disabilities in institutions helps us understand how people are able to survive isolation and dehumanizing treatment, and resist them. In writing about the strategies used by institutionalized people, O'Brien (2005) draws our attention to the agency and creativity of those living in institutions and warns against viewing them merely as passive victims waiting to be rescued. Instead, he suggests we adopt a more nuanced view to understand the ways people carve out moments of meaning and freedom, and urges us to understand how to see people's capacities for resistance as critical in order to move beyond oppressive conditions.

## Resistance and Parents with Intellectual Disabilities

Historically, people with intellectual disabilities have been judged unfit to be parents and various actions have been taken to prevent them from having children. The ideology behind institutionalization was the eugenics movement, which demanded that people with intellectual disabilities (then called morons, feeble-minded, or mentally retarded) were sent to institutions where they were segregated by sex to prevent them from having children (Scheerenberger, 1983). Another measure to prevent people with intellectual disabilities from having children was the mass sterilization carried out in most western countries and practiced into the 1970s in many places (Brantlinger, 1995). Efforts to prevent women with intellectual disabilities from having children continue. In our research and interactions with women with intellectual disabilities, we have come across a number of women, some of whom are young women, who have been sterilized. We have also met women who have had to resist being sterilized and others who have been coerced into having an abortion. There continue to be many barriers against women with intellectual disabilities having and raising children. These barriers are widely documented in the literature on parents with intellectual disabilities (Booth & Booth, 1994; Danish Ministry of Social Affairs, 1996; Sigurjónsdóttir, 2005; Tarleton, Ward, & Howarth, 2006).

Women with intellectual disabilities are aware of this history of prejudice and discriminatory practices and the widespread belief that they should not have children. In this context it is easy to understand their fear and resistance to the power of social services, and many studies have accounted for parents' conflicts with the service system (Booth & Booth, 1994, 1995, 1998a; Danish Ministry of Social Affairs, 1996; Espe-Sherwindt & Crable, 1993; McConnell, 2001; Tarleton et al., 2006; Taylor, 1995).

It is important to acknowledge that there are a number of professionals working with parents with intellectual disabilities who provide good and em-powering support and assist parents in many ways. The literature, however, indicates that this is the exception rather than the rule and that parents are more likely to encounter services that regard people with intellectual disabili-ties as not fit to be parents (Booth, Booth, & McConnell, 2005; Edgerton, 1999; Espe-Sherwindt & Crable, 1993; McConnell & Llewellyn, 2002). Their wish to have and raise children is commonly seen as unrealistic and unacceptable, and their attitude and behavior are interpreted as difficult for the service system and potentially harmful for their children (Danish Ministry of Social Affairs, 1996; Tarleton et al., 2006).

Detailed accounts of family life in families headed by parents with intellectual disabilities, presented from their own point of view, are rare. However, one such insider view is presented by Taylor (1995, 2000) in his writings about a family he calls the Duke family. Taylor's in-depth descriptions of the Duke family offer a rare insight into the lives of families headed by parents with intellectual disabilities, their ways of thinking about their lives, their understanding of their situation, and the strategies they use to deal with extended family as well as with services and professionals.

In light of the strong opposition to their parenting, it is interesting to examine how people with intellectual disability have managed to have children and what strategies they have employed to deal with a system that has such a profound distrust of their ability to be parents and that suspects children may be harmed by being raised in such families.

## Strategies in Dealing with Services and Professionals

Below we examine the strategies parents employ to overcome barriers to having children and describe their attempts to ensure their children will not be taken away.

### Concealing the pregnancy

Many of the mothers with intellectual disabilities we have encountered knew their pregnancy would not be received positively by their extended family and professionals, and some of them had to fight for their right to continue the pregnancy. In order to avoid being pressured into having an abortion, some mothers did not tell anyone about the pregnancy until it was too late for an abortion to occur. This is not unique for the mothers we have met as a similar strategy has been used by other parents with intellectual disabilities in other countries (Pixa-Kettner, 1996).

## Refusing to accept support and services

Many parents with intellectual disabilities have had negative experiences of the service system and there is a long history of difficult relations between parents and professionals (Booth & Booth, 1994; Booth et al., 2005; Danish Ministry of Social Affairs, 1996; McConnell et al., 2002; Tarleton et al., 2006). This is also true for the parents who have taken part in our research projects. Many of them have described problematic encounters with services. In addition, even if some of the parents had not had personal encounters with professionals, they knew about other people's negative experiences. As a result there was a widespread fear of the service system and parents frequently felt powerless in their dealings with professionals. Many of the professionals they encountered had neither the knowledge nor the experience of working with people with intellectual disabilities. These professionals commonly assumed that people with intellectual disabilities did not have the competence to be parents and would be unable to understand their children's developmental needs.

Knowing that the professionals often regarded them as incompetent, many parents were reluctant to ask for assistance, were afraid to receive services, and some refused to accept the assistance they were offered. This adversarial position and lack of response to services was in some instances counterproductive for the parents because their actions fed into the concerns professionals had about their parenting ability. The fear of engaging with services is widely documented in the literature on parents with intellectual disabilities and a refusal to accept support seems to be a common strategy used by parents in their attempts to avoid losing their children (Booth & Booth, 1993, 1994; Tarleton et al., 2006; Whitman, Graves, & Accardo, 1989).

## Pretending to conform

The parents who have participated in our research projects frequently received services from a variety of agencies such as child and family services, disability services, and health and social services. We have sometimes been present when support workers have visited parents' homes to provide support in taking care of their children. This support is important for the parents and their children, but it is not problem free. The parents did not always agree with the advice given by the support workers because it was not consistent with their values. Even more problematic was that professionals sometimes gave different, even conflicting, advice about raising the child. This had the potential to create anxiety in the parents, who knew they were required to act in accordance with the instructions from professionals but found it impossible to follow the conflicting advice they received. Another difficulty was that the instructions and advice provided were sometimes complicated and hard for the parents to understand. The parents were often frustrated in these situations but were afraid to ask for clarifications or argue with the professionals since they feared that this would be seen as evidence of their lack of competence and cooperation.

A common strategy parents used in these situations was to pretend to understand and to accept and cooperate with the support workers. The parents did not say much except "yes" and nodded their heads in agreement to what the support worker said, pretending they understood everything and trying to convince the support worker they would conform. After the worker left, however, they did what they themselves judged was best or, if needed, called on people they trusted to give them sound advice. By doing this, the parents were attempting to please the system and behave as they thought the system wanted them to. This was one of their strategies to keep support workers happy with their performance as parents.

## Establishing a parent group

The most proactive move on behalf of the parents we have encountered in Iceland was to establish a group of parents with intellectual disabilities. They contacted Hanna Björg and asked for her help to establish a group. This was in the autumn of 2002 and the group has met every other week since then. Hanna Björg has taken part in the parent group as a support person and an advocate. The group has two main purposes: first, to be a place where parents with intellectual disabilities come together, share experiences, and support each other; and second, to be a self-advocacy group that can speak up on behalf of parents with intellectual disabilities and their families, and work toward more rights for parents. The group has been empowering for the parents who take part in it and has increased their self-esteem and ability to advocate on their own behalf. Other studies have found that parent groups are regarded positively by parents with intellectual disabilities as a valuable resource where they can share helpful information and support one another (Tarleton et al., 2006).

## Recruiting advocates

The importance of advocacy to assist parents with intellectual disabilities to engage with child and family services is documented in the research literature (Booth & Booth, 1998b, 1999; Tarleton et al., 2006; Taylor, 1995). Despite this we found that advocacy support was not readily available for most parents in our studies. The parents expressed most need for assistance from advocates in dealing with child protection services and in going to meetings with professionals.

In some of these meetings parents had to face a number of professionals and other people from the services who had gathered to discuss their "case." Some of the parents found it difficult to follow what was going on in these meetings and even more difficult to argue with the professionals. Many of them tried to find an advocate to go with them to these meetings, often a family member or someone else they trusted. Parents said they were treated with more respect and were listened to when they were accompanied by an advocate. One of the mothers does not have an advocate to go to meetings with her and often feels she is talked down to and not taken seriously in these meetings. She has attempted to change this by taking a tape recorder with her and told the professionals she was recording the meeting. This strategy worked and the professionals treated her with more respect in meetings when they knew that what they said was "on the record."

## Staying in the public eye – being visible

The parents with intellectual disabilities who took part in our research projects usually tried to avoid drawing attention to themselves. Other researchers have also noted that parents keep a low profile in order to avoid problems with professionals (Booth & Booth, 1998b). One young couple we met, however, chose a different method of resisting the power of the system. Instead of trying to keep out of sight, they have tried to protect themselves by being highly visible. They have done this by appearing in the media, both in newspapers and on the television. This couple lost custody of their first child. They had been under the supervision of social services during the pregnancy and social workers were worried they would not be able to take care of the baby. In order to receive support in taking care of their newborn son, the parents stayed in the maternity ward at the hospital for a couple of weeks after their son was born. The parents, however, did not know they were being observed and evaluated by the staff in the maternity ward. This was the first time the hospital staff had come into contact with parents with intellectual disabilities. They were unsure what to do and did not want to be responsible "if something went wrong" with the baby after the parents left the hospital. So they decided at the last minute to report the parents to child protection services, saying they did not believe the baby would be safe in their care after they left the hospital. As the young parents were about to leave the hospital and take their baby son home, child protection workers suddenly showed up and took the baby away. The young parents had not been told this was going to happen and were devastated. They have fought to have their son returned but without success.

A few months after their son was taken from them, the mother became pregnant again, this time with twins. After their experience with professionals the parents feared the twins would also be taken away. In a desperate move to protect themselves from the system, they went public with their story. They believed that if they were highly visible, explained publicly how they were treated, and openly expressed their fear of the system, the child protection workers would hesitate to remove their new babies. This young couple has appeared regularly in the media. They have kept custody of their twins but their first son has remained in the custody of others. Other young parents have also appeared in the media, although this has not been a deliberate strategy to keep custody of their children; rather, it has been to make the public more aware of parents with intellectual disabilities.

## Participating in research

Due to our involvement with parents with intellectual disabilities, we are known in their circles. Some new parents with intellectual disabilities believe they would probably be protected if their lives were being observed and their story recorded by someone the service system respects. They thought that if they were known to a researcher who was involved with their lives, it would increase the likelihood of their keeping their children. As a result, some of them have approached us as early as during their pregnancy and asked if they could be a part of our research projects. Taking part in the research provided a guarantee for them that someone would be there to witness how they were treated by the services and the professionals.

## Gendered strategies of resistance

The diverse ways of interacting with professionals discussed above were common to both mothers and fathers. There were, however, gender differences in the parents' dealings with professionals. Women had a tendency to adopt a strategy of obedience and cooperation. They tried to please the professionals and keep them happy by doing what they were told by their support workers. They were more likely than the men to accept the power of the professionals and tried to be "good girls" as well as good clients. Men, on the other hand, had a tendency to challenge the service system and openly defy the service workers. They found it difficult and humiliating when service workers talked down to or did not listen to them and assumed they were incompetent. The men sometimes argued and protested, were angry and resentful. Some of their partners found these confrontations difficult and tried to act as mediators in order to keep the peace between the family and the service system.

# Recognizing Resistance

It is well documented in the research literature that parents with intellectual disabilities fear losing custody of their children and may therefore be likely to avoid encounters with services and resist the power of professionals in their lives. Yet, professionals rarely interpreted the parents' avoidance as resistance and, instead, were more likely to view their behavior as a part of their inability to be responsible parents. Based on our knowledge of families headed by parents with intellectual disabilities, we have come to the conclusion that many of the actions of parents are logical reactions to a situation in which they feel powerless. Many times during the course of our research we have witnessed anger, frustration, desperation, fear, and powerlessness on the part of the parents in their encounters with professionals. We have come to understand many of the parents' behaviors as acts of resistance against the power the service system exercises over them.

Although resistance by people with intellectual disabilities has mostly been discussed in relation to institutional life and deinstitutionalization, a few accounts have documented resistance to some of the oppressive practices found in community services. Thus, O'Brien (2005) argues that we are still "trapped" in the institution in the sense that many institutional practices have been brought into the community, where services still exercise power and control over people's lives. Other authors have expressed similar criticism of community services. In a discussion of deinstitutionalization in Australia, Gardner and Glanville (2005) argue that although moving out of institutions has been positive for many people, there are those for whom life in the community has meant "a move to accommodations that have some or all of the features of an institution," and that people continue "to experience restrictions upon their freedom of movement and other freedoms of decision-making" (p. 223). Tøssebro (2005) draws a similar conclusion based on his experiences of 12 years of research on deinstitutionalization in Norway. He states that although there have been positive changes and developments in community living for people with intellectual disabilities, there are also still similarities to institutional life.

Current community services have some of the characteristics of the institutions in that they still exercise power and control over people's lives. This is also true for many of the services encountered by parents with intellectual disabilities. Their resistance is, therefore, a reaction to stressful and oppressive conditions and should not be understood as a part of the intellectual impairment. Instead of being passive and incompetent, parents' actions present them as active agents in shaping their environment and being in control of their lives. In our analysis, they exhibit various methods of resistance as individuals or as a group in their attempts to protect their families, keep their children, and realize their right to family life.

## Conclusion

A common theme in the stories parents with intellectual disabilities tell is the struggle to resist powerful services, professionals, and staff who presume they should be in control of their lives. We find parallels in their stories and

ts of people who have lived in institutions and whose lives were
ed by oppression, power, and control by others. A closer look at
parents with intellectual disabilities helps us understand that they,
ing to resist oppressive conditions. Inspired by John O'Brien (2005),
we want to draw attention to the agency and creativity of parents and the
ways in which they attempt to carve out moments of freedom. We believe
it is important to understand parents' capacities for resistance as a critical
component of moving beyond oppressive conditions.


## Principles for Practice

There are important lessons we can draw from this chapter.

- It is important that professionals and practitioners recognize resistance
  for what it is and do not interpret the actions of parents with intellectual
  disabilities as a sign of their incompetence or as "defects."
- Professionals and practitioners need to be aware of the history of oppression
  and discrimination against people with intellectual disabilities and view their
  actions in light of their long struggle for the right to a regular community
  life, including family life.
- It is important to understand and encourage parents' capacities for resistance as critical to moving beyond oppressive conditions and continuing
  discrimination.
- Professionals and practitioners play an important role in the lives of many
  parents with intellectual disabilities and their support often makes a critical
  difference in assisting parents to realize their right to have children and live
  a family life.
- Professionals and practitioners should be aware of gender differences in
  parents' reactions to services and professionals they view as overpowering,
  oppressive, and controlling.


## References

Booth, T., & Booth, W. (1993). Parenting with learning difficulties: Lessons for practitioners. *British Journal of Social Work, 23*(5), 459–480.

Booth, T., & Booth, W. (1994). *Parenting under pressure: Mothers and fathers with learning
difficulties.* Buckingham: Open University Press.

Booth, T., & Booth, W. (1995). Unto us a child is born: The trials and rewards of
parenthood for people with learning difficulties. *Australian and New Zealand Journal
of Developmental Disabilities, 20*(1), 25–39.

Booth, T., & Booth, W. (1998a). *Growing up with parents who have learning difficulties.* London: Routledge.

Booth, W., & Booth, T. (1998b). *Advocacy for parents with learning difficulties: Developing advocacy support.* Brighton: Pavilion Publishing/Joseph Rowntree Foundation.

Booth, T., & Booth, W. (1999). Parents together: Action research and advocacy support for parents with learning difficulties. *Health and Social Care in the Community, 7*(6), 464–474.

Booth, T., Booth, W., & McConnell, D. (2005). Care proceedings and parents with learning difficulties: Comparative prevalence and outcomes in an English and Australian court sample. *Child and Family Social Work, 10*(4), 353–360.

Brantlinger, E. (1995). *Sterilization of people with mental disabilities: Issues, perspectives, and cases.* Westport, CT: Augurn House.

Dale, P. (2006). Assistance and resistance: Making sense of inter-war caring strategies. In D. Mitchell, R. Traustadóttir, R. Chapman, L. Townson, N. Ingham, & S. Ledger (Eds.), *Exploring experiences of advocacy by people with learning disabilities: Testimonies of resistance* (pp. 191–201). London: Jessica Kingsley.

Danish Ministry of Social Affairs. (1996). *Parenting with intellectual disability.* Copenhagen: Author.

Edgerton, R. B. (1999). Foreword. *Journal of Intellectual and Developmental Disability, 24*(1), 1–2.

Espe-Sherwindt, M., & Crable, S. (1993). Parents with mental retardation: Mowing beyond the myths. *Topics in Early Childhood Special Education, 13*(2), 154–174.

Gardner, J., & Glanville, L. (2005). New forms of institutionalization in the community. In K. Johnson & R. Traustadóttir (Eds.), *Deinstitutionalization and people with intellectual disabilities: In and out of institutions* (pp. 222–230). London: Jessica Kingsley.

Johnson, K., & Traustadóttir, R. (Eds.). (2005). *Deinstitutionalization and people with intellectual disabilities: In and out of institutions.* London: Jessica Kingsley.

McConnell, D. (2001). *Parents with intellectual disability and justice in the child protection process.* Unpublished doctoral dissertation, University of Sydney, Sydney.

McConnell, D., & Llewellyn, G. (2002). Stereotypes, parents with intellectual disability and child protection. *Journal of Social Welfare and Family Law, 24*(3), 297–317.

McConnell, D., Llewellyn, G., & Ferronato, L. (2002). Disability and decision-making in Australian care proceedings. *International Journal of Law, Policy and the Family, 16*(2), 270–299.

Mitchell, D., Traustadóttir, R., Chapman, R., Townson, L., Ingham, N., & Ledger, S. (Eds.). (2006). *Exploring experiences of advocacy by people with learning disabilities: Testimonies of resistance.* London: Jessica Kingsley.

Nind, M. (2006). Stereotyped behaviour: Resistance by people with profound learning difficulties. In D. Mitchell, R. Traustadóttir, R. Chapman, L. Townson, N. Ingham, & S. Ledger (Eds.), *Exploring experiences of advocacy by people with learning disabilities: Testimonies of resistance* (pp. 202–215). London: Jessica Kingsley.

O'Brien, J. (2005). Out of the institution trap. In K. Johnson & R. Traustadóttir (Eds.), *Deinstitutionalization and people with intellectual disabilities: In and out of institutions* (pp. 259–273). London: Jessica Kingsley.

Owen, K. (2006). Restriction and resistance: The experience of life on a locked ward for people with learning disabilities. In D. Mitchell, R. Traustadóttir, R. Chapman, L. Townson, N. Ingham, & S. Ledger (Eds.), *Exploring experiences of advocacy by people with learning disabilities: Testimonies of resistance* (pp. 20–26). London: Jessica Kingsley.

Pixa-Kettner, U. (1996). Can we or shall we prevent intellectually disabled people from becoming parents? In Danish Ministry of Social Affairs, *Parenting with intellectual disability* (pp. 93–105). Copenhagen: Danish Ministry of Social Affairs.

Scheerenberger, R. C. (1983). *A history of mental retardation.* Baltimore: Paul H. Brookes.

Sigurjónsdóttir, H. B. (2004). Intellectually limited fathers, their families and formal support services. In K. Kristiansen & R. Traustadóttir (Eds.), *Gender and disability research in the Nordic countries* (pp. 239–254). Lund: Studentlitteratur.

Sigurjónsdóttir, H. B. (2005). *Family support services and parents with learning difficulties.* Unpublished doctoral dissertation, University of Sheffield, Sheffield.

Sigurjónsdóttir, H. B., & Traustadóttir, R. (2001). *Ósýnilegar fjölskyldur: Seinfærar/þroskaheftar mæður og börn þeirra* [Invisible families: Mothers with intellectual limitations and their children]. Reykjavík: University of Iceland Press.

Tarleton, B., Ward, L., & Howarth, J. (2006). *Finding the right support? A review of issues and positive practice in supporting parents with learning difficulties and their children.* London: Baring Foundation.

Taylor, S. J. (1995). "Children's division is coming to take pictures": Family life and parenting in a family with disabilities. In S. J. Taylor, R. Bogdan, & Z. M. Lutfiyya (Eds.), *The variety of community experience: Qualitative studies of family and community life* (pp. 23–45). Baltimore: Paul H. Brookes.

Taylor, S. J. (2000). "You are not a retard, you're just wise": Disability, social identity, and family networks. *Journal of Contemporary Ethnography, 29*(1), 58–92.

Tøssebro, J. (2005). Reflections of living outside: Continuity and change in the life of "outsiders." In K. Johnson & R. Traustadóttir (Eds.), *Deinstitutionalization and people with intellectual disabilities: In and out of institutions* (pp. 186–202). London: Jessica Kingsley.

Traustadóttir, R., & Sigurjónsdóttir, H. B. (2008). The "mother" behind the mother: Three generations of mothers with intellectual disabilities and their family support networks. *Journal of Applied Research in Intellectual Disability, 21*(4), 331–340.

Walmsley, J., & Johnson, K. (2003). *Inclusive research with people with learning disabilities: Past, present and futures.* London: Jessica Kingsley.

Whitman, B. Y., Graves, B., & Accardo, P. J. (1989). Training in parenting skills for adults with mental retardation. *Social Work, 34*(5), 431–434.

# PART II

# HUMAN SERVICES ENABLING AND DISABLING PARENTS WITH INTELLECTUAL DISABILITIES

# 8

# Parenting Education Programs

*Maurice Feldman*

## Introduction

A strong focus of concern about parenting by people with intellectual disabilities from the earliest reported research literature to the present is whether or not women and men with intellectual disabilities can be competent parents. This concern arises from the view that intellectual ability is a necessary requirement to being a competent parent and, conversely, that intellectual disability is an impediment to competent parenting. In earlier times, this assumption was closely linked with eugenic policies and practices in which people with intellectual disabilities were sterilized to prevent them having children. Over the latter half of the 20th century, following the cessation of eugenic practices and with the realization that people with intellectual disabilities were indeed having children, attention turned to investigating sound and reliable methods to assist parents with intellectual disabilities to be competent parents.

This chapter begins by exploring the development of parent education programs for parents with intellectual disabilities. We then turn to elucidating the principles and practices that have been shown to be effective in teaching parenting skills to parents with intellectual disabilities. We describe in some detail how to implement efficacious parent education programs, acknowledging that parents learn in many ways, not only through parent education programs designed to teach parenting skills. Parents learn informally from their own parents and family members, from other parents, and from their friends (Llewellyn, 1997). Influences in parents' lives which also have an impact on what and

*Parents with Intellectual Disabilities: Past, Present and Futures*   Edited by Gwynnyth Llewellyn, Rannveig Traustadóttir, David McConnell, and Hanna Björg Sigurjónsdóttir   © 2010 John Wiley & Sons, Ltd

how they learn about parenting include social, contextual, and environmental factors. This chapter, however, focuses only on behavioral and self-directed instructional approaches to teaching parenting skills. We conclude by proposing directions for the next generation of research into parent education programs for parents with intellectual disabilities.

## Development of Parent Education Programs

The ability of parents with intellectual disabilities to provide adequate nutrition and stimulation, a clean and safe home environment, and to keep their children out of harm's way is often questioned. Parent education programs are premised on the assumption that parents with or without disability need to have certain knowledge, skills, and behaviors to raise their children successfully. The overall purpose of such programs is to ensure that children receive appropriate parenting. A useful way to think about parenting from this "raising children" perspective was proposed by Greenspan and Budd (1986). They suggest that parenting is about promoting child socialization so that the dependent child can develop and learn to take their place, as an adult and as a participating member of society. Within this approach three modes of child socialization can be distinguished.

The first mode of child socialization is teaching or the socialization of linguistic and cognitive development. Parent education programs that address this aspect of parenting aim to teach parents the skills and behaviors that will promote their child's cognitive development and language ability (e.g., Feldman, Sparks, & Case, 1993, 2004). The second mode of socialization is childcare or the socialization of healthy physical development. This area of parenting is most frequently found in parent education programs for parents with intellectual disabilities; these programs focus on teaching parents how to keep their children healthy and safe (e.g., Llewellyn, McConnell, Honey, Mayes, & Russo, 2003). The third mode of child socialization is self-regulation or socialization of personality and socioemotional development. Behaviorally oriented researchers in particular have concentrated on developing parent education programs to foster socially appropriate behavior in children, although to date few such studies have been conducted with parents with intellectual disabilities (Mildon, Wade, & Matthews, 2008).

At local and national levels, many curricula have been developed to teach parenting skills to parents with intellectual disabilities. For example, an innovative program in the early 1990s by the New York State Developmental Disability Services led to the development of several different types of parent education programs and a subsequent evaluation report (Ray, Rubenstein, & Russo, 1994). Much earlier, the National Institute of Mental Retardation in Canada published *Child Care Training for Adults with Mental Retardation Vol. I for Infants and*

*Vol II for Toddlers* (Dickerson, Eastman, & Saffer, 1984; Eastman, Saffer, & Dickerson, 1987). Although off-the-shelf curricula and innovative local programs are interesting and informative, we need well-designed studies to determine whether a program is effective in increasing parenting knowledge, skills, and behaviors.

The International Association for the Scientific Study of Intellectual Disability (IASSID), Special Interest Research Group on Parents and Parenting with Intellectual Disabilities published a position paper in 2008 (IASSID SIRG on Parents and Parenting with Intellectual Disabilities, 2008). An important conclusion of the position paper is the following:

> A consistent research finding is that many parents labeled with intellectual disability can learn, apply new knowledge and maintain new skills . . . Maurice Feldman in Canada, Alexander Tymchuk in the USA, and Susan McGaw in England pioneered the use of applied behavioral methods in teaching skills to parents labeled with intellectual disability. Their studies and others since, including a randomized controlled trial . . ., have demonstrated positive parent skill gains . . . (p. 301)

This summary statement demonstrates that as early as 1985 there was acceptable evidence that parents could learn new skills and apply these appropriately. Feldman (1994) reviewed 20 published studies with adequate outcome data on parenting education for parents with intellectual disabilities. A total of 190 parents (188 mothers, 2 fathers) were involved in the 20 published studies. The intelligence quotients of these parents ranged from 50 to 79. The parenting skills training included basic childcare, safety, nutrition, problem solving, positive parent–child interactions, and child behavior management. These areas correspond to the three modes of child socialization teaching, childcare, and self-regulation noted above. The majority of studies focused on childcare and teaching modes of child socialization with fewer that directly addressed child self-regulation. This emphasis is not surprising given that most of the studies only included parents of infants and young children up to four years old. The Feldman (1994) review demonstrated that changes in parent skills and behaviors were achieved following initial training and maintained at follow-up. Feldman noted that more research was needed in programming generalization of parenting skills to new situations (particularly as the child becomes older) and demonstrations of positive effects of parent education on the children.

An updated review by Wade, Llewellyn, and Matthews (2008) confirmed the Feldman (1994) conclusion that home-based, individualized, behaviorally oriented, parent education significantly improves parenting skills in parents with intellectual disabilities. With three independent randomized clinical trials (Feldman, Case, & Sparks, 1992; Feldman et al., 1993, 2004; Llewellyn et al., 2003), and numerous independent replications using single-case experimental designs (e.g., Bakken, Miltenberger, & Schauss, 1993; Feldman et al., 1986; Tymchuk, Andron, & Rahbar, 1988), behaviorally oriented parenting education for parents with intellectual disabilities meets Chambless and Hollon's (1998) criteria for empirically supported efficacious interventions.

Behaviorally based parent education programs are, however, not a panacea for the challenges that many parents with intellectual disabilities face in bringing up their children. Often these families require a variety of services and supports. Walton-Allen and Feldman (1991) showed that parents with intellectual disabilities in Canada felt that they were getting sufficient services related to childcare, but wanted more services for their own self-improvement (e.g., vocational training, academic upgrading, counseling). Their workers, on the other hand, felt that the families needed more services in all areas including childcare. Llewellyn, McConnell, and Bye (1998) found that mothers with intellectual disabilities in Australia thought, in similar fashion to the Canadian parents, that they were getting adequate services related to childcare but wanted more help with meeting people, making friends, and accessing resources and opportunities in their local communities.

The need to consider the family as a whole and provide coordinated, comprehensive services is the basis of two-generation programs, originally developed in the United States of America to support families living in poverty (Smith, 1995). Aunos and Feldman (2007, 2008) describe typical child and parent/family components of two-generation programs and their adaptations for families headed by parents with intellectual disabilities. In brief, the child component would include interventions to promote child development (e.g., parent education, specialized preschool, school-based). The child's health and safety could be monitored by child protection, visiting nurses, and other services. The parent/family component would include parent education and other services and supports as needed such as crisis intervention, advocacy, counseling, health care, nutrition, community living, financial advice, accommodation, and vocational supports. A service to help the parents form and maintain a natural support network would reduce the dependency on short-term funded services. A successful two-generation program relies on coordination, collaboration, and communication among the different workers, agencies, and unpaid support systems involved in supporting the family so that the child's and parents' needs can be addressed effectively and efficiently (Booth & Booth, 2005; Gilson, Bricourt, & Baskind, 1998; Lemieux, 2001; Matava, 1994).

## Principles and Practice in Efficacious Parent Education Programs

Efficacious parenting education is based primarily on behavioral teaching principles that are effective ways of teaching skills to persons with intellectual disabilities. The focus is on building competence and self-reliance. Cultural and family values and context are respected and guide application. Empirical evidence suggests that programs are more efficacious when they are home-based, skill-focused, and individualized, use behavioral teaching strategies, and are coordinated with other supports and services. Audiovisual materials need to be concrete and also utilize a step-by-step approach (Feldman & Case, 1993). In many cases, audiovisual materials presented in this manner can be used successfully in a self-directed learning paradigm (Feldman, 2004).

## Home-based

Feldman (1994) reported that programs that took place in the home or home-like settings produced better outcomes than classroom- or clinic-based instruction. For instance, Bakken et al. (1993) found that parents with intellectual disabilities did not perform newly acquired interaction skills learned in the clinic at home until they received training at home. Feldman et al. (1986) was able to show improvement in the home when the parents received training both in a group format and during individual home visits. In this study, the group training took place in a house rather than at a clinic or classroom. It is recommended that parent education programs for parents with intellectual disabilities offer childcare training at home or in a home-like setting (and wherever else training is needed, for example, in the street or playground).

A parent training-focused home visit usually lasts one to two– hours. It starts with a review of events of the previous week related to opportunities to practice the skills being learned. Then the parent is observed performing previously learned skills in maintenance mode. Their performance on maintained skills is not interrupted in order to see if they remember to do the entire task correctly. Upon completion of the task, feedback is given on maintenance of skills and coupons (if used) are awarded. Then current skills are observed and training given. We usually do not work on more than one or two trained skills at a time. Sometimes, parents will wish to talk about events unrelated to parent training (e.g., help completing forms, personal issues). We find it is best to defer these discussions until the "work" is done. Then, over a cup of tea, we will spend time addressing the parent's agenda. In this manner the parents learn the routine of our visits and eagerly participate in our training and the follow-up discussions.

## Skill-focused

Parenting can be viewed as a large set of behavioral skills that change as the child grows older. The number of skills a parent needs to learn to care for and nurture a child can be daunting (see Table 38.5 in Aunos & Feldman, 2007). Most parents with intellectual disabilities who are referred to parent education programs, however, already have a partial skill set (Feldman, 1998). A variety of observational checklists have been developed to identify parenting skills in

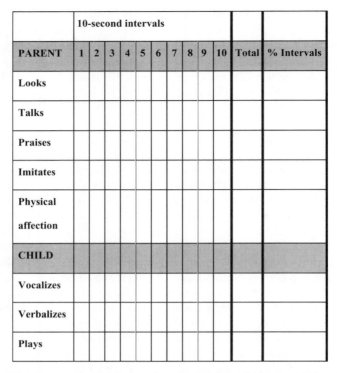

**Figure 8.1.** An example of an interaction checklist from Feldman and Case (1993).

need of training and to evaluate the effects of parent training programs (e.g., Feldman & Case, 1993). These checklists cover essential childcare skills in areas of newborn and infant care, home and street safety, nutrition, child health and medical emergencies, toilet training, positive interactions, and child behavior management.

Most available material applies to children from newborn to five years old. Below is a childcare checklist and Figure 8.1 presents an interaction checklist, both from the Feldman and Case (1993) manual.

1.  Food is room temperature or slightly warmer.
2.  Foods are presented separately on dish.
3.  Child is tied in or held securely in highchair.
4.  Seat position allows eye contact between mother and child.
5.  Uses positive coaxing strategies, if necessary.
6.  Remains calm if child refuses food.
7.  Makes four attempts but does not force feed.
8.  Allows child to touch food at least once.
9.  Talks to child.

10. Meal includes vegetable or fruit or protein, or protein substitute.
11. No junk food served.
12. Washes baby's face when done.

Checklists from the Feldman and Case manual have been designed with the input of pediatric health care professionals and have been validated in numerous studies (Feldman, 1998). Note that the skill is broken down into smaller steps (task analysis) and each step can be observed and scored. In this manner, a precise assessment can be made of which skills the parent already demonstrates and which skills (or sub-skills) need further training. This skills assessment should be done *in situ* with the parent being asked to perform the task the way she or he would normally do so. It is preferable to obtain several observations on different days to examine stability of performance. Of course, it is expected that the parents may be a bit anxious about being observed, but in our experience most parents with intellectual disabilities are motivated to show what they can do. For skills that cannot be readily observed (e.g., handling emergencies), role playing can be used (i.e., with a doll).

Once the skills assessment is completed, training will focus on teaching those skills and sub-skills that the parent needs to learn. For the Feldman and Case (1993) childcare checklists, a criterion of 80% correct was set, based on observations of parents without intellectual disabilities for whom there were no concerns about their parenting (Feldman, 1998). For interaction skills (e.g., praising, physical affection, imitating and expanding child vocalizations), a criterion of 30% of a five-minute play period (using 10-second observation intervals) was established (see Feldman et al., 1993, 2004). Skills that score lower than these criteria are earmarked for training.

## Individualized

Parent training for parents with intellectual disabilities appears to be more effective when the specific skill deficits of each parent are addressed. The skill assessment approach described above promotes individualization because it is often the case that parents have different skill strengths and weaknesses. Training in a group format becomes difficult when parents have different training needs because of their idiosyncratic skill set, the ages of their children, or the family context. In our experience, it is often difficult to find common ground in group training for child-related parenting skills, and some parents may not be getting what they need or what they want in the group.

Although current research supports individualized, home-based parent education, small group instruction has potential. In particular, parents may enjoy a game format (Bakken et al., 1993; Fantuzzo, Wray, Hall, Goins, & Azar, 1986). The crucial issue is how to design the group instruction to maximize the likelihood of generalization of parenting skills learned in class to real-life situations (Bakken et al., 1993).

## Behavioral teaching strategies

Behavioral teaching is based on the principles of applied behavior analysis. It is a competence-enhancing approach (Tucker & Johnson, 1989) and there is considerable research supporting its use in teaching a wide range of adaptive and community living skills to adults with intellectual disabilities. The basic format of behavioral teaching is to present the task or instruction, use prompts as needed to promote correct responding, reinforce correct responding, and provide error correction for incorrect responses and programming for generalization and maintenance. Adjunctive methods that are often used include task analysis and shaping, errorless procedures, generalization, and maintenance strategies. It is beyond the scope of this chapter to detail all these methods and we refer the reader to two excellent texts in applied behavior analysis that provide the principles and applications of behavior instruction, namely, Martin and Pear (2007) and Miltenberger (2007).

Here we will present how we use behavioral methods to teach childcare skills to parents with intellectual disabilities. Before we do that, see below for a list of teaching strategies that are neither consistent with effective behavioral instruction nor competence enhancing.

- Didactic instruction: reading materials and discussions of abstract concepts.
- Teaching too much at one time or too quickly.
- Focusing only on mistakes.
- Assuming correspondence between knowledge and skills.
- Not objectively monitoring individual progress.
- Talking down.
- Doing things for participants.

Unfortunately, we have seen workers use ineffective approaches with little success and then blame the parent's cognitive limitations for his or her failure to learn. As can be seen from this list, these strategies would be considered competence inhibiting (Tucker & Johnson, 1989). Not only are they ineffective ways of teaching parents with intellectual disabilities, they also can result in parents being totally unreceptive to advice and becoming frustrated and angry.

A list of behavioral strategies that have been used successfully with parents who have intellectual disabilities is given below (Feldman, 1994; Wade et al., 2008).

- Concrete discussion.
- Step-by-step approach.

- Pictorial posters and manuals.
- Audio and videotapes.
- Modeling.
- Practice.
- Positive feedback and reinforcement.
- Corrective feedback.
- Role playing.
- Game formats.
- Self-monitoring.

While discussions and instructions alone are not usually effective, we do explain to the parents the reasons why they need to carry out certain routines (Feldman, Case, Rincover, Towns, & Betel, 1989). For instance, we explain in simplified language why it is important to sterilize baby bottles (e.g., "There are germs in the bottle that we cannot see that will make your baby sick, but boiling water kills those germs"). However, knowing this fact has little to do with parents' ability to actually correctly sterilize baby bottles. Sometimes, workers will confuse knowledge with skills. Being able to describe what they are supposed to do does not mean the parent with intellectual disability can actually do it (Bakken et al., 1993; Fantuzzo et al., 1986). Conversely, not being able to clearly verbalize what to do does not mean that the parent cannot do it. Hence, it is crucial that assessments of parenting skills include direct observation and do not rely on verbal report.

The step-by-step or task-analysis approach was described earlier. It is not only useful for identifying specific skills and sub-skills in need of training, but also helps to give the parents specific feedback during training. We have used pictorial posters and manuals as well as audio and videotapes to augment practitioner-directed training and to serve as reminders to engage in correct parenting practices. Feldman, Garrick, and Case (1997) illustrate some visual materials we used to improve feeding and nutrition skills (and child weight) for parents with intellectual disabilities who had failure-to-thrive children. The use of audiovisual materials as self-learning aids will be discussed in the recent initiatives section below.

Modeling can be quite helpful, especially if it focuses on the specific sub-step the parent is missing. As the mother is practicing the skill, we may stop her and ask her to watch what we do. We then ask her to copy what we did. Sometimes we use exaggerated modeling to get the parent's attention. For instance, when showing a parent how to praise her young child, we may go a bit overboard with enthusiastic positive praise (e.g., "I REALLY, REALLY liked the way you helped clean up!"). The parent's (and child's) reaction is to laugh, so we know we have caught their attention. Luckily, parents do not mimic exactly, and their praise becomes quite appropriate with further training (Feldman et al., 1986, 1989, 1993, 2004).

Practice with positive feedback and reinforcement and corrective feedback are key elements of effective training. Just like we will not learn to drive well unless we get behind the wheel, parents with intellectual disabilities need to actually have opportunities for hands-on practice and to receive feedback. Because of their past failure experiences, many parents are not receptive to criticism, even if it is given with the intention of correcting errors. We see their eyes glaze over and they once again feel like failures. Therefore, when starting to teach a new skill, we provide considerably more positive feedback and praise than corrective feedback. Indeed, sometimes, the first session or two is devoid of correction. By using the step-by-step checklists, we usually can find several sub-steps that the parent is performing correctly that we can praise. While we try to provide more positive than corrective feedback, we increase the use of corrective feedback over sessions. When corrective feedback is embedded within positive feedback, parents with intellectual disabilities seem to be more receptive to correcting errors.

We alert the parent to the availability of natural reinforcers (e.g., "Look how your baby is smiling when you cuddle her," "See, the diaper rash is going away since you've started following the diaper rash checklist"). We also have used tangible reinforcers and token economies. We have awarded parenting coupons contingent on attendance (which can sometimes be a problem for highly stressed families) and improved performance on the parenting checklists. The coupons are exchangeable for small gift items for the child and the parent that the parent chooses. Each coupon is worth about 50 cents and favorite rewards include rail transit tickets, baby clothing, toys and accessories, restaurant gift certificates, and lottery tickets. We find that the coupons are highly motivating, but as the parents improve they find their success and their child's reactions (as described above) to be reinforcing as well. Once the skill is acquired, we reinforce maintenance of the skill and then we gradually reduce the coupon reinforcement to promote maintenance in the absence of tangible reward (Feldman et al., 1992). We do this by telling the parents that if they achieve their maintenance score (e.g., 8 out of 10 steps correct), then they can pick three numbers. They then roll a die or spin a wheel (with numbers one to six), and if their number comes up they win their coupons. At the next visit they can only choose two numbers, and so on (we also increase to two dice or a wheel with more numbers). Although they are not getting as many tickets as before, they do not seem to mind and enjoy the thrill of introducing an element of chance.

We program for generalization using several of the strategies recommended by Stokes and Baer (1977), such as sufficient exemplars and instructions to generalize. For instance, we conduct interaction training in various rooms in the home as well as outside so that the parent learns to provide positive inter-actions to the child regardless of location. Although we have found that verbal instruction alone is not an effective training technique, once parenting skills are trained using modeling, feedback, and reinforcement, then instructions to generalize (e.g., "praise your baby when she does something you like wherever you are") may promote use of the skills in a variety of situations that have not been explicitly trained (Feldman et al., 1989).

When it is not feasible to train a skill with the child, we may opt for role play. For instance, we use role play to practice handling medical emergencies. We use a life-like doll and fake blood and vomit. We would put some blood on the doll's arm and ask the parent to show us how they would treat bleeding. Unbeknown to the parent, we put the doll on the kitchen floor, with an opened bottle of bleach next to her. We then scream, "Where is your baby?" The parent has to demonstrate how she would handle a poisoning emergency (we provide a script as to what to say to the emergency line dispatcher). For parents with older children, we have found it easier to have the parent practice child behavior management strategies with us in a role-play format before attempting to try them with their children. We also do group role playing using game formats.

We occasionally use self-monitoring as a memory aide. For example, we may give the parent a pictorial checklist of examples of nutritious foods that they post on their fridge. We ask them to check off what foods they served for each meal that week. We find that even if parents do not record all the time, the posted checklist may still act as a reminder to serve healthy foods. For parents who understand time, we teach them how to time manage using a day-timer. We teach the parents not only to schedule appointments, but also to schedule daily routines, including playing with their children and other childcare activities. The parents check off when they have accomplished the scheduled tasks, and will show us what they have accomplished when we come for a visit.

## Qualifications of a parent education practitioner

Effective interventions are only as good as the competencies of the practitioners. Parent education practitioners need a unique set of competencies. They need to know how to build rapport and teach adults with intellectual disabilities. They also require expertise in child development and care. They should have experience in conducting behavioral observations and in behavioral teaching skills. Importantly, they need to be able to put aside any biases and preconceptions they may have about working with parents with intellectual disabilities. They need to be empathic and sensitive to working with persons with disabilities. There are few, if any, postsecondary programs that teach all these skills and knowledge. We find that practitioners with a background in psychology, nursing, early childhood education, social work, occupational therapy, and behavior analysis are able to learn quickly to supplement their missing expertise by working with an experienced parent education therapist.

# Recent Initiatives in Parent Education Programs

## Self-instructional approaches

The parent training approach described above, while efficacious, is labor-intensive and requires a worker with expertise. Not all locations have access to a parent education service for parents with intellectual disabilities. This scenario may result in children being permanently removed unnecessarily because no one is able to effectively improve the parents' childcare skills. What if a low-cost, easily disseminated intervention could be developed that does not require a highly trained parent education practitioner, but empowers the parents to learn on their own? Indeed, in a series of studies, Feldman and his associates demonstrated that parents with intellectual disabilities could improve their childcare skills through the use of self-instructional audiovisual materials (Feldman, 2004; Feldman & Case, 1997, 1999; Feldman, Ducharme, & Case, 1999). The manuals were prepared based on the step-by-step checklists described earlier (Feldman & Case, 1993). Each step of a childcare checklist was illustrated using tracings of photographs as this medium was preferred and most understandable to the parents. The illustrations are not all self-explanatory, so simple text describing the step is placed to the left of each picture. Audiotapes of someone reading the text and directing the parent to look at each picture were recorded for parents who could not read the accompanying text. A variety of childcare, health, and safety skills appropriate for newborns to 3-year-olds was depicted in these manuals (e.g., feeding, bathing, treating diaper rash, crib safety). After conducting baseline observations to identify skills in need of training, we asked the parent to read the manual to a worker once. The worker corrected any oral reading errors and asked several comprehension questions to make sure the parent understood the contents of the manual. We then observed the parent performing the skill about once a week. Unlike the full training described above, during these observations we passively observed and did not provide modeling, performance feedback, reinforcement, or any other training.

The combined results of the published studies with 33 parents with intellectual disabilities, including some fathers, showed that about 80% of them learned 80% of the skills to levels seen in parents without intellectual disabilities (Feldman, 2004). These findings are comparable to full training outcomes. Parents who readily accepted the manuals reached the criterion a little sooner than parents who initially were somewhat resistant to trying them. While reading ability was negatively correlated with success in using the manual, this relationship was no longer significant when parents were given the audiotapes that read the text to them. Very few parents needed reminders to use the manuals, and we replicated the findings when another service used them with a couple of their parents with intellectual disabilities, but only provided monthly in-home observation checks (Feldman & Case, 1999). Interestingly, follow-up observations indicated good maintenance of the skills in all our studies, although the parents claimed that they no longer needed to look at the manuals to remember how to perform the childcare skill. Consumer satisfaction was uniformly high, and most of them preferred the picture books without the audiotapes. Thus, we now routinely start with a self-directed learning approach, and only offer audiotapes and full training if the parent needs or requests it. The Feldman and Case (1993) *Step-by-Step Child-Care Manual* contains these pictorial manuals for a wide range of childcare skills and is available from M. Feldman.

## Conclusion

This chapter documents the now well-established evidence that parents with intellectual disabilities can and do learn parenting skills, building on their existing repertoire and acquiring new knowledge, behaviors. and skills. We have described the principles and practices that are necessary for this learning to take place. The evidence about successful parent learning comes mainly from parent education programs that focus on a raising children perspective; that is, ensuring that parents learn the knowledge, skills, and behaviors that will ensure that their children receive appropriate parenting. It is no longer necessary to ask the question whether parents with intellectual disabilities can learn. It is no longer necessary to ask how we should teach parents with intellectual disabilities the knowledge, skills, and behaviors they need to learn to raise their young children. In this chapter we have reported the answers to these questions.

There are, however, many questions that require answers. There are some beginning research efforts to design and test parent education programs to increase parent confidence and competence in accessing the local community as a first step to increasing social participation and decreasing social isolation. A concerted effort is needed to build the evidence base to ensure positive program effects on social participation. We commented earlier in this chapter that most programs focus on the early years, typically for newborns up until about the ages of six to seven years old. Raising children into adolescence and young adulthood can be challenging for many parents, and no less so for parents with intellectual disabilities (Llewellyn, McConnell, Grace, & Dibden, 1999). A new generation of research specifically addressing the particular challenges of raising children in late childhood and the adolescent years is urgently needed.

## References

Aunos, M., & Feldman, M. (2007). Parenting by persons with an intellectual disability. In I. Brown & M. Percy (Eds.), *A comprehensive guide to intellectual and developmental disabilities* (pp. 593–603). Baltimore: Paul H. Brookes.

Aunos, M., & Feldman, M. (2008). There's no place like home: The child's right to family. In T. O'Neill & D. Zinga (Eds.), *Children's rights: Multidisciplinary approaches to participation and protection* (pp. 137–162). Toronto: University of Toronto Press.

Bakken, J., Miltenberger, R. G., & Schauss, S. (1993). Teaching parents with mental retardation: Knowledge versus skills. *American Journal of Mental Retardation, 97*(4), 405–417.

Booth, T., & Booth, W. (2005). Parents with intellectual disabilities in the child protection system: Experiences and perspectives. *Journal of Intellectual Disabilities, 9*(2), 109–129.

Budd, K., & Greenspan, S. (1985). Parameters of successful and unsuccessful interventions with parents who are mentally retarded. *Mental Retardation, 23*(6), 269–273.

Chambless, D. L., & Hollon, S. D. (1998). Defining empirically supported therapies. *Journal of Consulting and Clinical Psychology, 66*(1), 7–18.

Dickerson, M., Eastman, M., & Saffer, A. (1984). *Child care training for adults with mental retardation. Vol. II for toddlers.* Toronto: National Institute of Mental Retardation in Canada.

Eastman, M., Saffer, A., & Dickerson, M. (1987). *Child care training for adults with mental retardation. Vol. I for toddlers.* Toronto: National Institute of Mental Retardation in Canada.

Fantuzzo, J. W., Wray, L., Hall, R., Goins, C., & Azar, S. (1986). Parent and social-skills training for mentally retarded mothers identified as child maltreaters. *American Journal of Mental Deficiency, 91*(2), 135–140.

Feldman, M. A. (1994). Parenting education for parents with intellectual disabilities: A review of outcome studies. *Research in Developmental Disabilities, 15*(4), 299–332.

Feldman, M. A. (1998). Parents with intellectual disabilities: Implications and interventions. In J. Lutzker (Ed.), *Child abuse: A handbook of theory, research, and treatment* (pp. 401–419). New York: Plenum.

Feldman, M. A. (2004). Self-directed learning of child-care skills by parents with intellectual disabilities. *Infants and Young Children, 17*(1), 17–31.

Feldman, M. A., & Case, L. (1993). *Step-by-step child-care: A pictorial manual for parents, child-care workers, and babysitters.* Toronto: Authors.

Feldman, M. A., & Case, L. (1997). The effectiveness of audiovisual self-instructional materials in teaching child-care skills to parents with intellectual disabilities. *Journal of Behavioral Education, 7*(2), 235–257.

Feldman, M. A., & Case, L. (1999). Teaching child-care and safety skills to parents with intellectual disabilities through self-learning. *Journal of Intellectual and Developmental Disability, 24*(1), 27–44.

Feldman, M. A., Case, L., Garrick, M., MacIntyre-Grande, W., Carnwell, J., & Sparks, B. (1992). Teaching child-care skills to parents with developmental disabilities. *Journal of Applied Behavior Analysis, 25*(1), 205–215.

Feldman, M. A., Case, L., Rincover, A., Towns, F., & Betel, J. (1989). Parent education project III: Increasing affection and responsivity in developmentally handicapped mothers: Component analysis, generalization, and effects on child language. *Journal of Applied Behavior Analysis, 22*(2), 211–222.

Feldman, M. A., Case, L., & Sparks, B. (1992). Effectiveness of a child-care training program for parents at-risk for child neglect. *Canadian Journal of Behavioral Science, 24*(1), 14–28.

Feldman, M. A., Ducharme, J. M., & Case, L. (1999). Using self-instructional pictorial manuals to teach child-care skills to mothers with intellectual disabilities. *Behavior Modification, 23*(3), 480–497.

Feldman, M. A., Garrick, M., & Case, L. (1997). The effects of parent training on weight gain of nonorganic-failure-to-thrive children of parents with intellectual disabilities. *Journal of Developmental Disabilities, 5*(1), 47–61.

Feldman, M. A., Sparks, B., & Case, L. (1993). Effectiveness of home-based early intervention on the language development of children of parents with mental retardation. *Research in Developmental Disabilities, 14*(5), 387–408.

Feldman, M. A., Sparks, B., & Case, L. (2004). Effectiveness of home-based early intervention on the language development of children of parents with mental retardation (reprint). In M. A. Feldman (Ed.), *Early intervention: The essential readings* (pp. 134–150). Oxford: Blackwell.

Feldman, M. A., Towns, F., Betel, J., Case, L., Rincover, A., & Rubino, C. A. (1986). Parent education project II: Increasing stimulating interactions of developmentally handicapped mothers. *Journal of Applied Behavior Analysis, 19*(1), 23–27.

Gilson, S. F., Bricout, J. C., & Baskind, F. R. (1998). Listening to the voices of individuals with disabilities. *Families in Society: The Journal of Contemporary Human Services, 79*(2), 188–202.

Greenspan, S., & Budd, K. (1986). Research in mentally retarded parents. In J. J. Gallagher & P. M. Vietze (Eds.), *Families of handicapped persons: Current research, programs and policy issues* (pp. 115–128). Baltimore: Paul H. Brookes.

IAASID Special Interest Research Group on Parents and Parenting with Intellectual Disabilities. (2008). Parents labelled with intellectual disability: Position of the IASSID SIRG on Parents and Parenting with Intellectual Disabilities. *Journal of Applied Research in Intellectual Disabilities, 21*(4), 296–307.

Lemieux, C. (2001). The challenge of empowerment in child protective services: A case study of a mother with mental retardation. *Families in Society: The Journal of Contemporary Human Services, 82*(2), 175–185.

Llewellyn, G. (1997). Parents with intellectual disability learning to parent: The role of informal learning and experience. *International Journal of Disability, Development and Education, 44*(3), 243–261.

Llewellyn, G., McConnell, D., & Bye, R. (1998). Perception of service needs by parents with intellectual disabilities, their significant others and their service workers. *Research in Developmental Disabilities, 19*(3), 245–260.

Llewellyn, G., McConnell, D., Grace, R., & Dibden, M. (1999). *Parents with intellectual disability and older children: Strategies for support workers.* Melbourne: Victorian Government Department of Human Services.

Llewellyn, G., McConnell, D., Honey, A., Mayes, R., & Russo, D. (2003). Promoting health and home safety for children of parents with intellectual disability: A randomised controlled trial. *Research in Developmental Disabilities, 24*(6) 405–431.

Martin, G., & Pear, J. (2007). *Behavior modification: What it is and how to do it* ( 8th ed.). Upper Saddle River, NJ: Prentice-Hall.

Matava, M. (1994). The implications of parenting standards in child protection: A paradox in disability policy. *Policy Studies Journal, 22*(1), 146–151.

Mildon, R., Wade, C., & Matthews, J. (2008). Considering the contextual fit of an intervention for families headed by parents with an intellectual disability: An exploratory study. *Journal of Applied Research in Intellectual Disabilities, 21*(4), 377–387.

Miltenberger, R. (2007). *Behavior modification: Principles and procedures* (4th ed.). Belmont, CA: Wadsworth.

Ray, N. K., Rubenstein, H., & Russo, N. J. (1994). Understanding the parents who are mentally retarded: Guidelines for family preservation programs. *Child Welfare, 73*(6), 725–743.

Smith, S. (1995). *Two generation programs for families in poverty: A new intervention strategy.* Westport, CT: Ablex.

Stokes, T. F., & Baer, D. M. (1977). An implicit technology of generalization. *Journal of Applied Behavior Analysis, 10*(2), 349–367.

Tucker, M. B., & Johnson, O. (1989). Competence promoting versus competence inhibiting social support for mentally retarded mothers. *Human Organization, 48*(2), 95–107.

Tymchuk, A. J., Andron, L., & Rahbar, B. (1988). Effective decision-making/problem-solving training with mothers who have mental retardation. *American Journal on Mental Retardation, 92*(6), 510–516.

Wade, C., Llewellyn, G., & Matthews, J. (2008). Review of parent training interventions for parents with intellectual disabilities. *Journal of Applied Research in Intellectual Disabilities, 21*(4), 351–366.

Walton-Allen, N., & Feldman, M. A. (1991). Perceptions of service needs by parents who are mentally retarded and their workers. *Comprehensive Mental Health Care, 1*(2), 137–147.

# 9

# Supported Decision Making for Women with Intellectual Disabilities

*Sue McGaw and Sue Candy*

## Introduction

Becoming pregnant can open up a world of opportunities for a woman with intellectual disability who has been labeled and treated differently as a young girl and now, as an adult, is still being told what to do (Finucane, 1998). Having the baby is a liberating experience. Deciding to have a baby ideally occurs in the context of informed decision making. There are still significant constraints, however, on women with intellectual disabilities participating in decisions that affect their lives. There is a lack of accessible information and support. The processes used by decision-making "authorities" exclude people with cognitive disabilities. In addition, there are a limited range of "decisions" or choices that are deemed acceptable by society, professionals, governments, and in some instances, statute. In this chapter, we examine a number of decision points that occur in relation to everyday decisions as well as life-altering ones in the lives of women with intellectual disabilities. We identify barriers to informed decision making and present strategies and promising practices that will help promote the full participation of women with intellectual disabilities and those who become mothers in the decisions that affect their lives.

## Ways of Thinking about Decision Making

Decision making is usually thought of as an internal cognitive process. Perhaps not surprisingly, then, it is generally assumed that people with low cognitive

*Parents with Intellectual Disabilities: Past, Present and Futures*   Edited by Gwynnyth Llewellyn, Rannveig Traustadóttir, David McConnell, and Hanna Björg Sigurjónsdóttir   © 2010 John Wiley & Sons, Ltd

ability or intellectual disability will have weaker decision-making abilities. Research examining the relationship between intellectual disability and decision making conducted in a laboratory setting (and referred to as *in vitro* decision making) has generally found this to be the case, although the differences are not discrete and there is some variation (Suto, Clare, Holland, & Watson, 2005). Similarly, in a sample of mothers with intellectual disabilities, Tymchuk, Yokota, and Rahbar (1990) reported that those with higher intelligence quotients tended to understand more and made better *in vitro* decisions than those mothers with lower intelligence quotients. On closer examination, however, people with intellectual disabilities are found to have strengths as well as limitations in the decision-making process. The hardest part for people with intellectual disabilities appears to be understanding which information is relevant in making a decision and the reasoning behind this information. By contrast, the parts of the process generally easier for people with intellectual disabilities are identifying the decision to be made, appreciating who is affected by the decision, and communicating their chosen outcome (Suto et al., 2005).

Advocates of the supported decision-making model (e.g., Bach & Rock, 1996; Dye, Hendy, Hare, & Burton, 2004) propose an alternative way of thinking about decision making. They see decision making as a process that is both cognitive and contextual. That is, decisions are made within a present context, taking past and future contexts into account. This means that good decision making depends not only on one's cognitive abilities (e.g., reasoning), but also on the context of our lives (past experiences, family opinion, friends) and, more specifically, on the quality of information and support that is available to the person making the decision. From this perspective, it is not sensible to measure decision-making ability in laboratory settings. Rather, measuring decision-making ability and outcomes requires the context and the person's capacity to be taken into account. Competent or adequate decision making therefore is defined as a combination of context and cognitive processing. We can no longer simply attribute poor decision making to an individual's cognitive limitations. Contextual influences make all the difference. In examining decisions in the lives of women with intellectual disabilities, the question is under what circumstances are women and mothers enabled to participate fully in decision-making situations, not whether they can participate in decisions that affect their lives and the lives of their children.

In the next section we highlight some contextual influences and barriers to informed decision making and autonomy for women with intellectual disabilities in relation to their health and safety as women, and if and when they wish to become mothers. These barriers include opposition from others and their low expectations; experiencing maltreatment in their own upbringing; social and economic deprivation; and inaccessible information and support. It is important to note that such barriers do not automatically result in poor decision making. Research in the field demonstrates that many women with intellectual disabilities can make positive, "healthy" decisions (despite the often difficult circumstances of their lives), but many more would probably do so if they had improved access to specialized health information and services (Llewellyn, McConnell, & Mayes, 2003; Willis, Kennedy, & Kilbride, 2008).

## Barriers to informed decision making

### Opposition from others

In the past, institutionalization and involuntary sterilization denied many women with intellectual disabilities the opportunity of deciding whether or not to become a mother. In high-income countries today, institutionalization and involuntary sterilization are no longer common practices. However, in some countries forced sterilizations and/or abortions are still conducted on some girls and women with disabilities, and even in countries where involuntary sterilization is more tightly controlled, for example in Australia, there have been reports that unauthorized sterilizations are being performed (Dowse & Frohmader, 2001). Current guidelines concerning involuntary sterilization in the United Kingdom (UK) are presented in Box 9.1.

---

**Box 9.1.** Involuntary sterilization and "consent" in the United Kingdom

In the United Kingdom, involuntary sterilization can only be conducted following multi-disciplinary consultation and after applying to an ethical committee (Department of Health and Social Security, 1975). The present guidelines, described by Roy and Roy (1988) regarding applications for sterilization of girls under 18 years, are that (1) sterilization must be with the leave of a High Court judge; (2) the girl will be represented by the official solicitor or other appropriate guardian (and, where appropriate, parents and the local authority will be made parties); and (3) expert evidence will be adduced, giving reasons for the application, the history and foreseeable future of the girl, the risks and consequences of pregnancy and of sterilization, and the practicability of alternative precautions. For women over 18 years of age who are unable to give personal consent, medical practitioners can proceed with sterilization in accordance with "good medical practice" in "exceptional circumstances, where there was no provision in law for consent and no one who could give consent and where the patient was suffering from such mental abnormality as to be unable to give consent" (Dyer, 1987, p. 258).

Consent is an essential prerequisite for any electric surgical procedure (Sklar, 1980). However, assessing the degree of competence, whether a reasoned decision has been arrived at, and whether that decision is

*(continued)*

---

truly voluntary is fraught with difficulties (Roy & Roy, 1988). Adults in the UK can exercise their right to make decisions affecting their own life, whether the reasons for that choice are rational, irrational, or even non-existent, and this right remains even if the outcome of the decision might be detrimental to the individual or to a viable fetus (Grisso, 1986). Self-determination is meaningful only if the individual is appropriately informed, has the ability (capacity) to make the decision, and is free to decide without coercion.

Today, most women with intellectual disabilities grow up in the community and have more opportunity to decide to start a family of their own. However, as young women they may still face resistance to their sexual development and transition to adulthood from those closest to them. Research conducted in the early 1980s found that many parents of children and young people with intellectual disabilities were uneasy about the sexual development of their offspring and attempted to restrict their child's sexual expression (Craft & Craft, 1981). Approximately 75% of parents surveyed in one study were against their children marrying and raising children, fearing that they would be incapable of parenting without help (Wolf & Zarfas, 1982). More recent research suggests that attitudes may not have changed, with many parents and teachers of persons with intellectual disabilities reportedly still supporting involuntary sterilization as a form of contraception (Aunos & Feldman, 2002).

When women with intellectual disabilities overcome this resistance and become mothers, they all too often run into opposition from child protection authorities. This opposition is also driven, at least in part, by a false assumption. In this instance the false assumption is that women with intellectual disabilities are not capable of making good decisions or learning to do so, and so are not capable of childrearing. Researchers from a number of different countries have found that the outcome of this type of thinking is that women with intellectual disabilities lose custody of their children who are removed from their care (e.g., McConnell & Llewellyn, 2002). A disproportionately large number of parents with intellectual disabilities have their parental rights terminated compared to the general parenting population (Booth, Booth, & McConnell, 2004a; McConnell, Llewellyn, & Ferronato, 2000). The literature bears witness to the unfair treatment and discriminatory attitudes shown to parents with intellectual disabilities within the child protection system and courts (Glaun & Brown, 1999; McConnell et al., 2000).

### Childhood experience and social and economic deprivation

Because decision making is contextually based, it is influenced by childhood experience. Childhood experience also informs understanding and expectations of ourselves including our worth, wants, and needs, and our expectations of others. These early experiences influence the decisions we make, for example, in the partner we choose, the way we decide to parent our own children, and so on. Similarly, our decision making is influenced by the people who are involved in our lives. For instance, if we live solitary lives, there is limited opportunity to meet potential partners. In addition, if our social circle is small, there will be limited opportunities to observe and learn from other parents and their experiences.

The childhood experience and social networks of many women with intellectual disabilities are a constraint or barrier to informed (as opposed to misinformed) decision making. To an observer, their decision making may seem indiscriminate with respect to their choice of partners. Many report trauma in the form of abuse and violence within relationships. The vulnerability of women and mothers with intellectual disabilities to exploitation and abuse from partners, some of whom they have lived with over a long period of time, is well documented (Booth & Booth, 2002; Booth, Booth, & McConnell, 2005). We must be wary, however, of making generalizations because not all male partners are violent or exploitative, and many provide positive support in the form of personal skills and accomplishments that can strengthen the family's coping responses (Booth & Booth, 2002).

Assuming that a causal relationship exists between intellectual disability and poor relationship choices is overly simplistic. Contextual influences and constraints must be taken into account. Many women with intellectual disabilities have suffered abuse or other maltreatment in their own upbringing. Several studies have found that women and mothers with intellectual disabilities are more likely than other women to report being abused as children, and those who do so are, in turn, more likely to report being victims of domestic violence in adult life (Ray, Rubenstein, & Russo, 1994; Sobsey, 2000; Wilson & Brewer, 1992). Women with intellectual disabilities typically have smaller social networks than other women (Emerson, Malam, Davies, & Spencer, 2005). Opportunities to meet a range of potential partners and to experience different relationships, positive as well as negative, are therefore limited. Moreover, women and mothers with intellectual disabilities are more likely than their peers to be living in public housing and/or in low-income communities, which are often beset with social problems (Emerson et al., 2005). In such communities, women and mothers with intellectual disabilities may be more likely to meet men who, for whatever reason, would mistreat them.

### Inaccessible information and support

Another major barrier to informed decision making for the current generation of women and mothers with intellectual disabilities is a lack of good-quality, accessible information and support. In the information age, most of us have access to information on virtually any subject via the Internet or popular press. In any news agency or bookshop we can find numerous periodicals or books on pregnancy, childbirth, and parenting. Yet this information is not accessible to most women and mothers with intellectual disabilities. Many people also have an extended network of family and friends who will share information, usually from their own experience. In contrast, mothers with intellectual disabilities have less access to this kind of information and support (Llewellyn & McConnell, 2002). Most people can also turn to, and obtain information from, professional sources. However, services are not usually equipped to accommodate the particular information and learning needs of women and mothers with intellectual disabilities (Tarleton, Ward, & Howarth, 2006).

We now turn to two situations in which women with intellectual disabilities frequently lack the information and support they need to make informed decisions. These are the decision to become a mother and decisions that are required as part of the statutory child protection process.

## Deciding to Become a Mother

To make an informed decision about becoming a mother, women with intellectual disabilities need to have knowledge about family planning. The available evidence suggests that many women with intellectual disabilities receive little or no education and support from their own parents or within the school curriculum to make informed decisions about their sexual expression, the use of contraceptives, or about becoming a mother (Aunos & Feldman, 2002). Furthermore, most do not access generic family planning services, although many seek advice from community nurses (Taylor, Pearson, & Cook, 1998). The need to provide women with intellectual disabilities with family planning education, support, and advocacy was recently highlighted by McCarthy (2002), who interviewed 27 women with mild or moderate intellectual disabilities and found that few had been given any accessible information about contraception, and most had very limited knowledge of how contraception worked.

Despite the apparent lack of family planning education and support for women with intellectual disabilities, there is no indication that this results in more pregnancies (Baum, 2000; Levy, Perhats, Nash-Johnson, & Welter, 1992). Women with intellectual disabilities typically do not have more children, whether planned or unplanned, than other women in the community. Contrary to popular belief, the average family size for families headed by one or two parents with intellectual disabilities appears to be the same as that for the general population (Garber, 1988; Tymchuk, 1990). The reported average number of children residing in the household of parents with intellectual disabilities ranges from 1.05 to 3.7 per family (Booth, Booth, & McConnell, 2004b; Mørch, Skar, & Andersgard, 1997).

Genetic counseling and prenatal testing may also inform a woman's decision making about whether to become a mother. However, women with intellectual disabilities who seek genetic counseling or prenatal testing are heavily disadvantaged by traditional counseling models that tend to rely on a person's understanding of factual information (Finucane, 1998). Typically, in these approaches the information is too complex in content and delivery format. Consequently, women with intellectual disabilities are placed in a difficult decision-making situation when, for example, they may need to weigh up the risks of a miscarriage following invasive diagnostic tests or consider the possible alternatives following the diagnosis of a fetal anomaly (Marteau & Dormandy, 2001).

Most children born to women with intellectual disabilities will not have a disability, but there is a higher risk (Kelly, Morisset, Barnard, & Patterson, 1996; McConnell, Mayes, & Llewellyn, 2008; Mørch et al., 1997). In deciding to become a mother, however, women with intellectual disabilities appear to be less concerned than other women about this potential risk. There is evidence to suggest that women with intellectual disabilities tend to perceive their "condition" as less serious than peers without a disability (Finucane, 1998). This may explain, at least in part, why their uptake of genetic counseling appears to be low (Finucane, 1998), and why they are less likely to endorse termination of pregnancies affected by their "condition" than are non-disabled parents with affected children (Henneman et al., 2001).

The decisions women with intellectual disabilities can make during pregnancy are also limited when antenatal care is either not accessible or underutilized. Through antenatal care there is the opportunity to learn about choices to make to enhance both their own health and the health of their unborn child, for example, by stopping smoking. Many pregnant women with intellectual disabilities may be missing out on such important information, thereby limiting their ability to make informed, "healthy" decisions. Although it is generally recognized that women have particular health care needs in relation to their reproductive health, the health care needs of women with intellectual disabilities are often ignored or not adequately met (Atkinson & Walmsley, 1995). Older studies have reported on the inadequate antenatal care of pregnant women with intellectual disabilities (defined as fewer than four visits to the health clinic or making the first visit after the 28th week of gestation), and their vulnerability to hospital admission resulting from medical complications (Bohlin & Larsson, 1986; Larsson, 1980).

The need for appropriate, accessible antenatal care for pregnant women with intellectual disabilities is highlighted by recent research suggesting that these women experience poorer pregnancy and birth outcomes than other women. This research, conducted in Australia, found that pregnant women with intellectual disabilities experienced an unusually high rate of preeclampsia and preterm birth, and their babies more often had low birth weight and were more frequently admitted to neonatal intensive care or special care nurseries (McConnell et al., 2008). Further research is needed to establish which of the multiple factors identified (biomedical, nutrition, maternal health, smoking, medication, environmental stressors) influenced this outcome. Research is also needed to determine the level of assistance needed by women with intellectual disabilities to ensure that they receive quality antenatal care.

In other areas of health care, women with intellectual disabilities are also disadvantaged with respect to decision making. Women with intellectual disabilities are not gaining access to regular blood pressure monitoring, cervical screening, or breast screening programs at the same rate as other women and appear unaware and uninformed of their right to such screening (Cowie & Fletcher, 1998; Kerr, 2006; Langan, Russell, & Whitfield, 1993). Rectification of this discriminatory situation is slow, despite the increased vulnerability of people with intellectual disabilities to health conditions such as gastrointestinal tract cancer (Cooke, 1997; Duff, Scheepers, Cooper, Hoghton, & Baddeley, 2001), coronary heart disease, and respiratory disease (Hollins, Attard, von Fraunhofer, McGuin, & Sedgwick, 1998).

## Participating in the Child Protection Process

Many mothers with intellectual disabilities find themselves caught up in a legal process that will determine whether or not they retain custody of their child. Throughout this process, they are required to make a number of difficult decisions that have far-reaching implications. Mothers with intellectual disabilities, however, often receive little or no support, including accessible information and/or a clear and comprehensible explanation of what is occurring and what is being asked of them. Under these circumstances it is questionable whether the decisions they make are adequately informed, and whether the process of decision making could be said to be competent as defined previously as context and cognitive capacity.

Below we describe the process in the UK. Typically, in the UK, parents' first involvement with the legal process occurs when an initial child protection case conference is called. Under the Children Act of 1989 (Department of Children, Schools, and Families, 1989), the child protection case conference should include family members and, if appropriate, the child and any professionals involved with the family. Case conferences can be intimidating for mothers with intellectual disabilities, who may struggle with explaining themselves and their situation particularly amidst a group of seemingly articulate professionals. The local authority must advise parents to seek legal advice if they are pursuing legal proceedings. Many mothers with intellectual disabilities are faced with the daunting task of selecting a solicitor in the absence of accessible support to facilitate this important decision. Currently, few solicitors are available who can provide skilled legal advice and expertise in meeting the specific needs of this group of parents (Tarleton, 2008).

The function of the case conference is to consider the likelihood of the child suffering significant harm in the future and deciding upon a child protection plan to safeguard the child. The Adoption and Children Act (ACA) (Department of Health, 2002) provides the legal underpinning for Every Child Matters (Department for Education and Skills, 2003). Emphasis is on promoting children's safety, good health, enjoyment and achievement, and economic well-being and on providing a positive contribution to society. Interagency cooperation is central and child protection plans should increasingly reflect this. Although laudatory, the involvement of many agencies increases the complexity of the process and provides additional challenges for mothers with intellectual disabilities.

If the Child Protection Plan decides to "twin track," birth parents are informed that the local authority is considering two options, either rehabilitation within a strictly limited timescale or adoption. At this juncture, the local authority concurrently plans the reunification of the family, while at the same time developing an alternative permanent option in case reunification fails. While parents are reassured that twin tracking does not preempt the outcome, this is a difficult concept for any mother, including mothers with intellectual disabilities, to comprehend. Lawyers working with mothers with intellectual disabilities may require additional time to explain such complexities to their clients so that they can be assisted to make an informed decision. Again, the level of training, expertise, and motivation for this work among lawyers varies considerably (Family Rights Group, 2008).

If the local authority pursues a placement for adoption, the parent has to decide whether he or she will consent to or contest this application. Parental consent, under section 52 of the ACA (Department of Health, 2002), is described as "consent given unconditionally and with full understanding of what is involved." The issue of "full understanding" is of particular relevance. As yet there are no additional services to ensure that mothers with intellectual disabilities are provided with the time and resources to understand the legal implications of their decision. If a parent does not agree to adoption, then application must be made for the section 21 compulsory Placement for Adoption Order. This will only be granted if the "test of significant harm" is fulfilled. The adoption agency has a legal obligation to "counsel" parents, ensuring they understand the implications of their consent; however, for mothers with intellectual disabilities, this might require expertise beyond that ordinarily available within the agency.

One of the main changes from the Adoption Act of 1976 within the ACA is that it has dispensed with the "Freeing for Adoption Orders." The new placement provisions within the Act mean that "Freeing Orders" are, in effect, defunct. Birth parents maintain parental responsibility although, after an adoption placement has been agreed, this responsibility will be shared until an Adoption Order has been made. This prevents children drifting as "looked after" children without legal parents, as previously happened with children "freed" for adoption but not yet placed. The shifting legal status of birth parents through this process is particularly difficult to explain to parents with intellectual disabilities.

The ACA strengthens contact agreements and section 26 requires the legal carers of a child to allow that child to have contact with a named person. Applications can be made by the child, the agency, or birth-family members. Mothers with intellectual disabilities need to understand the importance of making decisions in respect to contact early in the proceedings. At the time when an Adoption Order is made, birth parents can apply for a section 8 CA post-adoption contact order. This right is explicitly protected within section 26 of the ACA. However, if the application is not heard at the time of the Adoption Order, the birth parent is not able to apply for a contact order at a later date as it requires the applicant to be the parent. If the mother with an intellectual disability is not aware or advised of this fact by her legal representative, she may miss taking this important action, which occurs at a time when she is most likely to feel extremely disempowered.

While the legal context for mothers with intellectual disabilities, as for all parents, has improved with the introduction of the ACA, there remains a short-fall in services to enable parents with intellectual disabilities to be supported and to express their views in the decision-making process. Achieving adequate support for parents with intellectual disabilities will require improvement to the format of case conferences to enable participation, increasing the number of advocates, and advancing the level of skill and sensitivity possessed by legal advisers. Specialist advocacy services for parents with intellectual disabilities involved in child protection proceedings, where these exist, have been found to be particularly helpful in facilitating parents' understanding of the child protection process, ensuring that the parent's voice is heard and providing parents with the support that they need if they wish to challenge child protection professionals' practice (Tarleton, 2008).

## Supported Decision Making for Women and Mothers

Supporting women with intellectual disabilities to participate in decisions that affect their lives needs to begin in childhood. Good practice in supported decision making needs to focus on the early years where young girls with intellectual disabilities can learn in a safe situation how to protect themselves from harm. In adolescence and adulthood, good practice will address providing opportunities to develop decision-making skills, again in a supported and safe environment, about sexual relationships, contraception, and parenting. In the parenting role, good practice will be based on research-proven strategies to assist mothers to make informed decisions and, when necessary, to help mothers seek appropriate advocacy support. In this section we briefly describe some research-based principles, strategies, and programs to support decision making for women and mothers with intellectual disabilities.

## General principles and strategies

To make deliberate, informed decisions, women and mothers with intellectual disabilities may need assistance to reduce stressors in their lives and/or distractions within the decision-making environment. It is difficult for anyone to make considered decisions when they are stressed, for example, by poverty, paperwork, or illness, or distracted by competing demands, for example, a crying baby or a controlling parent or partner. Once a "best possible" decision-making environment or situation is created, practitioners can assist women and mothers with intellectual disabilities by breaking information down and by using visual aids such as photographs and illustrations (Grisso & Applebaum, 1995; Wong, Clare, Holland, Watson, & Gunn, 2000). Quality decision making is also more likely to occur when women and mothers with intellectual disabilities are presented with specific situations rather than with information about alternative modes of action and their consequences (Bakken, Miltenberger, & Schauss, 1993; Tymchuk et al., 1990). It is also vital for practitioners who are supporting women and mothers with intellectual disabilities in their decision-making to be gentle, patient, and non-judgmental (Espe-Sherwindt & Kerlin, 1990). These principles have, in various ways, been incorporated into some specific programs that are described in the literature and below.

## Enhancing the decision making of children and young people

The five steps Self-Determination Program (Hoffman, 2003) is one example of how the decision making of children with intellectual disabilities may be enhanced within schools. This program is designed to help students prepare for the multiple roles of adulthood, including that of parenting (Wehmeyer, 2002). The facilitative framework teaches students to make effective choices and decisions by assessing their own strengths, weaknesses, and needs and preferences, based on a foundation of knowledge and positive affirmation about themselves (Field & Hoffman, 1994). While most of the program is delivered within schools, it extends beyond the school environment to include family members, professionals, and family support programs to promote generalization. It is designed to help people with intellectual disabilities in the following ways.

1. Acknowledge their disabilities, without having to take on the stigmatization associated with such ownership. When students choose to disclose their hidden learning difficulties, they must then deal with the perceptions and misperceptions that others may have about them.
2. Understand their strengths and weaknesses, and acceptance of self as the foundation for making effective choices and decisions (Field et al., 1994).

3. Recognize the difficulties associated with learned helplessness and self-deprecating attributions (Bos & Vaughn, 2002).
4. Understand that poor socialization skills ultimately restrict choice, in contrast to positive relationships, which rely on strong social skills, all of which is enhanced by self-determination and making choices.
5. Enhance their executive functioning skills, including organizational and planning abilities, mental flexibility, and task initiation, all of which are fundamental to effective decision making and choices.

## Specific programs and resources for pregnant women

To support women with intellectual disabilities to make healthy decisions during and after pregnancy, several studies have trialled different strategies. One study described a successful support program provided to a woman with a severe intellectual disability (intelligence quotient < 40) who was helped to make informed choices about her prenatal treatment during gestation and birth, using sign language and facial expressions (Baum, 2000). Another study in the United States of America evaluated a school-based program, Chicago's Children and Adolescent Pregnancy Project (CAPP), for pregnant teenage girls (11–19 years), about one-third of whom had mild intellectual disabilities (Levy et al., 1992). This study found that integrating pregnant teens with mild intellectual disabilities into a group with young pregnant teens without intellectual disabilities was an effective way of reducing risks, including, for example, subsequent pregnancies and school dropout.

Most recently, a new resource designed to promote the participation of pregnant women with intellectual disabilities in their pregnancy care was piloted in Australia (Australian Supported Parenting Consortium, 2007). This resource, called Healthy Start for Me and My Baby (HSMMB), has two components: a plain English booklet and a blank audiotape for recording consultations. The booklet includes essential information with illustrations and photographs; question prompt sheets (questions a woman may like to ask her doctor or midwife); tip sheets (things you can do); and it encourages women to use the workbook to document changes they have noticed. The pilot of HSMMB involved six sites, nine antenatal care providers, and 27 pregnant women with mild intellectual disabilities. The results showed that both pregnant women with learning difficulties and practitioners found the HSMMB resource to be unique, accessible, and useful. HSMMB was described as reassuring (helping the women to understand what is "normal" and what to expect), and it encouraged the women to think more about and express how they were feeling; it helped the women to participate more in their antenatal care consultations; and it gave the women ideas about what they can do to care for themselves and their babies during their pregnancy and immediately after the birth.

## Supported decision making in the parenting role

Processes that actively facilitate supported decision making are well demonstrated in four group-based programs for parents with intellectual disabilities described in the literature. One is the Supported Learning Project (SLP), developed and evaluated by Booth and Booth (2003) in Sheffield, England. Another is the Australian Supported Learning Program (McConnell, Dalziel, Llewellyn, Laidlaw, & Hindmarsh, 2009). The third group program is described by McGaw, Ball, and Clark (2002). This program, implemented in Cornwall, England, brought parents together weekly for two hours over a 14-week period, and employed a cognitive-behavioral approach to raise social awareness and to enhance interpersonal communications and listening in relationships. The fourth group-based program, called Parents Forever, was implemented and evaluated in Saskatchewan, Canada (Heinz & Grant, 2003). The program has three main components. These are the creation of a supportive and comfortable environment for group discussions, teaching parenting and self-care skills, and crisis management.

These four programs are quite different in many respects, but they also share some common principles and processes, and all four have demonstrated success. The common elements are (1) a person-centered approach, in which the participants make their own decisions about what to learn and discuss; (2) recognition and respect for participants' prior learning and life skills; (3) flexibility, allowing participants to participate on their own terms, although within the limits of rules set by the group; and (4) *in vivo* learning, with participants developing self-advocacy and decision-making skills by addressing issues arising in their own lives. Although these principles were applied in group-based interventions, they could also be applied by practitioners in their individual casework to support the decision making of women and mothers with intellectual disabilities.

# Conclusion

To support women and mothers with intellectual disabilities and promote their full participation in the decisions that affect their lives, information and services need to be more accessible. These women and mothers need and have a right to accessible health screening, sex health education, and parenting support services. Accessible information and support need to be available across a range of settings, including schools, GP practices, statutory service settings, and family support units to optimize decision making through informed, supported guidance and self-determination (Fraser, 1994). On occasions, when another person needs to make a decision on a woman's or mother's behalf by acting in her best interests and/or the best interests of her children, each woman's values and preferences need to be taken into account along with her psychological health, well-being, quality of life, relationships with family or other carers, spiritual and religious welfare, and her own financial interests (Department of Health, 2001; Dye et al., 2004).

In the UK there are encouraging signs of government commitment to improving services and access to information for women and mothers with intellectual disabilities. For example, the National Service Framework for Children, Young People, and Maternity Services (Department of Health, 2004) proposes a fundamental change in the delivery of services relating to children's health. Services are to become more child-, young person-, and family-centered, preventive, and better integrated. Greater emphasis will be placed on mothers having the support and the information they need to make the best health choices for them and their baby. In particular, parents and carers will be enabled to receive the information, services, and support that will help them to care for their children and will, reportedly, be equipped with the skills they need to ensure that their children have optimum life chances and are healthy and safe (Standard 2). Further, useful guidance is now available on how to enhance decision making for people who have difficulty deciding for themselves (Lord Chancellor's Department, 2003a, 2003b, 2003c, 2003d, 2003e). The range of leaflets available provides information about where they can access help to support them in their decision making, how to make their voice heard, and the options available to them in terms of day-to-day decisions, friendships and relationships, getting medical treatment, and managing their money.

In the UK, the challenge will be in turning what appears to be genuine commitment, reflected in these policy documents, into action. The translation of policy and research into practice will take more than a call from government. It will require the commitment of each individual agency and practitioner to ensure that women and mothers with intellectual disabilities are supported to make their own decisions rather than being ignored, as currently happens all too often, or constrained in the decision-making process.

# References

Atkinson, D., & Walmsley, J. (1995). A woman's place? Issues of gender. In T. Philpot & L. Ward (Eds.), *Values and visions: Changing ideas in services for people with learning difficulties* (pp. 218–231). Oxford: Butterworth Heinemann.

Aunos, M., & Feldman, M. A. (2002). Attitudes towards sexuality, sterilization and parenting rights of persons with intellectual disabilities. *Journal of Applied Research in Intellectual Disabilities, 15*(4), 285–296.

Australian Supported Parenting Consortium. (2007). *Healthy start for me and my baby: Preliminary findings report.* Sydney: University of Sydney.

Bach, M., & Rock, M. (1996). *Seeking consent to participate in research from people whose ability to make an informed decision could be questioned: The supported decision-making model.* An occasional paper from the Roeher Institute. Ontario: Roeher Institute.

Bakken, J., Miltenberger, R. G., & Schauss, S. (1993). Teaching parents with mental retardation: Knowledge versus skills. *American Journal on Mental Retardation, 97*(4), 405–417.

Baum, S. (2000). Interventions with a pregnant woman with severe learning disabilities. *Clinical Psychology Forum, 137,* 16–20.

Bohlin, A. B., & Larsson, G. (1986). Early identification of infants at risk for institutional care. *Journal of Advanced Nursing, 11*(5), 493–497.

Booth, T., & Booth, W. (2002). Men in the lives of mothers with intellectual disabilities. *Journal of Applied Research in Intellectual Disabilities, 15*(3), 187–199.

Booth, T., & Booth, W. (2003). Self-advocacy and supported learning for mothers with learning difficulties. *Journal of Learning Disabilities, 7*(2), 165–193.

Booth, T., Booth, W., & McConnell, D. (2004a). Parents with learning difficulties, care proceedings and the family courts: Threshold decisions and the moral matrix. *Child and Family Law Quarterly, 16*(4), 409–421.

Booth, W., Booth, T., & McConnell, D. (2004b). Family trials. *Disability, Pregnancy and Parenthood International, 45* (Winter), 12–13.

Booth, T., Booth, W., & McConnell, D. (2005). The prevalence and outcomes of care proceedings involving parents with learning difficulties in the family courts. *Journal of Applied Research in Intellectual Disabilities, 18*(1), 7–17.

Bos, C. S., & Vaughn, S. (2002). *Strategies for teaching students with learning and behavior problems* ( 5th ed.). Boston: Allyn & Bacon.

Cooke, L. B. (1997). Cancer and learning disability. *Journal of Intellectual Disability Research, 41*(4), 312–316.

Cowie, M., & Fletcher, J. (1998). Breast awareness project for women with a learning disability. *British Journal of Nursing, 7*(13), 774–778.

Craft, A., & Craft, M. (1981). Sexuality and mental handicap: A review. *British Journal of Psychiatry, 139*(6), 494–505.

Department for Education and Skills. (2003). *Every child matters.* London: The Stationery Office.

Department of Children, Schools, and Families. (1989). *Children's Act.* London: The Stationery Office.

Department of Health. (2001). *Valuing people: A new strategy for learning disability for the 21st century.* London: The Stationery Office.

Department of Health. (2002). *Adoption and Children Act 2002.* London: HMSO.

Department of Health. (2004). *National service framework for children, young people and maternity services.* London: HMSO.

Department of Health and Social Security. (1975). *Sterilisation of children under 16 years of age.* Discussion paper 1–4. London: HMSO.

Dowse, L., & Frohmader, C. (2001). *Moving forward: Sterilisation and reproductive health of women and girls with disabilities.* Rosny Park: Women with Disabilities Australia.

Duff, M., Scheepers, M., Cooper, M., Hoghton, M., & Baddeley, P. (2001). *Helicobacter pylori*: Has the killer escaped from the institution? A possible cause of increased stomach cancer in a population with intellectual disability. *Journal of Intellectual Disability Research, 45*(3), 219–225.

Dye, L., Hendy, S., Hare, D. J., & Burton, M. (2004). Capacity to consent to participate in research – a recontextualization. *British Journal of Learning Disabilities, 32*(3), 144–150.

Dyer, C. (1987). Consent and the mentally handicapped. *British Medical Journal, 295*(6592), 257–258.

Emerson, E., Malam, S., Davies, I., & Spencer, K. (2005). *Adults with learning difficulties in England 2003/04.* London: Office of National Statistics.

Espe-Sherwindt, M., & Kerlin, S. (1990). Early intervention with parents with mental retardation: Do we empower or impair? *Infants and Young Children, 2*(4), 21–28.

Family Rights Group. (2008). *Supporting disabled parents: Social care services for parents and adults in a parenting role.* Retrieved July 2009, from http://www.frg.org.uk/pdfs/6.%20ssfor%20disabled%20parents.pdf.

Field, S., & Hoffman, A. (1994). Development of a model for self-determination. *Career Development for Exceptional Individuals, 17*(2), 159–169.

Finucane, B. (1998). Acculturation in women with mental retardation and its impact on genetic counseling. *Journal of Genetic Counseling, 7*(1), 31–47.

Fraser, J. (1994). Brook Advisory Centres: Responding to the needs of young people with learning disabilities. *Mencap News, 47,* 18–19.

Garber, H. (1988). *The Milwaukee Project.* Washington, DC: American Association on Mental Retardation.

Glaun, D. E., & Brown, P. F. (1999). Motherhood, intellectual disability and child protection: Characteristics of a court sample. *Journal of Intellectual and Developmental Disability, 24*(1), 95–105.

Grisso, T. (1986). *Evaluating competencies: Forensic assessments and instruments.* New York: Plenum Press.

Grisso, T., & Appelbaum, P. S. (1995). The MacArthur treatment competence study. III. Abilities of patients to consent to psychiatric and medical treatments. *Law and Human Behavior, 19*(2), 149–174.

Heinz, L. C., & Grant, P. R. (2003). A process evaluation of a parenting group for parents with intellectual disabilities. *Evaluation and Program Planning, 26*(3), 263–274.

Henneman, L., Bramsen, I., Van Os, Th. A. M., Reuling, I. E. W., Heverman, H. G. M., Van der Laag, J., Van der Ploeg, H. M., & ten Kate, L. P. (2001). Attitudes toward reproductive issues and carrier testing among adult patients and parents of children with cystic fibrosis (CF). *Prenatal Diagnosis, 21*(1), 1–9.

Hoffman, A. (2003). Teaching decision making to students with learning disabilities by promoting self-determination [Electronic version]. *ERIC Digest.* Retrieved July 2009, from www.ericdigests.org/2004-2/self.html.

Hollins, S., Attard, M. T., von Fraunhofer, N., McGuin, S., & Sedgwick, P. (1998). Mortality in people with intellectual disabilities: Risks, causes, and death certification findings in London. *Developmental Medicine and Child Neurology, 40*(1), 50–56.

Kelly, J. F., Morisset, C. E., Barnard, K. E., & Patterson, D. L. (1996). Risky beginnings: Low maternal intelligence as a risk factor for children's intellectual development. *Infants and Young Children, 8*(3) 11–23.

Kerr, M. (2006). Assessment in primary care. *Psychiatry, 5,* 351–354.

Langan, J., Russell, O., & Whitfield, M. (1993). *Community care and the general practitioner: Primary health care for people with intellectual disabilities.* Bristol: Norah Fry Research Centre.

Larsson, G. (1980). The amphetamine-addicted mother and her child. *Acta Paediatrica Scandinavica, 69*(S278), 7–24.

Levy, S. R, Perhats, C., Nash-Johnson, M., & Welter, J. F. (1992). Reducing the risks in pregnant teens who are very young and those with mild mental retardation. *Mental Retardation, 30*(4), 195–203.

Llewellyn, G., & McConnell, D. (2002). Mothers with learning difficulties and their support networks. *Journal of Intellectual Disability Research, 46*(1), 17–34.

Llewellyn, G., McConnell, D., & Mayes, R. (2003). Health of mothers with intellectual limitations. *Australian and New Zealand Journal of Public Health, 27*(1), 17–19.

Lord Chancellor's Department. (2003a). *Making decisions: Helping people who have difficulty deciding for themselves. A guide for legal practitioners.* London: The Stationery Office.

Lord Chancellor's Department. (2003b). *Making decisions: Helping people who have difficulty deciding for themselves. A guide for social care professionals.* London: The Stationery Office.

Lord Chancellor's Department. (2003c). *Making decisions: Helping people who have difficulty deciding for themselves. A guide for healthcare professionals.* London: The Stationery Office.

Lord Chancellor's Department. (2003d). *Making decisions: Helping people who have difficulty deciding for themselves. A guide for family and friends.* London: The Stationery Office.

Lord Chancellor's Department. (2003e). *Making decisions: Helping people who have difficulty deciding for themselves. Planning ahead. A guide for people who wish to plan for possible future incapacity.* London: The Stationery Office.

Marteau, T. M., & Dormandy, E. (2001). Facilitating informed choice in prenatal testing: How well are we doing? *American Journal of Medical Genetics, 106*(3), 185–190.

McCarthy, M. (2002). Responses to women with learning disabilities as they go through the menopause. *Tizard Learning Disability Review, 7*(1), 4–12.

McConnell, D., Dalziel, A., Llewellyn, G., Laidlaw, K., & Hindmarsh, G. (2009). Strengthening the social relationships of mothers with learning difficulties. *British Journal of Learning Disabilities, 37*(1), 66–75.

McConnell, D., & Llewellyn, G. (2002). Stereotypes, parents with intellectual disability and child protection. *Journal of Social Welfare and Family Law, 24*(3), 297–317.

McConnell, D., Llewellyn, G., & Ferronato, L. (2000). *Parents with a disability and the NSW Children's Court.* Sydney: University of Sydney.

McConnell, D., Mayes, R., & Llewellyn, G. (2008). Women with intellectual disability at risk of adverse pregnancy and birth outcomes. *Journal of Intellectual Disability Research, 52*(6), 529–535.

McGaw, S., Ball, K., & Clark, A. (2002). The effect of group intervention on the relationships of intellectually disabled parents. *Journal of Applied Research in Intellectual Disabilities, 15*(4), 354–366.

Mørch, W., Skar, J., & Andersgard, A. B. (1997). Mentally retarded persons as parents: Prevalence and the situation of their children. *Scandinavian Journal of Psychology, 38*(4), 343–348.

Ray, N. K., Rubenstein, H., & Russo, N. J. (1994). Understanding the parents who are mentally retarded: Guidelines for family preservation programs. *Child Welfare, 73*(6), 725–743.

Roy, M., & Roy, A. (1988). Sterilisation for girls and women with mental handicaps: Some ethical and moral considerations. *Mental Handicap, 16* (September), 97–100.

Sklar, C. (1980). You and the law. Consent, sterilisation and mental incompetence: The case of "Eve." *The Canadian Nurse, 78*(1), 14–16.

Sobsey, D. (2000). Faces of violence against women with developmental disabilities. *Impact, 13*(3), 2–27.

Suto, W. M., Clare, C. H., Holland, A. J., & Watson, P. C. (2005). Capacity to make financial decisions among people with mild intellectual disabilities. *Journal of Intellectual Disability Research, 49*(3), 199–209.

Tarleton, B. (2008). Specialist advocacy services for parents with learning disabilities involved in child protection proceedings. *British Journal of Learning Disabilities, 36*(2), 134–139.

Tarleton, B., Ward, L., & Howarth, J. (2006). *Finding the right support? A review of issues and positive practice in supporting parents with learning difficulties and their children.* London: Baring Foundation.

Taylor, G., Pearson, J., & Cook, H. (1998). Family planning for women with intellectual disabilities. *Nursing Times, 94*(40), 60–61.

Tymchuk, A. (1990). Parents with mental retardation: A national strategy. *Journal of Disability Policy Studies, 1*(4), 43–55.

Tymchuk, A., Yokota, A., & Rahbar, B. (1990). Decision-making abilities of mothers with mental retardation. *Research in Developmental Disabilities, 11*(1), 97–109.

Wehmeyer, M. (2002). Self-determination and the education of students with disabilities [Electronic version]. *ERIC Digest.* Retrieved July 2009, from http://www.eric.ed.gov/ERICWebPortal/custom/portlets/recordDetails/detailmini.jsp?_nfpb=true&_&ERICExtSearch_SearchValue_0=ED470036&ERICExtSearch_SearchType_0=no&accno=ED470036.

Willis, D., Kennedy, C., & Kilbride, L. (2008). Breast cancer screening in women with learning disabilities: Current knowledge and considerations. *British Journal of Learning Disabilities, 36*(3), 171–184.

Wilson, C., & Brewer, N. (1992). The incidence of criminal victimization of individuals with an intellectual disability. *Australian Psychologist, 27*(2), 114–117.

Wolf, L., & Zarfas, D. E. (1982). Parents' attitudes toward sterilization of their mentally retarded children. *American Journal of Mental Deficiency, 87*(2), 122–129.

Wong, J. G., Clare, I. C. H., Holland, A. J., Watson, P. C., & Gunn, M. (2000). The capacity of people with a "mental disability" to make a health care decision. *Psychological Medicine, 30*(2), 295–306.

# 10

# Turning Policy Into Practice

*Beth Tarleton*

## Introduction

Current policy in England asserts that services should support parents with intellectual disabilities in order "to ensure their children gain maximum life chance benefits" (Department of Health, 2001). The same national policy, *Valuing People: A New Strategy for Learning Disability in the 21st Century*, states that:

> People with learning disabilities can be good parents and provide their children with a good start in life, but may require considerable help to do so. This requires children and adult social care teams to work closely together to develop a common approach. (Department of Health, 2001, para 7.40)

This policy is supported by the publication of a *Good Practice Guidance on Working with Parents with a Learning Disability* (Department of Health/Department for Education and Skills, 2007). The *Guidance* is aimed at professionals and others working with parents with intellectual disabilities and provides examples of good practice in supporting parents and their children. While the *Guidance* is not statutory and therefore not enforceable by law, it is supported by recent legislation such as the Disability Equality Duty under the Disability Discrimination Act (2005). The Disability Equality Duty requires services to make appropriate adjustments in order to accommodate

*Parents with Intellectual Disabilities: Past, Present and Futures*   Edited by Gwynnyth Llewellyn, Rannveig Traustadóttir, David McConnell, and Hanna Björg Sigurjónsdóttir   © 2010 John Wiley & Sons, Ltd

people with disabilities and has been confirmed in the report, *A Life Like Any Other? Human Rights and Adults with Learning Disabilities* (Joint Committee on Human Rights, 2008). In this report the Committee states that if services do not provide support to parents with intellectual disabilities, they could be violating children's right to live with their family. The recent updating of the national strategy for adults with intellectual disabilities, *Valuing People Now* (Department of Health, 2009), also recognizes that services should work together to provide more appropriate supports for parents with intellectual disabilities.

Other national policies in England concerning children and families, such as *Every Child Matters* (Department for Education and Skills, 2003) and *The National Service Framework for Children, Young People and Maternity Service* (Department for Education and Skills/Department of Health, 2004), provide a context in which it is presumed that children should be supported to stay with their families, and that parents who require special assistance should receive the support they need.

Although there are no definite figures regarding the number of parents with intellectual disabilities in England, it is generally acknowledged that their number is steadily rising (Booth, 2000). The difficulties with establishing the prevalence of parents with intellectual disabilities include that many parents with mild intellectual disabilities do not self-define as having intellectual disability. They are also not eligible for support services and only come into contact with services responsible for the protection of children when others are concerned about their parenting. The national survey of adults with intellectual disabilities in England found that one in 15 of the 2,898 adults interviewed were parents, and among those interviewed as a part of the survey, 48% were not living with their children (Emerson, Malam, Davies, & Spencer, 2005). Some of these children may have grown up and left home. However, these findings are consistent with other studies reporting that parents with intellectual disabilities are at a high risk of having their children removed. Thus, while national policy states the rights of children to grow up in their families and the rights of parents with intellectual disabilities to appropriate support, in practice, children are being removed from their parents in disproportionate numbers. Clearly, there is a gap between policy and practice.

This chapter reports on a study titled *Finding the Right Support?* (Tarleton, Ward, & Howarth, 2006). Its aim was to provide a review of existing services for parents with intellectual disabilities in the United Kingdom (UK) in order to identify and describe examples of positive practice in supporting parents. The chapter begins by providing background information from the literature and from parents' organizations about the current state of support for parents with intellectual disabilities in the UK. This is followed by a description of the study and presentation of some of the findings. The chapter concludes with a set of principles drawn from this research to inform practice.

# The Policy and Practice Gap

The literature on parents with intellectual disabilities and their children confirms the gap between policy and practice when it comes to the provision of support and services. Parents with intellectual disabilities still report that they are discriminated against when involved with services concerned with the welfare of their children (Booth, 2000; McGaw & Newman, 2005; Morgan & Goff, 2004). They feel they are expected to be "perfect parents" and to attain standards of parenting that are of a much higher level than those applied to non-disabled parents, and that they are not allowed to make mistakes or to move on from, in many cases, a negative history (McConnell & Llewellyn, 2002; Sellars, 2002). The *Good Practice Guidance* (Department of Health/Department for Education and Skills, 2007) points out that the relationships between parents and children's social care services have often been difficult, particularly if children have been previously removed from the parents' care. Parents often feel powerless and hostile and are reluctant to engage with services they fear will take their children. Parents commonly also lack knowledge about their rights and have limited information about support services that are available. The literature reflects that it is well known what kinds of support are needed to assist parents with intellectual disabilities in successfully bringing up their children (McGaw & Newman, 2005; Tarleton et al., 2006). This support, however, is not commonly or widely available to parents and their children.

CHANGE is an organization of and for disabled people that runs a network for parents with intellectual disabilities. In a national gathering of parents with intellectual disabilities, parents outlined the barriers they face and provided strategies for positive engagement with services. Their demands included:

- Accessible information about their own health and the health of their baby, and how to look after their baby.
- Self-advocacy groups and coming together with other parents.
- Getting support before things go wrong and become a crisis.
- Being assessed in parents' own homes, not in an unfamiliar residential family center.
- Assessment and support by people who understand learning disabilities.
- Advocacy.
- Making courts more accessible.
- Support for fathers.
- Support for women and men experiencing violent relationships.

(CHANGE, 2005, pp. 6–7)

The *Good Practice Guidance* stresses the importance of empowering parents through accessible information, communication, and independent advocacy.

It also states that support should be provided in a multi-agency manner to both parents and children for the long term, if necessary. It draws on recent literature, including the report of the *National Gathering* (CHANGE, 2005), which highlights that parents with intellectual disabilities can be supported to be "good-enough parents" through proactive, empowering, multi-agency support that is sensitive to the changing needs of the baby or child (Llewellyn & McConnell, 2005; McGaw & Newman, 2005; Social Care Institute for Excellence, 2007; Tarleton et al., 2006).

In 2007, parents with intellectual disabilities regrouped and acknowledged that improvements had been made, particularly in publishing the *Good Practice Guidance*. However, they emphasized that there was still a long way to go and that many parents "still have their children taken away." The parents updated their demands as follows:

- Support should be given as soon as parents know they are pregnant. There should be money for this.
- Parents should have more time – and more chances to understand why things are happening and why decisions are made.
- Look at skills and strengths and be positive rather than take a negative approach.
- Promote choice, value, and respect in education about sex and relationships, and have clear guidelines.
- All information to be made accessible using a national database which is free!
- Give children back and give the right and continuous support.

(CHANGE, 2007a, pp. 32–33)

## Finding the Right Support?

The *Finding the Right Support?* project was undertaken in 2004 and 2005. It was a mapping study which sought to investigate the issues around providing support to parents with learning difficulties and its main aim was to locate and share positive practice around the United Kingdom. Positive practice was defined as new or innovative practice that was regarded as supportive by parents with intellectual disabilities.

The research was guided by a group of 13 parents with intellectual disabilities who were located through a voluntary support organization. The parents acted as expert consultants providing information and insight into the issues at hand. The parents met four times with the researchers during the life of the project, and for over half a day on each occasion. During the meetings the parents shared:

- their detailed stories, including the ages and current home location of their children;

- the history of their interactions with services;
- the support they were currently receiving, if any, and what they felt consti- tuted, "good" and "bad" support;
- what, in their view, positive support would look like and their opinions on the emerging findings;
- their views on how the research should be undertaken with parents with intellectual disabilities.

The advice and personal information provided by the parents was used as a basis for developing the interviews with parents and to develop criteria through which positive practice was evaluated. The research had four strands:

1. A review of the literature and resources in the area of parenting with intellectual disability.
2. An exploratory web-based questionnaire for professionals.
3. Follow-up telephone interviews with 20 professionals identified as provid- ing examples of positive practices.
4. Case study visits to six services in different parts of the UK identified as exhibiting positive practice in supporting parents with intellectual disabil- ities.

The web-based questionnaire was developed using the information provided by the parent consultants and through discussions with services already known to be providing positive support to parents with intellectual disabilities.

The questionnaire was piloted and disseminated widely through intellec- tual disability networks in order to try to locate services that were supporting parents with intellectual disabilities, either as their core role or as part of their wider mission. The questionnaire was completed by 85 professionals including community nurses, advocates, psychologists, workers in adult services, and oc- cupational therapists working in 73 services providing direct support to parents with intellectual disabilities. These services were mainly services for adults with intellectual disabilities, a small number of family support services, and services specifically for parents with intellectual disabilities.

Telephone interviews were then undertaken with 20 professionals who had completed the online questionnaire. They were employed in a range of services across the UK and were selected on the basis of examples of positive practice described in their web questionnaire. The interviews investigated in detail how parents with intellectual disabilities were supported by the service. This sup- port included the development of care pathways or protocols, parents' groups, specialist parenting services, and successful multi-agency support, including working closely with mainstream services and services supporting vulnerable families.

Case study visits were then made to six areas of the UK to further explore different examples of positive practice that had been described in the telephone interviews and had appeared particularly innovative. The aim of these two-day visits was to gain further insight that could be shared with other services. During these visits, 17 parents who received support from these services were interviewed about the support they received and their opinions of this support. Individual and focus group interviews were also undertaken with a range of professionals and front-line workers who were directly involved in supporting parents.

Below are some of the findings from the study. For a more detailed report, see Tarleton et al. (2006).

## Barriers to positive support

One of the striking findings was how many barriers there are to parenting with intellectual disabilities and to positive support for parents to bring up their children. Although the Children's Act 1989 and wider policy context indicate that children should be supported within their family whenever possible, the parents with intellectual disabilities we met during the study, and the professionals supporting them, felt that professionals in mainstream, generic, or child protection services had no experience of working with adults with intellectual disabilities. One professional, who also acted as an advocate for parents, said:

> There is, in general, a negative attitude from many professionals involved with these parents. That having a learning disability prevents them from being "good-enough" parents. That the parents will not be able to learn to parent more effectively, or that it will take more time and children cannot wait. Also that giving families additional support will be prohibitively expensive. (Tarleton et al., 2006, p. 23)

Professionals supporting parents with intellectual disabilities felt that other professionals commonly presumed that people with intellectual disabilities would not be able to understand their children's developmental needs or learn the necessary skills quickly enough to meet these needs. They also said that the lack of awareness regarding adults with intellectual disabilities, and the support they required, was responsible for parents' late referral, frequently at crisis point, to adult and specialist support services. One professional remarked:

> Too many of our parents are referred only at the point at which the Child Protection team has decided to place the matter before the court. At this point they receive few services geared to assist them to become more effective parents. Hearing the chronology of these parents' problems leaves me feeling that if they were referred earlier it might have been possible to gain them access to effective services which helped them keep their children. (Tarleton et al., 2006, p. 27)

Many professionals also recognized that lack of resources inhibited the provision of support for parents with intellectual disabilities. Any support that was available to parents was short term, through which parents were expected to learn the skills they needed and then apply them on their own once the intervention was completed. One psychologist noted that children and family services "do not have a concept of ongoing support to mitigate the effects of a disability. Neither do they have mechanisms or funds to mitigate this" (Tarleton et al., 2006, p. 24). As a result, professionals involved with protecting children wanted to ensure a "concrete outcome" for children by placing them with other carers. This was a way of preventing the children from being exposed to *any* level of risk. As one parent said: "They hear what they want to hear, they don't listen to your side. They don't understand what you are saying. They are only interested in taking the kids" (Tarleton et al., 2006, p. 26).

Professionals providing positive support to parents with intellectual disabilities said the lack of clarity about what constituted "good parenting" contributed to parents' lack of confidence in their skills and in their ability to prove that they were "good-enough" parents. Parenting is not an "exact science" and each of the often numerous professionals who came into contact with parents with intellectual disabilities had his or her own concept of "good parenting." "The social worker says, 'Don't cuddle the baby too much'. The foster carer says, 'You can't love a baby too much'" (Tarleton et al., 2006, p. 25). As a result, the parents often did not know what standards they should be working toward. This confusion ranged from simple issues such as whether a dummy was acceptable to whether pursuing their own personal development was a good thing or not. One professional noted that a mother had been both praised and criticized by different professionals for leaving her child with her mother one day a week in order to attend college.

These conflicting messages were particularly problematic for the parents when their child's social worker from child and family services changed, requiring the parent to form a new relationship and perhaps conform to new values around parenting. A social worker providing support to parents acknowledged this and said:

> Families can often move through three or four teams in a space of three or four months, with frequent changes of social workers or being unallocated for periods of time. The direction of the case is influenced by the individual social worker and leaves the parent feeling very confused. (Tarleton et al., 2006, p. 25)

Compounding this, professionals supporting parents with intellectual disabilities felt these parents were, unhelpfully, expected to be "perfect parents" and to meet "impossibly high standards." Parents and the professionals supporting them also said that families were not allowed to move on from previous negative circumstances, such as having children removed from their care in the past, but judgments on their current circumstances and capabilities were made on the basis of past events. One parent observed: "Social workers assume you can't do it. They talk about your history and baggage, they don't let you change

... They use the same evidence against you ten years later" (Tarleton et al., 2006, p. 26).

A small number of professionals also felt that parents with intellectual disabilities did not get the support other families received in the event of a crisis or unfortunate life event. One of them said:

> How other parents known to social services receive information to access support and help systems or assistance to deal with issues doesn't seem to happen to parents with a learning difficulty – in one case a mum's distraction from learning new skills because of benefit, housing and relationship problems was given as a reason why she wouldn't be able to change her parenting skills to meet the needs of her daughter. (Tarleton et al., 2006, p. 24)

The parents expressed anxiety and fear, which derived from the combination of all the factors outlined above and their belief that others judged them for having a social worker. This often resulted in a fear of engaging with services. In fact, some parents took a deliberate stance against services. This was particularly the case when they had previously had children removed from their care. This seemingly adversarial position, and lack of responsiveness to services, could subsequently feed into children and family services' concerns about their parenting ability.

## Parenting with support

The term "parenting with support" aptly describes how professionals involved in this study conceptualized the way in which they were endeavoring to support parents with intellectual disabilities. They recognized that having an intellectual disability was a lifelong impairment and that the parents would need ongoing support to help them parent to the best of their ability. One of the intellectual disability social workers in the study explained: "We know they have a learning difficulty. You don't wake up and not have a learning difficulty. We have a mindset within learning disability services – we are generally there for life" (Tarleton et al., 2006, p. 29). One advocate also recognized:

> That people with a learning difficulty can be "good enough" parents, but may need more support and time to learn new skills than parents without a learning disability. Parents with a learning difficulty are disabled people in their own right and should be eligible for resources and support when needed, to assist them in their role as a parent. (Tarleton et al., 2006, p. 29)

Similarly, parents with intellectual disabilities involved in this research recognized their need for ongoing support and the benefits to them and their family from involvement with positive service provision, frequently praising the individual workers who were supporting them. Comments from parents included:

> We've got a nice social worker. She does what you ask. We get proper support in what to do . . . they trust in me and Kylie. (Tarleton et al., 2006, p. 34)
>     If Alison hadn't spotted me I wouldn't have a child now. (Tarleton et al., 2006, p. 33)

This supportive practice was developed by professionals who had recognized parents' personal difficulties, the barriers within society that further impaired their ability to parent to the best of their ability, and who had witnessed poor practice in relation to this group of parents. They had begun to champion the parents' cause locally and were acting as interpreters or mediators, supporting parents to engage with children and family services and to break the vicious cycle that had developed in their interactions so that parents could prove that, with support, they could be "good-enough" parents.

There are three themes integral to the emerging concept of "parenting with support." These are:

1.  empowering support for parents with intellectual disabilities;
2.  raising awareness of parents with intellectual disabilities and their support needs;
3.  developing multi-professional and multi-agency support for parents with intellectual disabilities and their families.

In the following sections these three themes will be addressed.

### Empowering support

Parents with intellectual disabilities involved in this study and the professionals supporting them discussed ways in which empowering support was provided to parents. This support included helping parents learn the skills they needed, and in the way they needed, developing more confidence, and assisting the parents in having their voices heard. Parents also needed to be able to support each other and understand the child protection and judicial systems.

Positive relationships with professionals underpinned parental empowerment. Parents developed confidence and self-esteem through positive relationships with professionals who spent time listening to them and praised their achievements. The professionals also strove to maintain a non-judgmental attitude and communicate clearly and honestly with parents about their expectations in terms of the parenting knowledge or skills that were required. These professionals also tried to ensure that parents remained in control of their parenting through supporting them to do things for themselves. They were supporting parents to learn new skills by breaking tasks down into small steps and "thinking outside the box" to find creative and innovative strategies to facilitate parents' learning. Parents were supported to follow picture prompts, for example, in making a baby's bottle and to use an appropriately sized container to measure milk rather than to have to measure the water when making up formula milk.

Central to the empowerment of parents was the provision of easy-to-understand information about the stage of parenting they were at and, if relevant, about the child protection or court processes. Professionals ensured that relevant information was provided in a suitable format for parents, whether this was in short, clear sentences with no jargon and explanatory pictures or on audio tape, video, or DVD. In at least one area of the UK, all of the relevant information about the antenatal pathway had been produced in an easy-to-understand format. Professionals also used and adapted easy-to-understand information about the parenting process that was available, such as the books *You and Your Baby* (Affleck & Baker, 2004) and *You and Your Little Child 1–5* (CHANGE, 2007b) and the "I Want to Be a Good Parent," one of the *Parenting Skills Cards* (McGaw, Smith, & Tomabene, 1999). A review of the resources available to parents with intellectual disabilities (Marriott & Tarleton, 2009) can be downloaded from the Working Together with Parents Network website (www.right-support.org.uk). The actual practical support to learn and implement new skills was often evaluated using a competency-based assessment such as the *Parent Assessment Manual* (McGaw, Beckley, Connolly, & Ball, 1998).

Through the empowering relationships and practices described here, parents were supported to engage with children and family services, including the child protection system when appropriate, and to work with the requirements made of them to improve their parenting. The study also revealed that many of the professionals supporting parents with intellectual disabilities attempted to advocate for them when they were involved in child protection proceedings. This situation was, however, confusing for the parents because these professionals were supporting them to be involved in proceedings in which they were also reporting on their progress. The professionals acknowledged that the parents should be supported by an independent advocate and that their advocacy could conflict with their role as professionals helping parents. However, due to the shortage of advocates, the professionals took on an advocacy role to try to ensure the parents had a voice in the proceedings.

Belonging to parent groups was empowering for the parents. They enjoyed belonging to the group and felt supported and empowered by being with other parents, in an environment where they could learn from each other and develop friendships. They also benefited from information shared by visiting "experts," who were invited to the group, such as dentists and dieticians. Some areas provided specific training courses for parents, such as an adapted Webster Stratton Parenting course or cookery courses that result in accreditation through non-standard assessment via photographs and other alternative measures. In some cases the parents also received assistance to access family support services such as children's centers or baby, breastfeeding, or parenting groups in the community.

Many parents needed support to overcome issues such as poor housing, harassment, debt, or mental health support needs which detracted from their ability to parent. The parents were grateful to be supported to get rid of "loan sharks," to understand their finances, and to budget appropriately. In particular they found it helpful to be assisted to move closer to supportive family members.

The support outlined in this section was proactive and flexible, and tailored to the individual needs of the family. It was provided in a respectful way, taking into account the individual parents and their needs. It focused on the parents' strengths, enabling them to demonstrate they could be "good-enough parents," and also ensured their children's needs were met. The ongoing involvement of professionals allowed them to address any potential difficulties before they became real issues. Professionals from intellectual disability backgrounds who were supporting adults in their parenting role maintained an awareness of child protection issues and were willing to report any issues to child and family services. This joint emphasis on protecting children furthered their positive relationship with child and family services and contributed to the development of positive multi-agency collaboration.

### Raising awareness

Lack of awareness about parents with intellectual disabilities and their needs has been identified as one of the barriers to appropriate support for them and their children. Part of the positive practice identified in this study was the raising of awareness about parents with intellectual disabilities and their support needs. This awareness was raised at a variety of levels. Locally, professionals involved with parents with intellectual disabilities were advocating for their needs by networking with colleagues and attending or developing relevant forums, such as maternity alliances, in order to raise the profile of parents with intellectual disabilities in the local area. These professionals were also providing information and assistance to colleagues who did not have any experience working with adults with intellectual disabilities. In one area, the intellectual disabilities team had provided information boxes to other services containing relevant factual information about the types of support services available. In other areas simple assessment strategies had been developed so that professionals who did not have a background in intellectual disabilities could determine whether the parents might have an intellectual disability.

The professionals were also offering, generally in collaboration with parents, training for professionals in mainstream and children's services. The training discussed the impact of having intellectual disabilities on an adult's life and how support could be provided to empower adults to meet their children's ever-changing needs appropriately.

*Multi-agency support*

Multi-agency support is considered to be one of the keys in developing comprehensive support for parents with intellectual disabilities. Many of the professionals who took part in this study were working hard to develop coordinated multi-professional and multi-agency support for parents with intellectual disabilities. This strategy is in line with *Valuing People* (Department of Health, 2001), which stresses that there should be effective partnerships between adults' teams and children's services. This is also consistent with the recent guidance regarding multi-agency support published by the Social Care Institute for Excellence (2007). The professionals have, among other things, developed joint protocols and pathways that describe how, and by whom, the support needs of parents with intellectual disabilities will be met.

In some localities, when a number of professionals and/or agencies were supporting a family, a "key-worker" system had been implemented. This entails one worker being responsible for liaising with the parents as well as with the other professionals involved. In order to facilitate this, consent procedures were developed with parents so that information shared with the key worker could be passed on to colleagues. Clear communication strategies were put in place, such as regular telephone calls between workers, communication books, and meetings of all professionals involved in supporting a family.

Teams of professionals supporting a particular family were also working to develop a shared concept of "good-enough" or acceptable parenting through discussions involving the parents about the standards that were appropriate for their family. Each of the professionals would then use these shared understandings in their interactions with parents. For instance, in one area, parents with intellectual disabilities and all of the professionals involved with them had attended the same course on behavior management and were then all able to work toward maintaining the same standards and responses to the children's behavior. Professionals involved in multi-agency collaboration were also developing a wider understanding of, and respect for, each other's roles through shared training. An example of this was that professionals with a background in working with adults with intellectual disabilities were undertaking training in child protection, and professionals with a background in children and family services received training in supporting adults with intellectual disabilities.

# Conclusion

The overarching policy framework regarding family support and maintaining children in their birth family and the *Good Practice Guidance on Working with Parents with a Learning Disability* (Department of Health/Department for Education and Skills, 2007) heralds the way to a better, and more inclusive, future for parents with intellectual disabilities and their families. However, policy is currently ahead of practice and the positive developments reported in this study were emerging in pockets across the UK against a backdrop of negative assumptions held by people with little experience with people with intellectual disabilities, in services as well as in society in general. There is clearly a need for change at an attitudinal level and there are many factors that can contribute to changing views and understanding of parents with intellectual disabilities and wider concepts of parenting. For instance, we need to change the notion that asking for help with parenting is admitting failure, move away from a culture of crisis intervention, and promote the benefits of ongoing preventive support to all families who need it. A much needed attitudinal change would mean that all parents with intellectual disabilities who require it would be provided with proactive support, easy-to-understand information, and an advocate. In addition, all relevant professionals would be trained to be able to meet parents' individual communication and support needs. Changes would be required in the way services and resources are allocated and provided. Widespread implementation of the *Good Practice Guidance* would support this attitudinal change, although challenges in the courts, using the Disability Discrimination Act, may initially be necessary to ensure that supportive services are provided to enable parents with intellectual disabilities to demonstrate they can, with appropriate support, be "good-enough" parents.

Nationally, a number of key organizations have formed the Working Together with Parents Network, which is raising awareness of parents with intellectual disabilities and promoting the implementation of the existing positive national policy as well as enabling professionals in the field to network and share positive practice (www.right-support.org.uk). There is now also a larger groundswell of interest in the support needs of parents with intellectual disabilities. Many local and national conferences are being organized to raise awareness of parents with intellectual disabilities and the service developments required to support them to be successful parents. These new initiatives are promoting the implementation of existing policies and the *Good Practice Guidance* and call for multi-agency support, which is a key principle for good practice.

## Principles for Practice

- It is important to actively reach out to professionals and others working with parents with intellectual disabilities and make them aware of the *Good Practice Guidance on Working with Parents with a Learning Disability* (Department of Health/Department for Education and Skills, 2007) and other important resources such as the guidance on multi-agency working for disabled parents published by the Social Care Institute for Excellence in 2007.
- It is equally important to actively reach out to parents with intellectual disabilities and make them aware of the easy-to-understand versions of the

*Good Practice Guidance* and other similar resources relevant for parents with intellectual disabilities.

- Parents with intellectual disabilities face many barriers in their role as parents. There are also many barriers that can get in the way of providing positive support to this group of parents. Most of these barriers have nothing to do with the parents' impairment. Instead they derive mostly from negative and stereotypical attitudes toward parents on the part of professionals as well as the general public. Part of removing these barriers is attitudinal change, achieved primarily by providing more information about the everyday lives of parents with intellectual disabilities and their children.
- There is an urgent need for the provision of independent advocates for parents involved in child protection proceedings and the judicial process. Further information on advocacy for parents with learning difficulties can be found in Mencap (2007).
- Parents with intellectual disabilities are often supported by a range of different professionals. To avoid confusion, conflicting advice, and to ensure consistency, it is important to provide a "key worker" for each family who can coordinate services and supports from various agencies and professionals.
- Parents' groups have been identified as particularly empowering and supportive for parents. In these groups, parents share experiences and support each other, learn new skills, and develop their self-esteem. It is important to encourage parents to establish parents' groups and support them in doing so.
- When working with parents to increase their skills and competence in their parenting role, it is important to base this work on each parent's strengths and competences. Tasks should be broken down into small, manageable steps.

## Acknowledgment

Thanks to the Baring Foundation for permission to quote extensively from *Finding the right support? A review of issues and positive practice in supporting parents with learning difficulties and their children* (Baring Foundation, 2006)

## References

Affleck, F., & Baker, S. (2004). *You and your baby.* Leeds: CHANGE.

Booth, T. (2000). Parents with learning difficulties, child protection and the courts. *Representing Children, 13*(3), 175–188.

CHANGE. (2005). *Report of national gathering of parents with learning disabilities.* Leeds: Author.

CHANGE. (2007a). *Moving forward – Parents with learning difficulties want a better future.* Leeds: Author.

CHANGE. (2007b). *You and your little child 1–5.* Leeds: Author.

Department for Education and Skills. (2003). *Every child matters.* London: The Stationery Office.

Department for Education and Skills/Department of Health. (2004). *National service framework for children, young people and maternity services.* London: Author.

Department of Health. (2001). *Valuing people: A new strategy for learning disability for the 21st Century.* London: The Stationery Office.

Department of Health. (2009). *Valuing people now: A new three-year strategy for people with learning disabilities.* London: Author.

Department of Health/Department for Education and Skills. (2007). *Good practice guidance on working with parents with a learning disability.* London: Author.

*Disability Equality Duty under the Disability Discrimination Act.* (2005). London: The Stationery Office.

Emerson, E., Malam, S., Davies, I., & Spencer, K. (2005). *Adults with learning difficulties in England 2003/4.* London: Office of National Statistics.

Joint Committee on Human Rights. (2008). *A life like any other? Human rights of adults with learning disabilities.* London: The Stationery Office.

Llewellyn, G., & McConnell, D. (2005). You have to prove yourself all the time: People with learning disabilities parenting. In G. Grant, P. Goward, M. Richardson, & P. Ramcharan (Eds.), *Learning disability: A life cycle approach to valuing people* (pp. 441–467). Buckingham: Open University Press.

Marriott, A., & Tarleton, B. (2009). Research unpacked. *Learning Disability Today, 9*(6), 32–33.

McConnell, D., & Llewellyn, G. (2002). Stereotypes, parents with intellectual disability and child protection. *Journal of Social Welfare and Family Law, 24*(3), 296–317.

McGaw, S., Beckley, K., Connolly, N., & Ball, K. (1998). *Parent assessment manual.* Truro: Trecare NHS Trust.

McGaw, S., & Newman, T. (2005). *What works for parents with learning disabilities?* Ilford: Barnardo's.

McGaw, S., Smith, K., & Tomabene, A. (1999). *The parenting skills cards.* Kidderminster: British Institute of Learning Disabilities.

Mencap. (2007). *Providing the right support for parents with a learning disability: Evaluating the work of the north-east parents' support service and the Walsall parents' advocacy service.* London: Author.

Morgan, P., & Goff, A. (2004). *Learning curves: The assessment of parents with a learning disability – a manual for practitioners.* Norwich: Norfolk Area Child Protection Committee.

Sellars, C. (2002). *Risk assessment in people with learning disabilities.* Oxford: Blackwell Publishing.

Social Care Institute for Excellence. (2007). *Working together to support disabled parents.* London: Author.

Tarleton, B., Ward, L., & Howarth, J. (2006). *Finding the right support? A review of issues and positive practice in supporting parents with learning difficulties and their children.* London: Baring Foundation.

# 11

# Caught in the Child Protection Net

*David McConnell and Hanna Björg Sigurjónsdóttir*

The brutal reality is that many parents labeled with intellectual disability will have their children taken from them by child protection authorities. Persons labeled with intellectual disability today enjoy freedoms that past generations could hardly have imagined, including greater opportunity to form relationships and start a family of their own (Mayes, Llewellyn, & McConnell, 2008). At the same time, the routine practice of seizing their children has remained unchecked, unchallenged, and unchanged for the greater part of a century (Booth, Booth, & McConnell, 2005; Lightfoot & Laliberte, 2006).

In 1957, Brandon protested about the "inhumane and expensive administration process whereby an allegedly feeble-minded mother is permanently separated from her child" (p. 710). Four decades passed before researchers began systematically investigating this process. Investigations in a growing number of high-income countries have produced disturbing evidence of widespread service system failure and outright systems abuse. The evidence supports Booth and Booth's (2003) conclusion that "[s]ystems abuse, more than child abuse, is a crucial precipitating factor behind the high rates of child removal," and "[u]ntil we recognize its destructive effects, parents with learning difficulties will continue to receive rough justice and their children will get a raw deal" (p. 206).

The research shows that parents with intellectual disabilities are short-changed with respect to justice in the child protection system and courts. They are presumed incompetent and have their competence as parents judged against harsher standards than other parents (Hayman, 1990; Levesque, 1996; Watkins,

*Parents with Intellectual Disabilities: Past, Present and Futures* Edited by Gwynnyth Llewellyn, Rannveig Traustadóttir, David McConnell, and Hanna Björg Sigurjónsdóttir © 2010 John Wiley & Sons, Ltd

1995). They are presumed incapable of learning to overcome any perceived deficiencies, and are less likely to receive appropriate support with parenting before and after child protection authorities intervene (Booth, Booth, & McConnell, 2004; McConnell, Llewellyn, & Ferronato, 2006). They are excluded from decision making, and rarely receive any support to understand what is happening in the care and protection process (Booth & Booth, 2005; McConnell, Llewellyn, & Ferronato, 2002). They are also many times more likely than other parents to have their parental responsibility terminated and their children permanently placed in someone else's care (Booth & Booth, 2004a; Booth et al., 2005; Llewellyn, McConnell, & Ferronato, 2003; Taylor et al., 1991).

In this chapter, we draw on the available research from Australia, England, Iceland, Canada, and the United States of America to describe the unfair and discriminatory processes that result in the permanent separation of parents from their children.

We begin by reviewing the literature on parents with intellectual disabilities and the allegations made against them by child protection authorities. Key influences on the process and outcomes for parents with intellectual disabilities and their children, and the parents' experiences of the care and protection process, are then discussed.

## The Parents

Knowledge about parents with intellectual disabilities, including those with and without custody of their children, comes from several independent sources. These include qualitative case studies (e.g., Sigurjónsdóttir & Traustadóttir, 2000; Taylor, 1995; Traustadóttir & Sigurjónsdóttir, 2008), correlational studies in clinical populations (e.g., Aunos, Goupil, & Feldman, 2004; Tymchuk & Andron, 1990), reviews of child welfare court records (Booth et al., 2005; Llewellyn, McConnell, & Ferronato, 2003; Taylor et al., 1991), and a secondary analysis of a large Canadian child welfare data set (McConnell, Feldman, & Aunos, 2008). These sources reveal a diversity of family types, circumstances, and scenarios. No systematic relationship between parent characteristics and child removal has been found. Two North American studies, however, suggest that parents who have had a child taken away are more likely to report a lack of support from extended family members and dissatisfaction with services (Aunos et al., 2004; Tymchuk & Andron, 1990).

Many, but not all, parents with intellectual disabilities have to contend with the difficult circumstances of poverty, poor housing in low-income communities, exposure to abuse and/or neglect in their own upbringing, violence in one form or another in adult life, and poor physical and/or mental health (Booth & Booth, 1994; Ehlers-Flint, 2002; Llewellyn, McConnell, & Mayes, 2003; Tymchuk & Andron, 1990). In some locations, parents with intellectual disabilities are relatively advantaged, including, for example, Icelandic parents who do not have to deal with abject poverty and poor housing (Sigurjónsdóttir, 2005; Sigurjónsdóttir & Traustadóttir, 2001). The fact remains that whether parents with intellectual disabilities are advantaged or not, many will lose custody of their children and these children will be placed permanently in the care of others.

The reason is that child protection workers and other professionals all too often presume that parents with intellectual disabilities are incapable of raising their children regardless of whether there is evidence of neglect or maltreatment (Booth et al., 2005; McConnell & Llewellyn, 2002). Parents with intellectual disabilities are often regarded as children themselves, "children" who cannot be entrusted with the care of another (Hayman, 1990). This presumption is so deep-seated that any perceived parenting deficiencies are routinely attributed to the parent's intellectual impairment (Booth & Booth, 2003; McConnell et al., 2006). Alternative explanations, such as the difficult circumstances of parents' lives including, for example, poverty, poor health, or social isolation, are frequently overlooked (McConnell & Llewellyn, 2005). In addition, because intellectual disability is a permanent condition, workers readily assume that any perceived parenting problems are also permanent (Booth, McConnell, & Booth, 2006; McConnell et al., 2002).

## The Child Protection Concerns

In court affidavits, child protection authorities typically report a long list of perceived concerns about the parenting difficulties of parents with intellectual disabilities (McConnell et al., 2002). This is despite the following admission from one Australian lawyer who represents the child protection authority in court matters: "If you look at the evidence in all the cases we run before the court, in 50 per cent of them there is evidence there. In 50 per cent there isn't . . . we don't have the evidence" (McConnell et al., 2002, p. 285). Lawyers representing parents in the Australian courts argue that contesting the "evidence and claims" made by the child protection authority is usually a futile exercise. This is because: (1) the authority only has to prove its case to a very highly probable standard; (2) the authority "throws everything [they can think of] into their affidavit," and it is difficult to challenge each and every concern, especially when the rules of evidence do not apply; and (3) any doubts usually go in favor of the authority, with court magistrates "erring on the side of caution" (McConnell et al., 2002).

Common allegations listed by child protection authorities include: a dirty and unhygienic home, developmental deprivation for the child or children, a chaotic lifestyle with frequent changes of residence, exposure to a volatile and/or violent parental relationship, and perceived parental non-cooperation. Physical and/or sexual abuse allegations are rare. So too is any evidence of harm to the child or children. More often, the child protection case and course of action are based on the perceived "risk" of harm (Booth & Booth, 2004a). Analysis of child protection concerns in Canadian, Australian, and English samples suggests several common case types or profiles based on the allegations made by the child protection authorities. These are inadequate provision (or "presumed neglect"); inadequate protection ("perceived risk of abuse"); prior history of child removal ("newborn at risk"); and lack of effective parental control.

## Inadequate provision – presumed neglect

The most common case type is based on the child protection authority alleging that the child is being deprived of an adequately stimulating environment. The parent's capacity to provide for the child's basic needs is called into question. For infants and toddlers, the concerns are usually about the parent's capacity to provide physical and emotional care. In the middle years, the issues raised typically focus on observed or perceived risk of developmental delay based on an underlying assumption that the child or children are not realizing their potential. For example, in one court report filed in England, the authority declared that the parents are "unable to keep up with and anticipate the child's developing and changing demands and needs." If the child is developmentally delayed, this is typically attributed to the parents being unable to provide intellectual stimulation and/or their inability to be emotionally available and responsive to the child. With older children, the issues are more often about behavioral difficulties and the lack of "effective parental control."

Although allegations are made about the ability of parents with intellectual disabilities to provide a stimulating environment, there is no evidence to suggest that they are unable to do so. Several studies report that the quality of the home environment provided by parents with intellectual disabilities, including maternal warmth and responsiveness, is not significantly different from the environments provided by other similarly socioeconomically disadvantaged parents (Feldman, Case, Towns, & Betel, 1985; McConnell, Llewellyn, Mayes, Russo, & Honey, 2003). Furthermore, McConnell et al. (2003) found in their study that the variation observed in the children's development was associated with poor pregnancy and birth outcomes and not with differences in the quality of the home environment. The findings from a recent birth cohort study support this association (McConnell, Mayes, & Llewellyn, 2008). In this study, pregnant women with intellectual disabilities were found, on average, to suffer high levels of stress, anxiety, depression, and a high rate of preeclampsia; they were significantly more likely to deliver preterm and/or low birth weight babies; and their infants were significantly more likely to be admitted to neonatal intensive care or special care nurseries after their birth.

## Inadequate protection – perceived risk of abuse

The second case type is based on the child protection authority alleging that the mother is unable to protect her child from unsafe adults. In some cases, the primary concern is the risk of physical harm posed by a partner who is perceived to be volatile, unpredictable, violent, and/or exploitative. In other cases, the primary concern is the risk of sexual abuse: The mother's partner may have been previously investigated or charged with a child sex offense, or a known offender (perhaps an uncle or a grandfather) may have unsupervised access and/or contact with the child. Typically, the mother is said to be isolated, passive, and dependent, and, in many instances, dominated by a male partner or "string of male partners." In one English report the child protection authority asserted that the mother was "targeted by men who use her and put her children at risk." In another, the child protection authority concluded that "the mother is unable to protect herself or her children from risks posed by other adults . . . and it appears that she has been exploited by virtually every 'friend'" (Booth & Booth, 2004b).

Although these mothers may be seen as "victims," they are rarely thought of as blameless by the child protection authority. Indeed, in many cases the mothers are regarded as complicit in, or even responsible for, putting their child at risk. Some accounts, taken from the Australian and English studies (Booth et al., 2005; McConnell et al., 2002), follow: The mother "failed to acknowledge the risk posed to the child"; "put(s) her own needs first"; "tends to deny or minimize the risks and dangers to the child"; "lacks recognition of her role in the abuse that her other children have suffered and how she could alter her behavior to avoid repetition"; "indicates an inability to grasp that she puts the children at risk"; has "exposed him to persons known to pose a threat of physical and sexual abuse to children"; has "repeatedly been told that if she wishes her children to be returned to her that she must separate from him (her partner), but to date she has failed to do so"; and "is still refusing assessment as a lone parent."

## Previous child removal – newborn at risk

The third case type is when the child protection authority decides that a newborn child is at risk and removes the baby soon after birth. In countries where there is a two-step process in removing children, such as Australia, Canada, and England, these cases go straight to the care and protection court; no alternative to removal of the baby is explored. In many of these cases, the mother (and in some cases the father) has had at least one other child taken away previously. In these cases, a primary assertion is that the mother or father is unlikely to be able to change. In some cases this conclusion is based on the mother's or father's perceived failure to learn and demonstrate change despite receiving services in the past. In other cases it is based on the mother's perceived lack of insight. For example, in one case the child protection authority in England observed that "(the mother) has been unable to see her own failure as the cause of her older children being removed from her care and placed elsewhere." Experts may be brought in to give an opinion to the court about the likelihood of change; they base their views on what they believe about intellectual disability. As one "expert" put it in a report to an English court, "the children's needs would change at a faster rate than the parents' abilities to learn the new skills necessary, with the children ultimately outsmarting their parents." If parents are thought to be uncooperative, this can also lead to the conclusion that they are unlikely to be able to change their parenting behaviors. This is likely to occur, for example, if the parents refuse to be assessed or to allow professionals to visit them in their home (Booth et al., 2005).

## Perceived lack of effective parental control

Allegations in proceedings involving older children constitute the fourth case type. These are less common. The child protection authority typically alleges that the parents are unable to maintain effective parental control, resulting in the children experiencing behavioral difficulties or irregular school attendance, or a combination of both. For example, in one Australian case, the child protection authority reported that "the child has been seen to be out of (his mother's) control, and has run away on occasions." In another case the child was seen "wandering the streets." In a couple of cases, concerns were raised about the child taking on an inappropriate level of responsibility for siblings.

These four case types are based on the range of allegations documented by child protection authorities in their position put to the care and protection court. The other side of this coin is invisible. We do not know what the parents' views are on the allegations that have been made against them. This is because the parents' perspective is rarely heard or documented in child protection or court records. In Australia, for instance, McConnell et al. (2002) found that, in just one-quarter of all cases, an affidavit or report had been submitted by the lawyer acting for the parents. Moreover, we do not know whether the allegations made by the child protection authority would hold up if they were tested in a court of law. That is because, as noted above, lawyers who represent parents in the care and protection court do not typically contest the claims made by the child protection authority as the likelihood of a successful outcome is very low.

Only when the child is perceived to be at risk of imminent harm, which happens only in extreme cases, is there a direct relationship between the allegations made by the child protection authority and the child being removed and placed away from home (McConnell et al., 2002). This type of case is the exception rather than the norm. In most cases "the evidence" provided by the child protection authority is more ambiguous or uncertain (McConnell & Llewellyn, 2005; Parton, 1995; Thorpe, 1994).

## The Child Protection Process and Outcomes

Usually child protection authorities and child welfare courts take a number of factors into consideration in deciding the future of the child. These include child age or perceived vulnerability, complexity and intensity of the parenting and childcare load, and perceived hope of improving the child's home situation (McConnell et al., 2006).

### Child age or perceived vulnerability

In the English court study, if the child was older when he or she was removed by the child protection authority, the child was more likely to be allowed to return home (Booth et al., 2004). This is because older children are generally regarded as less vulnerable, and their wishes may also be given more credence. It is also the case that in most places, it is more difficult to find suitable and willing foster carers or adoptive parents. Harry's story illustrates this point.

Harry and his elder brother Keith (not their real names) were 11 and 12 years of age respectively when they came to the notice of the child protection authority after their father sent them to school with a note requesting that they be fostered. Their father, Clive, was alone at the time, he was depressed, and he had started drinking to excess. Clive may still have been grieving over the death of his wife some two years earlier. Before her death they had been separated for some time, but he never lost hope of reconciliation. Indeed, he had followed her from town to town, moving several times with the boys in tow. Such "instability" was highlighted by the child protection authority in their brief to the court. However, the turning point seems to have been Keith's challenging behaviors. The case record suggests that Keith, who has learning difficulties, was aggressive and violent toward Harry and that Clive was struggling to cope. After Clive sent the boys to school with "the note," he packed his bags and crossed the country to move in with a family member. Over the coming months Clive remembered the boys' birthdays and regularly asked after them. Harry's birthday wish was to be with his father. He bought a train ticket with the money his father had sent him, and without warning his foster family, school, or friends, he found his own way home. With Keith in care, the child protection authority and the court were satisfied that Clive would be able to cope with Harry alone and did not intervene.

## Perceived complexity and or intensity of parents' childcare workload

Many of the children in the English court sample who were restored to their parents' care had one or more siblings (and frequently a disabled sibling) who remained in out-of-home care (Booth & Booth, 2004b). The rationale, explicit in some cases and implicit in others, seemed to be that if one or more of the siblings, and particularly a sibling with special needs, was no longer in the parental home, the burden on the parents would be eased to a point where they would be better able to cope. Laura and Ashleigh's story is a case in point.

Two-year-old Laura and her older sister Ashleigh were removed from their parents' care along with their autistic brother Angus when he was four years old and Ashleigh six years old. The child protection authority first investigated this family when a childminder notified them of a bruise on Angus's face. Concern was heightened when their mother Debbie was observed to be having difficulties managing Angus's behavior. There was also concern about Laura's weight gain. Debbie was less than enthusiastic about the intervention of "the welfare," and with these three concerns her parenting capacity was called into question. The case turned when Debbie reconciled with her husband, who was also the children's father, and a consulting psychologist explained that managing Angus's behavior would be a struggle for any parent. The girls were restored with support to Debbie and her husband, although scrutiny of Debbie's parenting continued and the situation was observed to improve. Angus remained in care.

## Hope of improving the child's home situation

The major focus of deliberation for the child protection authority and the care and protection court is whether the alleged risk to the child can be ameliorated and the child's home situation improved (McConnell et al., 2002). This is irrespective of child age or perceptions of the parenting and childcare workload. There are two reasons for this. One is that legislation governing child protection practice typically, although not universally, requires that reasonable efforts are made to preserve the family unit. Another is that the supply of alternative care or foster care is finite and therefore this resource must be carefully rationed.[1]

Sometimes the outcome is predetermined because decision makers are "wired" to see the parent as the problem, and as parents with intellectual disabilities are presumed to be incapable of learning parenting skills, they are

---

[1] The threshold for court action and, later, out-of-home placement is a product of supply and demand: the more out-of-home care options, the more out-of-home care placements. The implication is that recruiting more foster carers or making it easier to release children for adoption will lower the "tolerance threshold" and likely increase the rate at which children are taken from parents with intellectual disabilities.

also presumed unable to adapt to the changing needs and demands of a child. This presumption of irremediable deficiency in the parents is illustrated by the following quotes from the Australian court study (McConnell et al., 2002). The first is from a senior child protection worker and the second is from a child welfare court magistrate.

> In some cases we do need to be tested. But in most cases, particularly those involving parents with disabilities, [we don't]. Like . . . in one case, they both had . . . IQ tests, and they were below 80 . . . So we all knew what was going to happen. (McConnell et al., 2006, p. 237)
>
> If they have got that disability, you can't fix it. If there is impairment to the brain there is nothing you can do to fix it. They don't know how to cook the child a meal . . . and this person is never going to learn because they can't. (McConnell et al., 2002, p. 292)

At other times, the child protection authority or the court may be influenced by several factors in making their decision about whether the child's situation might be improved. These factors are perceived parent cooperation, availability of suitable family support or preservation services, and the pressure of time.

Perceived cooperation from the parents was identified as a key determinant of case outcomes in the Canadian, English, and Australian studies. The child protection authority and the courts were influenced by their perception of the parent's cooperation, including open disclosure, perceived "insight" or acceptance of responsibility for any perceived maltreatment, and parent willingness to engage with assessments and services. In Iceland, Sigurjónsdóttir (2004, 2005) found that the parents who knew "the client's role," and who did not question the authority of "the welfare" to define their family's needs, were more likely to be thought of as cooperative. The same study revealed that fathers were more likely to challenge this authority than mothers, and when they did so, this affected how the family was perceived and treated, and sometimes the outcome of whether the families remained intact or not.

McConnell, Feldman, and Aunos (2008) reported that, in Canada, parents with intellectual disabilities are more than twice as likely to be classed as non-cooperative. Parental non-cooperation increased the odds fourfold of the case going to court. In Australia, McConnell et al. (2006) found that court action was often used as "the big stick" by the child protection authority to coerce parents into cooperation, or rather, compliance, as the following quotes from child protection workers illustrate.

> Going to court is not always to remove (the child), it can be a wake up call. So we've tried to put in the supports and it might just need the magistrate to say . . . you will . . . work with these people. And some people go okay, some don't. (McConnell et al., 2006, p. 235)
>
> (Going to court) triggers a crisis . . . and then you can engage, you can co-opt and you can work with the family . . . the family will realize we are serious, its

not just another lot of social work wankery, you know, "please be good," they've heard that all their lives. (McConnell et al., 2006, p. 235)

One reason why parents with intellectual disabilities may be classified as non-cooperative is that they may be unreliable timekeepers, and missed appointments are often interpreted as non-cooperation (Booth et al., 2006). Another reason is that child protection workers rarely have the time or skill required to deal with the parents' fear of "the welfare" and develop the necessary rapport with the parents (Booth et al., 2006). A third reason is that the parents may seem to acquiesce with what they are being told or asked to do without fully comprehending what they are being told. And when they do not follow through, this may be interpreted as non-cooperation.

I think that social workers have not got the . . . expertise in managing parents with learning disabilities . . . I think the other issue, which is not so talked about, is the fact that they don't get on with [them], they don't like working with them because of the time they take. (Child protection worker, Booth et al., 2006, p. 1001)

The perceived availability of suitable support services is another condition influencing whether the child protection authorities or courts believe there is hope of improving the child's situation. In Australia, McConnell et al. (2006) found that most child protection workers reported having no time or relevant training to do the necessary casework themselves. Consequently, they relied where possible on other supports and services to work with the parents, which they all agreed were not usually suitable for parents with intellectual disabilities. In the United Kingdom, services for parents with intellectual disabilities have been described as "patchy and undeveloped" (Department of Health, 2001, p. 81). McGaw (2000, p. 18) observes that "empirical research and clinical practice indicates that the majority of services are as yet inadequate in meeting the needs of these families."

Parents with learning difficulties aren't amenable to be made better . . . within a short period. If you are dealing with a child of six months old then a year is a long time . . . the phrase we use is, this child cannot go home within the child's time scales. (Child protection worker, Booth et al., 2006, p. 1009)

Hope of improving the child's situation is also influenced by the child protection authority and the courts' perspective on time. The prevailing wisdom, embedded in policy and child protection practice, is that any delay in care cases is bad for the child. The question, therefore, becomes whether the child's home situation can be improved in "the child's timeframe." As Booth et al. (2006) reported, time works against parents with intellectual disabilities. Services in England, for example, are increasingly offered on a time-limited basis. Parents have a brief window of opportunity to learn and then demonstrate that they can "stand alone." This short-term approach to service availability is particularly hard on parents with intellectual disabilities when the research suggests that many will succeed, but that this requires intermittent support over the long term (Booth et al., 2006). Sigurjónsdóttir (2005) made a similar observation in the Icelandic context, illustrated by the following quotes, the first from the mother of a mother with intellectual disability. The second quote comes from the lawyer who represented this mother.

> Overall we feel that the parents received rough and unjust treatment. The system giving hopes and promises and not fulfilling them. With a training period being both short and inadequate they never stood a chance. We as a family felt ill-informed, at times intimidated, and never given time to consider options or take decisions. (p. 116)
>
> [It was] . . . a battle to get it agreed that the parents would be given a chance . . . I am quite afraid that the short period of time they got to prove themselves indicates that the decision was already made. It was more a formality to pacify the parents and their lawyer . . . Looking back things were never discussed in detail nor action taken to work the case and continue the training from the viewpoint of the parents retaining custody (and) ascertaining the necessary support requirements. There were never any ideas forwarded on this. The assessment should have been aimed at their ability with support instead of their individual ability but this was never done . . . It looked like they were trying to sniff out the mistakes and most likely the parents needed longer time. (pp. 104–105)

## Parent Perspectives on the Child Protection Process

Although researchers have given little attention to how parents with intellectual disabilities themselves experience the child protection process, the findings are consistent in the available data (Booth & Booth, 2005, 2006; Sigurjónsdóttir, 2005; Taylor, 1995). In short, parents with intellectual disabilities typically experience the child protection process as bewildering and unjust. In this they are not alone. Hunt, Macleod, and Thomas (1999), for example, found that most parents, whether they have a disability or not, find the process to be intimidating, disabling, and depersonalizing.

Parents with intellectual disabilities often feel alone and unsupported. They report difficulty with understanding the process and procedures, and, once in court, many receive little or no support to understand the case against them. Many parents report that no one, not even their own lawyer, would listen to them. Consequently, they often perceive the whole child protection process, including the investigation, "expert" assessment, case conferences, and court proceedings, as something that was done to and not with them. They feel like spectators rather than participants. They understand that their fate and the future of their children hang in the balance but feel powerless to influence the course of events.

> It was so strange it was like he (the first lawyer) was representing the Child Protection Service and not my daughter and her partner. No one appeared to be supporting our side, although the Ombudsman was supposed to be there for us she said very little and appeared to be as much on their side as ours. (Mother of a mother with intellectual disability, Sigurjónsdóttir, 2005, p. 111)

Sigurjónsdóttir (2005) found that some parents resented what they perceived to be a lack of openness and honesty on the part of the child protection authority. The parents often felt that workers were going behind their backs and withholding information. Booth and Booth (2005) also report that many parents with intellectual disabilities feel a strong sense of injustice based on the conviction that they had been set up, misunderstood, and misrepresented by the child protection authority. Some express anger or indignation, others experience quiet despair or defeat over what they perceive to be "distorted evidence" that showcases their failings, however minor, and fails to give due credit for their strengths, however great. Across the world, it appears, parents with intellectual disabilities are experiencing similar disadvantage in the care and protection process. Booth and Booth's (2005) study was completed in England. The perceptions of the parents they interviewed correspond well with the "realities of the adversarial system" described by McConnell et al. (2002) in Australia. For instance, McConnell et al. (2002) cited one child protection worker who explained:

> I think unconsciously you tend to play down the parent's strengths because you are trying to sort of create a case that defends the child's rights . . . so you tend to play down the strengths, which you might have known are there and unconsciously you don't want to highlight it. (p. 280)

In summary, the evidence about parents with intellectual disabilities in the child protection system demonstrates that the processes are anything but fair. Prejudicial and demonstrably false presumptions about parents based on the label of intellectual disability have a major influence on parents being "accused" of neglect or abuse and their children being removed from their care. The most damaging and concerning outcome is that once a parent is labeled as intellectually disabled, the child protection authorities are likely to act irrespective of whether the child is at risk or the parents are having difficulties. When parents with intellectual disabilities do experience difficulty in raising their children, the child protection authorities are likely to attribute this to intellectual impairment, rather than to the challenges parents confront in the face of prejudicial attitudes about their capacity to parent and the "tears in the social fabric" of their everyday lives.

# Principles for Practice

The key lessons to be learned from this chapter lead to 10 practice points to promote natural justice for parents with intellectual disabilities and their children.

1. The determinants of parenting success are many, and with respect to parenting success, the population of parents with intellectual disabilities is diverse. Every parent has unique strengths, limitations, and potential. Therefore, we have to be slow to judge, and resist making inferences or "prognoses" based upon the label of intellectual disability.

2. Practitioners need to identify parental strengths and strengths in the parent's social and environmental context as well as possible constraints. This provides balance and fairness to any assessment of the child's situation. It also provides information about identified concerns and how these may be addressed as well as information about positive attributes on which future improvements in parenting capability and social and environmental supports can be built.

3. There needs to be a renewed focus on prevention. Social inequality and inequity have to be repoliticized and multi-level (from national to local) innovations developed to tackle poverty and social exclusion. This is because when parents with intellectual disabilities do experience difficulties in raising their children, these are deeply rooted in longstanding social inequities and all too often a lifetime of "violence" in one guise or another. Yet, in high-income countries, increasing portions of government funding (taxpayer dollars) are being pushed into the "sharp" or crisis-driven end of the child and family welfare system, that is, into child and youth protection. In crisis-driven practice, the "parent-as-problem" framework underpins workers' understanding of causation and consequently the only solution appears to be either parent reform or child removal. This is inappropriate and inadequate when the root cause of the parents' difficulties lies elsewhere.

4. Attention must be paid to supporting families of children with intellectual disabilities and to enriching these children's lives with positive learning opportunities and affirmation of their worth. Young people with intellectual disabilities must have the opportunity to learn about sexuality, healthy relationships, and parenting. This is because many children with intellectual disabilities will form relationships as they grow up and start a family of their own.

5. Rather than blaming parents with intellectual disabilities for their perceived shortcomings, attention needs to be focused on the shortcomings of human service systems. Concerted efforts are needed to build systems capacity to support these parents and their children in the community.

Since the 1980s, there has been a great deal of research about the support and service needs of parents with intellectual disabilities: We now know how to effectively support parents with intellectual disabilities. Yet, the translation of this knowledge into policy and practice is, at best, only partial. The Australian national strategy, known as *Healthy Start*, is a capacity-building model that other countries might consider adapting. Information about *Healthy Start* can be found at www.healthystart.net.au.

6. The capacity of parents with intellectual disabilities to raise their children is not a "locked-up," measurable parental quality. Parental capacity is a measure of fit between a parent and his or her life experiences, the environment, including extended family and social network, and the available supports and services. When the child of a parent with intellectual disability does have to be removed by child protection authorities, the record, including the court record, should "tell the truth," so that the child may know that she was separated from her mum or dad because the human service systems were unwilling or unable to support her parents.

7. Practitioners must ensure that when assessing parenting capacity, they do not use a yardstick based on "ideal" parenting that represents a particular privileged socioeconomic group. The appropriate yardstick is whether the child's basic needs are met within the child's broad social network. This is an appropriate definition of "good-enough" parenting. The contributions of grandparents, neighbors, and others who participate in the child's life to meet the child's basic health and development needs must all be taken into account.

8. Assessment of parenting capacity must also take into account whether supports and services have been or are being provided, and whether these were suitably targeted to meet the needs of the family. It is unreasonable to determine parental failure if the services and supports provided were inappropriate or inadequate to the task, including not being offered for the relevant period of time.

9. The support and service needs of parents with intellectual disabilities and their children change over time. Agencies and practitioners must regularly review the support and services provided to ensure these are appropriate to changing needs. Access to resources such as social support, transport, adequate housing, respite care, skills training, and babysitting can assist families in managing their parental tasks. Individual service planning, undertaken in consultation with the parents and family members, is more likely to be successful in supporting children and parents.

10. Ethically responsible practice demands that practitioners communicate with parents with intellectual disabilities in ways that they can understand so that parents know what is going on and can make their views known. Practitioners need to take the time to ensure that parents understand the

care and protection process (an advocate or interpreter may be needed to assist) so that their ongoing participation in decisions that affect their lives and the lives of their children is assured.

# References

Aunos, M., Goupil, G., & Feldman, M. (2004). Mothers with an intellectual disability who do and do not have custody of their children. *Journal on Developmental Disabilities, 10*(2), 65–79.

Booth, T., & Booth, W. (1994). *Parenting under pressure: Mothers and fathers with learning difficulties.* Buckingham: Open University Press.

Booth, T., & Booth, W. (2003) Parents with learning difficulties and the stolen generation. *Journal of Learning Disabilities, 7*(3), 203–209.

Booth, T., & Booth, W. (2004a). Findings from a court study of care proceedings involving parents with intellectual disabilities. *Journal of Policy and Practice in Intellectual Disabilities, 1*(3–4), 179–181.

Booth, T., & Booth, W. (2004b). *Parents with learning difficulties, child protection and the courts: A report to the Nuffield Foundation.* Sheffield: University of Sheffield.

Booth, T., & Booth, W. (2005). Parents with learning difficulties in the child protection system: Experiences and perspectives. *Journal of Intellectual Disabilities, 9*(2), 109–129.

Booth, T., & Booth, W. (2006). The uncelebrated parent: Stories of mothers with learning difficulties caught in the child protection net. *British Journal of Learning Disabilities, 34*(2), 94–102.

Booth, T., Booth, W., & McConnell, D. (2004). Family trials. *Disability, Pregnancy and Parenthood International, 45*, 13–14.

Booth, T., Booth, W., & McConnell, D. (2005). Care proceedings and parents with learning difficulties: Comparative prevalence and outcomes in an English and Australian court sample. *Child and Family Social Work, 10*(4), 353–360.

Booth, T., McConnell, D., & Booth, W. (2006). Temporal discrimination and parents with learning difficulties in the child protection system. *British Journal of Social Work, 36*(6), 997–1015.

Brandon, M. W. G. (1957). The intellectual and social status of children of mental defectives. *Journal of Mental Science, 103*(433), 710–724.

Department of Health. (2001). *Valuing people: A new strategy for learning disability for the 21st Century* (No. Cm 5086). London: The Stationery Office.

Ehlers-Flint, M. L. (2002). Parenting perceptions and social supports of mothers with cognitive disabilities. *Sexuality and Disability, 20*(1), 29–51.

Feldman, M. A., Case, L., Towns, F., & Betel, J. (1985). Parent Education Project 1: Development and nurturance of children of mentally retarded parents. *American Journal of Mental Deficiency, 90*(3), 253–258.

Hayman, R. (1990). Presumptions of justice: Law, politics and the mentally retarded parent. *Harvard Law Review, 103*(5), 1201–1271.

Hunt, J., Macleod, A., & Thomas, C. (1999). *The last resort: Child protection, the courts and the 1989 Children Act.* London: The Stationery Office.

Levesque, R. (1996). Maintaining children's relations with mentally disabled parents: Recognizing difference and the difference it makes. *Children's Legal Rights Journal*, *16*(2), 14–22.

Lightfoot, E., & Laliberte, T. (2006). The inclusion of disability as grounds for termination of parental rights in state codes. *Policy Research Brief*, *17*(2), http://ici.umn.edu/products/prb/172/default.html.

Llewellyn, G., McConnell, D., & Ferronato, L. (2003). Prevalence and outcomes for parents with disabilities and their children in an Australian court sample. *Child Abuse and Neglect*, *27*(3), 235–251.

Llewellyn, G., McConnell, D., & Mayes, R. (2003). Health of mothers with intellectual limitations. *Australian and New Zealand Journal of Public Health*, *27*(1), 17–19.

Mayes, R., Llewellyn, G., & McConnell, D. (2008). Active negotiation: Mothers with intellectual disabilities creating their social support networks. *Journal of Applied Research in Intellectual Disabilities*, *21*(4), 341–350.

McConnell, D., Feldman, M., & Aunos, M. (2008). Child welfare investigation outcomes for parents with cognitive impairment and their children in Canada. *Journal of Intellectual Disability Research*, *52*(8–9), 722.

McConnell, D., & Llewellyn, G. (2002). Stereotypes, parents with intellectual disability and child protection. *Journal of Social Welfare and Family Law*, *24*(3), 297–317.

McConnell, D., & Llewellyn, G. (2005). Social inequality, the deviant parent and child protection practice. *Australian Journal of Social Issues*, *40*(4), 553–566.

McConnell, D., Llewellyn, G., & Ferronato, L. (2002). Disability and decision-making in Australian care proceedings. *International Journal of Law, Policy and the Family*, *16*(2), 270–299.

McConnell, D., Llewellyn, G., & Ferronato, L. (2006). Context-contingent decision-making in child protection practice. *International Journal of Social Welfare*, *15*(3), 230–239.

McConnell, D., Llewellyn, G., Mayes, R., Russo, D., & Honey, A. (2003). Developmental profiles of children born to mothers with intellectual disability. *Journal of Intellectual and Developmental Disability*, *28*(2), 122–134.

McConnell, D., Mayes, R., & Llewellyn, G. (2008). Women with intellectual disability at risk of adverse pregnancy and birth outcomes. *Journal of Intellectual Disability Research*, *52*(6), 529–535.

McGaw, S. (2000). *What works for parents with learning disabilities?* Barkingside: Barnardo's.

Parton, N. (1995). Neglect as child protection: The political context and the practical outcomes. *Children and Society*, *9*(1), 67–89.

Sigurjónsdóttir, H. B. (2004). Intellectually limited fathers, their families and the formal support services. In K. Kristiansen & R. Traustadóttir (Eds.), *Gender and disability: Research in the Nordic countries* (pp. 239–254). Lund: Studentlitteratur.

Sigurjónsdóttir, H. B. (2005). *Family support services and parents with learning difficulties.* Unpublished doctoral dissertation, University of Sheffield, Sheffield.

Sigurjónsdóttir, H. B., & Traustadóttir, R. (2000). Motherhood, family and community life. In R. Traustadóttir & K. Johnson (Eds.), *Women with intellectual disabilities finding a place in the world* (pp. 253–270). London: Jessica Kingsley.

Sigurjónsdóttir, H. B., & Traustadóttir, R. (2001). *Ósýnilegar fjölskyldur. þroskaheftar/seinfærar mæður og börn þeirra* [Invisible families: Mothers with learning disabilities and their children]. Reykjavík: University of Iceland.

Taylor, C. G., Norman, D., Murphy J., Jellinek, M., Quinn, D., Poitrast, F., *et al.* (1991). Diagnosed intellectual and emotional impairment among parents who seriously mistreat their children: Prevalence, type, and outcome in a court sample. *Child Abuse and Neglect 15*(4), 389–401.

Taylor, S. J. (1995). "Children's division is coming to take pictures": Family life and parenting in a family with disabilities. In S. J. Taylor, R. Bogdan, & Z. M. Lutfiyya (Eds.), *The variety of community experience: Qualitative studies of family and community life* (pp. 23–45). Baltimore: Paul H. Brookes.

Thorpe, D. (1994). *Evaluating child protection.* Buckingham: Open University Press.

Traustadóttir, R., & Sigurjónsdóttir, H. B. (2008). The "mother" behind the mother: Three generations of mothers with intellectual disabilities and their family support networks. *Journal of Applied Research in Intellectual Disabilities, 21*(4), 331–340.

Tymchuk, A. J., & Andron, L. (1990). Mothers with mental retardation who do or do not abuse or neglect their children. *Child Abuse and Neglect, 14*(3), 313–323.

Watkins, C. (1995). Beyond status: The Americans with Disabilities Act and the parental rights of people labeled developmentally disabled or mentally retarded. *California Law Review, 83*(6), 1415–1475.

# 12

# Turning Rights into Realities in Québec, Canada

*Marjorie Aunos, Laura Pacheco, and Katherine Moxness*

## Introduction

Persons with intellectual disabilities have the right to make the decision to become parents. The United Nations (UN) Convention on the Rights of Persons with Disabilities (2006) mandates that they have "the right to marry and found a family .... to non-discriminatory treatment in all matters relating to marriage, family, parenthood and relationships" (Article 23 (1)) and "to appropriate assistance in the performance of their child-rearing responsibilities" (Article 23 (2)). They also have the same right as other people to make decisions about their own lives (Article 6, Montreal Declaration on Intellectual Disability, 2004, www.declarationmontreal.com/english/welcome.htm).

The reality is somewhat different from these statements. Despite the mandated rights in the UN Convention, many persons with intellectual disabilities, as parents, continue to suffer discrimination and rarely receive assistance that is appropriate or adequate to meet their needs (Goodringe, 2000; Tarleton, Ward, & Howarth, 2006). Furthermore, people with intellectual disabilities are exercising their right to become parents and then having their parental rights terminated and their children taken away (Booth, Booth, & McConnell, 2005a, 2005b). In this chapter we describe our strategy and initiatives to bridge the gap between the rights of persons with intellectual disabilities and the reality of the lives of parents with intellectual disabilities in Québec, Canada. This strategy is a work in progress. It does not have a name and we have no "master plan." It continues to evolve as we raise awareness, engage stakeholders, and

*Parents with Intellectual Disabilities: Past, Present and Futures*   Edited by Gwynnyth Llewellyn, Rannveig Traustadóttir, David McConnell, and Hanna Björg Sigurjónsdóttir   © 2010 John Wiley & Sons, Ltd

gather momentum to respond to the most pressing needs and priorities of the increasing number of parents with intellectual disabilities we are now serving.

## Our Starting Point

In 2003, a comprehensive study involving 50 mothers with intellectual disabilities and their children across Québec was completed by the first author (Aunos, Goupil, & Feldman, 2003). One finding from this study was that mothers with intellectual disabilities are often socially isolated and, on average, have poorer physical and mental health than mothers without intellectual disabilities. Another finding was that many of these mothers needed support to adapt their parenting style to be more consistent and positive. A third main finding was that mothers with intellectual disabilities relied heavily on professionals and formal services for support. These services were described by the mothers and professionals as being ill-equipped in terms of knowledge, skills, and resources to meet their needs.

This study highlighted the gap between the rights and reality of parents with intellectual disabilities in Québec. Canadian law and social policy in Québec recognize the rights of persons with intellectual disabilities and their entitlement to "different treatment," that is, the accommodation of difference to achieve equality of outcomes. But our study revealed that agencies and workers were not equipped to offer the support that parents with intellectual disabilities need. The recommendations based on the study findings called for appropriate training and support for workers, increased collaboration between agencies, and a more systemic approach to address the psychosocial and educational needs of all family members over the long term.

The study findings resonated with practitioners in Québec and their own clinical observations. In 2005, workers from a regional Centre de Réadaptation (West Montreal Readaptation Center) met together to discuss their experiences and ongoing professional development needs to better support parents with intellectual disabilities. The workers all had clinical experience in the intellectual disability field. However, they reported often feeling overwhelmed by the challenges that parents with intellectual disabilities faced. They were keen to learn more and get a better understanding of how to support them and their children. All who attended these meetings committed to working together to build systems capacity to support parents with intellectual disabilities and their children. Together, with the first and third author, goals based on the recommendations from the Québec study were set and preliminary plans were drafted.

Our starting point was building capacity within the specialized services for persons with intellectual disabilities offered by the readaptation center. There were a number of reasons for this. One is that this is where we ourselves are located. Another is that the readaptation centers in Québec, 23 in all, have an important role in providing "second–line" services. That is, they share expertise with mainstream services (our term in Québec is community partners) to enable them to offer services that are accessible to and appropriate for persons with intellectual disabilities. At that time, however, few readaptation center workers were knowledgeable about the literature and best practice in working with parents with intellectual disabilities. A third reason is that we thought that many of the parents with intellectual disabilities being referred to readaptation centers needed specialized assistance in addition to what our community partners were equipped to provide. The service pathway for persons with intellectual disabilities in Québec and the role of readaptation centers is outlined in Box 12.1. In the next section we describe the building blocks of our strategy. We then describe our progress to date.

---

**Box 12.1.** Role of readaptation centers

When a diagnosis of intellectual disability is made, families of persons with intellectual disabilities are referred to their local center for community services (CLSC – CSSS), where a basic psychosocial assessment of their needs is completed. This local center for community services has the mandate to coordinate services among other community and public organizations and, as such, will produce a report identifying the needs of the users. This report will be sent, accompanied by documents confirming the diagnosis of intellectual disability, to the regional readaptation center.

Readaptation centers must ensure that persons with intellectual disabilities or pervasive developmental disabilities "have their needs assessed and that the required services are offered to them in their natural living environment" (Act Respecting Health Services and Social Services 1996). Readaptation centers then have the mandate to offer services that include adaptation, readaptation, and social integration and to offer services to parents and families (Moxness & Dulude, 2003). Services include specialized educational support where an educator offers direct support to children with developmental delays and adults with intellectual disabilities and their families. This service includes early intervention strategies to support the social integration of these children into their community organizations, such as daycare and schools, and support in a work setting for adults with intellectual disabilities. Residential and respite services are also organized around readaptation centers. As part of a specialized agency, another mandate is organized around offering support to professionals in other health and social support agencies who do not have that expertise. Finally, specific services within each readaptation center are also organized to provide support in crisis situations when users have dual diagnosis and challenging behaviors. A team of professionals (i.e., social

*(continued)*

workers, nurses, psychologists, occupational therapists, psychiatrists) is then involved with the user, the user's family, and community partners in order to structure and plan for a comprehensive intervention plan.

Whatever service is provided by readaptation center workers, they are required to implement "best practices" ensuring that appropriate assistance is offered. These services then include the use of validated tools, are part of a continuous validation process through research, and have as their main objective to establish a proactive and consolidated partnership with community organizations and to provide supervision, consultation, and training to them.

## The Building Blocks of Our Strategy

To develop appropriate supports for persons with intellectual disabilities in the parenting role, there has to be an evidence-based framework for understanding what their needs might be. We use as our guide the interactional model of parenting by persons with intellectual disabilities proposed by Maurice Feldman (2002). This model synthesizes ecological systems theory (e.g., Belsky, 1984; Bronfenbrenner, 1986) with more than five decades of research on parents and parenting with intellectual disabilities. This model presents the multiple, interacting determinants and influences on parenting and child development. Such influences may include historical factors, such as the parent's own upbringing; characteristics of the parent and child, including, for example, the parent's mental health and the child's temperament; family and community resources, such as income, housing, neighborhood safety, and the availability of informal and formal supports; and more distal social and cultural influences, including societal norms, public policy, and social stigma. Hypotheses derived from this model have been tested with many samples of parents with intellectual disabilities. Associations have been found between social network characteristics (including support satisfaction) and quality of the home environment (including parent–child interactions), and between parent stress, parenting style, and child behavior outcomes (Aunos, Feldman, & Goupil, 2008; Feldman, Varghese, Ramsay, & Rajska, 2002).

Another crucial building block of our strategy is research about "what works" for parents with intellectual disabilities including evidence-based parenting education programs. Our operational objective is to implant best practices based on research into services throughout the province. The research suggests that appropriate parent education and support significantly reduce the likelihood of child removal, that is, the termination of parental rights. Some reports suggest that the rate of child removal from parents with intellectual disabilities who are clients of child and youth protection services may drop from around 80% to below 20% when appropriate assistance is provided (Feldman, 1997).

What is appropriate assistance? Appropriate assistance to parents with intellectual disabilities is responsive to the particular learning and support needs of each parent and family over time (Espe-Sherwindt & Kerlin, 1990; Feldman, 2002; Llewellyn, 1997; Llewellyn & McConnell, 2002). Many parents with intellectual disabilities will need intermittent support over the long term, as parenting must be constantly adapted to the needs of the developing child. Appropriate assistance promotes parental competence. Competence-promoting assistance (1) acknowledges and builds on parent strengths; (2) treats parents as partners in the process of developing, implementing, and evaluating a support plan; and (3) helps parents "learn and do" for themselves as opposed to others "doing for" the parents (Tucker & Johnson, 1989). A positive attitude on the part of professionals is one of the most powerful determinants of success for parents with intellectual disabilities using services (Tymchuk, 1991a). Appropriate assistance is also multi-faceted. That is, it addresses both the psychosocial disadvantage experienced by parents with intellectual disabilities, for example by strengthening social relationships or reducing stress, and their educational needs, for example through parenting skills training (Booth & Booth, 1999; Espe-Sherwindt & Kerlin, 1990; Feldman, 2002; Llewellyn, 1997; Llewellyn & McConnell, 2002; Tucker & Johnson, 1989).

Most of the research about what works for parents with intellectual disabilities has focused on parenting education and skills training. Since the early 1980s researchers have documented their successes in teaching parents with intellectual disabilities a wide range of skills. The research has shown improvements in parenting skills in areas such as basic childcare (Feldman et al., 1992), home safety and health (Llewellyn, McConnell, Russo, Mayes, & Honey, 2002; Tymchuk, 1991b; Tymchuk & Andron, 1992; Tymchuk, Hamada, Andron, & Anderson, 1990a, 1990b), problem solving and decision making (Tymchuk, Andron, & Rahbar, 1988; Tymchuk, Yokota, & Rahbar, 1990), parent–child interactions (Tymchuk & Andron, 1988, 1992), and parents' receptivity toward their children (Bakken, Miltenberger, & Schauss, 1993; Feldman, Case, Rincover, Towns, & Betel, 1989; Feldman et al., 1986). Parallel skills such as grocery shopping and planning, and cleaning and nutrition, have also been targeted with specific task analysis and programs, and the findings demonstrate positive results as well (Feldman, Garrick, & Case, 1997; Saber, Halasz, Messner, Bickett, & Lutzker, 1983). Some specific evidence-based programs designed for parents with intellectual disabilities are shown in Table 12.1. It is important, however, to note that most of these programs have been developed for English-speaking parents with young children. Translation and cultural adaptation for francophone and minority culture parents in Québec are therefore necessary, and new programs are needed for parents with older children.

**Table 12.1.** Parent education programs

| Title | Authors | Aims of program | Who it is for | How to get it |
|-------|---------|-----------------|---------------|---------------|
| Health and Wellness Program | Tymchuk | Promotes the development of knowledge and skills for managing home dangers, accidents, and childhood illness | Parents with intellectual disabilities with children under 6 years | Brookes Publishing |
| Parent Education Program | Feldman & Case | Promotes the development of basic childcare skills | Parents with intellectual disabilities with children under 4 years | Contact M. Feldman, mfeldman@brocku.ca |
| Healthy Start for Me and My Baby | Australian Supported Parenting Consortium | Promotes health and well-being during pregnancy | Pregnant women with intellectual disabilities | www.healthystart.net.au |
| Australian Supported Learning Program (ASLP): Me and My Community | Australian Supported Parenting Consortium | Promotes connections for parents with learning difficulties within their community | Parents with intellectual disabilities with children under 6 years | www.healthystart.net.au |
| Healthy and Safe: An Australian Parent Education Kit | Australian Supported Parenting Consortium | Promotes the development of knowledge and skills for managing home dangers, accidents, and childhood illness | Parents with intellectual disabilities with children under 5 years | www.healthystart.net.au |
| Parenting Young Children: A program for parents with learning disabilities | Australian Supported Parenting Consortium | Promotes positive parent–child interactions and parents' skills in childcare | Parents with intellectual disabilities aged 6 months through 6 years | www.healthystart.net.au |
| Step-by-Step Baby Care DVD | Australian Supported Parenting Consortium | Promotes the application of critical childcare tasks related to nutrition and daily care for new babies | Parents with intellectual disabilities and new babies | healthystart@parentingrc. org.au |

## Our First Step to Bridge the Gap between Research and Practice

Building on Feldman's (2002) interactional model and the research about what works for parents with intellectual disabilities, our first step was to develop and pilot a new parenting education program focusing on the needs of parents with older children. The program, called The Art of Parenting, was initially piloted with four mothers. It involved eight group-work sessions, "homework," and home visits. The group-work session content was based on the needs identified by 12 mothers with intellectual disabilities who were clients of the West Montreal Readaptation Center at that time. Eleven of these mothers had children aged six years and older and eight of these mothers had teenagers. The sessions included a verbal presentation of the skill to be learned, objectives and importance of learning this skill, demonstration of the skill, modeling, practice time, and feedback. Participants were asked to practice the skill during the week and to share their experience in the next session. Home visits were also made to support the application of new skills in the home setting. The outcomes were positive, and the program was deemed to be successful in teaching, informing, and supporting these mothers in their parenting role. Since 2005, the program curriculum has been expanded to 42 optional sessions with appropriate sessions selected on the basis of need. The success of The Art of Parenting program has been replicated many times over with different groups of mothers in Québec and a second organization has since joined the project (Lisette-Dupras Readaptation Center).

## Our Second Step: The Development of Standards of Practice

Our next step was the development of standards of practice to guide all readaptation centers within the province in the development of expert services for parents with intellectual disabilities. Under the auspices of the Québec Federation of Readaptation Centers, an expert group was assembled with three clinicians, a researcher-practitioner (the first author), and a facilitator. Each expert was experienced in working both with parents with intellectual disabilities and with other agencies and professionals in consultation, training, and mentoring roles. The group met monthly for one day at a time over a period of six months. Each day-long meeting began with tabling messages and recommendations from the research literature, which the expert group then applied to the Québec context. Using this process, we developed policy and practice standards. These standards were then reviewed by senior management at each readaptation center to ensure their financial viability and their clinical feasibility within current and future organizational structures. Four major policy standards and four practice standards were established. We describe the policy standards in the next section.

## Policy standards

### Standard 1. Establishing clear guidelines and internal policies

This first standard requires each readaptation center to develop and/or apply policies that (1) support the self-determination of persons with intellectual disabilities in matters relating to their sexuality, relationships, and parenting, and (2) promote a positive approach and timely delivery of services to parents with intellectual disabilities. Persons with intellectual disabilities are to be provided with the information they need to make informed decisions and to participate as partners in the process of planning support. Each center should already have a policy on sexuality (Richards et al., 2009). This standard requires centers to review and update this policy to include a specific section on pregnancy and parenting if it does not already do so. Translated into practice, this means that young people and adults with intellectual disabilities are to receive appropriate information and counseling on sexuality, relationships, family planning, and parenting. Further, center guidelines around access to services are to be reviewed and revised to limit any waiting time for services. Services are required to be preventive rather than crisis-driven whenever possible.

### Standard 2. Building partnerships with all organizations involved

The second standard requires each center to create positive and cooperative working partnerships with other agencies that are likely to be involved in the delivery of services for parents with intellectual disabilities. This standard recognizes that interventions with parents with intellectual disabilities are often multi-systemic. To establish those partnerships, potential partners (community organizations, public agencies, volunteer services) need to be identified. Once these are identified, the workers involved with any particular family are accountable for delineating their respective roles and responsibilities and their mode of collaboration. Signed service collaborations are suggested as beneficial in sealing the potential partnership agreement and facilitating any specific interventions with individual families.

### Standard 3. Enhancing collaboration with natural/informal support networks

Although many parents with intellectual disabilities are isolated, some have involved informal or natural support networks (Llewellyn & McConnell, 2002).

This third standard requires each center, with the parent's consent, to work with and support members of the parent's informal support network. The members of the parent's informal support network (e.g., extended family) are to be treated as important partners and potentially as support recipients. This is consistent with the mandate of readaptation centers to offer services to family members of persons with intellectual disabilities (Ministère de la santé et des services sociaux; http://www.msss.gouv.qc.ca/). Members of the extended family may benefit from information about the services that are put in place to support parents with intellectual disabilities and about grants and other financial programs and community organizations that could offer support to their family.

### Standard 4. Involving staff in training, continuing education, and supervision

The fourth standard requires each center to address the professional development, support, and supervision needs of their staff to work effectively with parents with intellectual disabilities. This standard acknowledges that staff need basic training and continuing professional education to achieve best practice. This includes support to stay informed about new research and resources.

In addition to these four policy standards, the four practice standards address the sequence of steps involved in the process of support planning and service delivery. We now describe the practice standards.

## Practice standards

### Standard 5. Assessing the request for services

The fifth standard provides a framework for readaptation centers to use to consider and act upon a request for a service for parents with intellectual disabilities from any community or public agency. Centers are advised to first ascertain the specific expectations of all stakeholders, including the referral source, the parent with intellectual disability, and, when appropriate, other family members. Based on these service expectations, the most appropriate member of the multi-disciplinary team is appointed as case manager. The case manager then gathers and reviews any existing documentation such as previous assessment reports, including but not limited to the results of intelligence tests, and any information about past and present service utilization. The objective is to develop a preliminary picture of potential support and service needs to orient future assessment and intervention planning. In reviewing the documents, the case manager is advised to look for indication of strengths and difficulties in information processing from the intelligence test or other assessment tools; the qualifications of the professional/s who conducted any previous assessment, the methods and tools they used, and their conclusions; and any information that may shed light on the relationship dynamics between any agencies and workers involved with the parent and their family. In reviewing all documents, case managers are advised to be wary of any biases or prejudices that may distort the picture that they develop of the parent's situation.

### Standard 6. Assessing parenting, parallel abilities, and quality of life

The sixth standard provides guidelines for the assessment conducted by center staff. Following the review of any existing documentation, the case manager presents "the findings" to the rest of the multi-disciplinary team and a comprehensive assessment is then planned and undertaken. Following the recommendations of Aunos and Feldman (2007), the assessment includes an evaluation of the appropriateness and outcomes of any past service provision; consideration of the parent and child's home environment, natural/informal support network, health and well-being, and quality of life; and an appraisal of the parent's adaptive behavior, parenting skills, and everyday routines. The assessment procedure should include parent interview, observations made in the home environment (e.g., parent–child interactions, home safety), and the administration of well-validated tools and measures. Parents are to be active partners in the assessment process, and the assessment findings are reviewed with the parents before they are presented to other agencies involved, or potentially involved, in supporting the family.

### Standard 7. Planning for services

Standard 7 provides guidelines for planning services. After the assessment findings are presented to parents and community partners, they are then used as the basis for joint service planning. Priorities are to be agreed and then a service and support plan (intervention plan) is created. The intervention plan includes psychosocial support and psychoeducational support as needed. Specific parent learning needs are specified so that, whenever possible, these can be matched to an existing, validated, research-proven program, such as one of the programs listed in Table 12.1. In addition, the service plan is to be reassessed at regular intervals to ensure that services are responsive to any change in parent and family circumstances and need.

### Standard 8. Offering and implementing specialized services

The eighth standard offers guidance for the development and provision of specialized services. Potential areas for intervention are presented as shown in the list below:

- offering support to families in accessing appropriate services;
- building and initiating functional partnerships with community, youth protection, and health services;

- providing training and clinical orientations based on evidence-based practices to basic support teams, community partners, and legal representatives (i.e., family court lawyers and judges);
- offering psychoeducational and psychosocial support to parents with intellectual disabilities;
- supporting the validation of new alternative residential resources for parents with intellectual disabilities (i.e., developing a residential model that would include elements of family reunification);
- guiding and supporting extended family members in their supportive role.

Readaptation centers are advised to take a lifespan perspective: Services are to start ideally in the teenage years and need to include counseling and support for young people with intellectual disabilities to make informed decisions with respect to family planning. A community and social participation model is required to underpin service provision so that parents are supported to access mainstream community and government resources. The importance of a systemic approach is emphasized to ensure links are created between informal and formal sources of support and mainstream and specialized services to exchange expertise and work together to support parents with intellectual disabilities. Services are to be research-informed and whenever possible utilize validated tools/program.

## Building on Success

Since 2005 the number of clients who are parents referred to our two readaptation centers has more than doubled. In 2005–2006, our two centers were serving 16 parents with intellectual disabilities. By 2009 this number had increased to 41. This growth, combined with increased awareness and confidence in supporting persons with intellectual disabilities in the parenting role, has given us some forward momentum. Our collaboration, initially around the pilot program, has now expanded into a multi-faceted and multi-disciplinary "center of excellence." We now provide psychosocial and psychoeducational support to parents with intellectual disabilities and their families. The range of services now offered is listed below:

- problem solving and decision making;
- understanding services and systems (i.e., school, community resources, youth protection system);
- emotion management (i.e., loss and bereavement, stress and anger management, communication skills);
- rights, self-esteem, and assertiveness in parents;

- child development (i.e., emotional development and attachment, development of sexuality, developing stress and anger management skills, self-esteem and assertiveness in children);
- parent–child interactions (i.e., play and imagination, language and communication, increasing parent's sensitivity to child);
- behavior management (i.e., establishing routines, rules, and consequences, reinforcing behaviors, techniques to decrease inappropriate behaviors);
- basic parental skills (i.e., nutrition, first aid, and medical issues);
- relationships within the family (i.e., role of each member in family, issues with divorce, separation, reconstitution, introducing a new member, father–child relationship, privacy, sexually transmitted diseases, pregnancies);
- support in accessing socioprofessional services if required or desired;
- financial planning (i.e., budgeting skills and work skills).

Moreover, we are now providing consultation, training, and support to an increasing number of workers and community partners and are working on developing inter-agency partnerships across the province. For instance, we recently conducted a one-day "knowledge exchange" workshop involving readaptation center staff and child and youth protection workers. These workers came together to learn about best practices, to exchange ideas, foster shared understanding, and promote future cooperation in serving parents with intellectual disabilities and their children.

## Challenges and Future Directions

Our efforts to bridge the gap between research and practice and between the rights and reality of parents with intellectual disabilities in Québec are ongoing. We believe that we have made progress. At the same time, we recognize that this is not a project or puzzle that can be completed or solved once and for all. The pieces of this puzzle, including the parents, the workers, the agencies, the human service system, and the research knowledge base, all change shape and form over time. We therefore have to solve the puzzle, fitting these pieces together time and time again. We do believe, however, that there are some essential keys to making progress whatever the context. Research is one of these keys. We believe that the best way to ensure that our efforts are informed and led by research is to be actively engaged in it. Another essential key is partnership. This means working in partnership with parents and their significant others. Parents are not merely the passive recipients of services. They are agents of change in their own lives, families, and communities. Working in partnership also means creating and nurturing relationships and networks between agencies and professional disciplines. We believe that this type of collaboration is the best way to facilitate knowledge transfer and exchange and to find creative solutions to what are often complex challenges in multi-agency service delivery.

## Conclusion

In other countries, too, researchers and practitioners are working together to bridge the gap. These initiatives vary greatly. They vary in scope and formality. What they share in common is the emphasis on research and partnership. The most formalized initiative is in Australia, with *Healthy Start: A National Strategy for Children of Parents with Learning Difficulties* (www.healthystart.net.au; McConnell, Matthews, Llewellyn, Mildon, & Hindmarsh, 2008). This initiative is bringing practitioners together, from different disciplines and agencies, and at local, state, and national levels. It intends to equip them with knowledge from research and research-proven programs and resources to support parents with intellectual disabilities and their children. No other country has a funded, planned, and systematic national strategy like *Healthy Start* – at least, not yet! However, there are groups in other countries who are working at local or state or national levels to bridge the gap between rights and reality and between research and practice, just as we have reported in this chapter. For instance, a coalition of researchers and practitioners has recently established the North American Association for Successful Parenting. The goal of this association is to ensure that evidence-based services are available to all parents with intellectual disabilities in Canada and the United States of America. To gather momentum, foster partnerships, and facilitate knowledge exchange, this coalition plans to continue and convene conferences and summits to advance knowledge sharing and collaboration across North America.

We must acknowledge that our efforts in Québec and initiatives such as *Healthy Start* are possible because there is now a critical mass of research about best practice in working with parents with intellectual disabilities. We also appreciate that there continues to be a significant gap in knowledge in this field. Some of the under-researched areas are highlighted in a position paper prepared by the International Association for the Scientific Study of Intellectual Disability Special Interest Research Group on Parents and Parenting (IASSID SIRG on Parents and Parenting with Intellectual Disabilities, 2008). Two areas of particular interest about which little is currently known are the influence of social and cultural factors on parenting and the experience and support needs of parents from minority cultural groups. As we look ahead, we anticipate that new research will generate insights crucial to improving services for parents with intellectual disabilities and, in so doing, contribute significantly to the ongoing project of bridging the gap between research and practice and rights and reality for parents with intellectual disabilities, worldwide.

# References

Aunos, M., & Feldman, M. (2007). Assessing parenting capacity in parents with intellectual disabilities. In C. Chamberland, S. Léveillé, & N. Trocmé (Eds.), *Des enfants à protéger, des adultes à aider: Deux univers à rapprocher* [Children to protect, adults to support: Two universes to link together] (pp. 223–240). Sainte-Foy: Presses de l'université du Québec.

Aunos, M., Goupil, G., & Feldman, M. (2003). Les parents présentant une déficience intellectuelle: Revue de littérature [Parents with intellectual disabilities: Literature review]. *Handicap: Revue des Sciences Humaines et Sociales, 97*, 32–54.

Aunos, M., Goupil, G., & Feldman, M. (2008). Mothers with intellectual disabilities who do or do not have custody of their children. *Journal on Developmental Disabilities, 10*(2), 65–79.

Bakken, J., Miltenberger, R. G., & Schauss, S. (1993). Teaching parents with mental retardation: Knowledge versus skills. *American Journal on Mental Retardation, 97*(4), 405–417.

Belsky, J. (1984). The determinants of parenting: A process model. *Child Development, 55*(1), 83–96.

Booth, T., & Booth, W. (1999). Parents together: Action research and advocacy support for parents with learning difficulties. *Health and Social Care in the Community, 7*(6), 464–474.

Booth, T., Booth, W., & McConnell, D. (2005a). Care proceedings and parents with learning difficulties: Comparative prevalence and outcomes in an English and Australian court sample. *Child and Family Social Work, 10*(4), 353–360.

Booth, T., Booth, W., & McConnell, D. (2005b). The prevalence and outcomes of care proceedings involving parents with learning difficulties in the family courts. *Journal of Applied Research in Intellectual Disabilities, 18*(1), 7–17.

Bronfenbrenner, U. (1986). Ecology of the family as a context for human development: Research perspectives. *Developmental Psychology, 22*(6), 723–742.

Espe-Sherwindt, M., & Kerlin, S. L. (1990). Early intervention with parents with mental retardation: Do we empower or impair? *Infants and Young Children, 2*(4), 21–28.

Feldman, M. A. (1997). Parents with intellectual disabilities: Implications and interventions. In J. Lutzker (Ed.), *Child abuse: A handbook of theory, research, and treatment* (pp. 401–419). New York: Plenum.

Feldman, M. A. (2002). Parents with intellectual disabilities and their children: Impediments and supports. In D. Griffiths & P. Federoff (Eds.), *Ethical issues in sexuality of people with developmental disabilities*. Kingston, NY: NADD Press.

Feldman, M. A., Case, L., Garrick, M., MacIntyre-Grande, W., Carnwell, J., & Sparks, B. (1992). Teaching child-care skills to parents with developmental disabilities. *Journal of Applied Behavior Analysis, 25*(1), 205–215.

Feldman, M. A., Case, L., Rincover, A., Towns, F., & Betel, J. (1989). Parent education program project III: Increasing affection and responsivity in developmentally handicapped mothers: Component analysis, generalization, and effects on child language. *Journal of Applied Behavior Analysis, 22*(2), 211–222.

Feldman, M. A., Garrick, M., & Case, L. (1997). The effects of parent training on weight gain of nonorganic-failure-to-thrive children of parents with intellectual disabilities. *Journal on Developmental Disabilities, 5*(1), 47–61.

Feldman, M. A., Towns, F., Betel, J., Case, L., Rincover, A., & Rubino, C. A. (1986). Parent education project II. Increasing stimulating interactions of developmentally handicapped mothers. *Journal of Applied Behavior Analysis, 19*(1), 23–37.

Goodringe, S. (2000). *A jigsaw of services: Inspection of service to support disabled adults in their parenting role.* London: Department of Health.

IAASID Special Interest Research Group on Parents and Parenting with Intellectual Disabilities. (2008). Parents labelled with intellectual disability: Position of the IASSID SIRG on Parents and Parenting with Intellectual Disabilities. *Journal of Applied Research in Intellectual Disabilities, 21*(4), 296–307.

Llewellyn, G. (1997). Parents with intellectual disability learning to parent: The role of experience and informal learning. *International Journal of Disability, Development and Education, 44*(3), 243–261.

Llewellyn, G., & McConnell, D. (2002). Mothers with learning difficulties and their support networks. *Journal of Intellectual Disability Research, 46*(1), 17–34.

Llewellyn, G., McConnell, D., Russo, D., Mayes, R., & Honey, A. (2002). Home-based programs for parents with intellectual disabilities: Lessons from practice. *Journal of Applied Research in Intellectual Disabilities, 15*(4), 341–353.

McConnell, D., Matthews, J., Llewellyn, G., Mildon, R., & Hindmarsh, G. (2008). "Healthy Start": A national strategy for parents with intellectual disabilities and their children. *Journal of Policy and Practice in Intellectual Disabilities, 5*(3), 194–202.

Moxness, K., & Dulude, H. (2003). L'intégration et le soutien en milieu communautaire [Integration and community support]. *La déficience intellectuelle* [Intellectual disabilities]. Montreal: Gaétan Morin.

Richards, D., Miodrag, N., Watson, S. L., Feldman, M. A., Aunos, M., Cox-Lindenbaum, D., & Griffiths, D. (2009). Sexuality and human rights of persons with intellectual disabilities. In F. Owen & D. Griffiths (Eds.), *Rights of persons with intellectual disabilities: Historical, legal, policy and theoretical issues.* London: Jessica Kingsley.

Sarber, R. E., Halasz, M. M., Messmer, M. C., Bickett, A. D., & Lutzker, J. R. (1983). Teaching menu planning and grocery shopping skills to a mentally retarded mother. *Mental Retardation, 21*(3), 101–106.

Tarleton, B., Ward, L., & Howarth, J. (2006). *Finding the right support: A review of the issues and positive practice in supporting parents with learning difficulties and their children.* London: Baring Foundation.

Tucker, M. B., & Johnson, O. (1989). Competence promoting versus competing inhibiting social support for mentally retarded mothers. *Human Organization, 48*(2), 95–107.

Tymchuk, A. (1991a). Parents with mental retardation: A national strategy. *Journal of Disability Policy Studies, 1*(4), 43–55.

Tymchuk, A. J. (1991b). Training mothers with mental retardation to understand general rules in the use of high-risk household products. *Journal of Practical Approaches to Developmental Handicap, 15*(2), 15–19.

Tymchuk, A. J., & Andron, L. (1988). Clinic and home parent training of a mother with mental handicap caring for three children with developmental delay. *Mental Handicap Research, 1*(1), 24–38.

Tymchuk, A. J., & Andron, L. (1992). Project parenting: Child interactional training with mothers who are mentally handicapped. *Mental Handicap Research, 5*(1), 4–32.

Tymchuk, A., Andron, L., & Rahbar, B. (1988). Effective decision-making/problem-solving training with mothers who have mental retardation. *American Journal of Mental Retardation, 92*, 24–38.

Tymchuk, A. J., Hamada, D., Andron, L., & Anderson, S. (1990a). Emergency training with mothers who are mentally retarded. *Child and Family Behavior Therapy, 12*(3), 31–47.

Tymchuk, A. J., Hamada, D., Andron, L., & Anderson, S. (1990b). Home safety training with mothers who are mentally retarded. *Education and Training of the Mentally Retarded, 25*, 142–149.

Tymchuk, A. J., Yokota, A., & Rahbar, B. (1990). Decision-making abilities of mothers with mental retardation. *Research in Developmental Disabilities, 11*(1), 97–109.

United Nations. (2006). *Convention on the rights of persons with disabilities.* New York: Author.

# 13

# Supporting Mothers' Community Participation

## David McConnell and Gwynnyth Llewellyn

## Introduction

In the early 1990s we conducted a study of the support and service needs of parents with intellectual disabilities. The study took us into the homes and lives of families from rural and metropolitan regions of New South Wales, Australia. Most of the parents we interviewed were mothers. The stories they shared, and the impression they made upon us, set the direction of a research program to identify ways to support mothers with intellectual disabilities to participate in the community. As newcomers to the field, we were struck by their apparent social isolation. Many received little support from their own families, few had friends, and even fewer were well connected in their local community. When we talked to these mothers about their support and service needs, many said their first priority was to meet people and make friends, and to get help to find opportunities and access resources in their local community. These needs were not being met by the professionals involved in their lives.

Research in Australia and other countries since that time confirms that mothers with intellectual disabilities, on average, have smaller social networks and report lower levels of social support than other mothers in the community (Feldman et al., 2002; Llewellyn & McConnell, 2002, 2004; Llewellyn, McConnell, Cant, & Westbrook, 1999; Stenfert-Kroese, Hussein, Clifford, & Ahmed, 2002). This social disconnect places these mothers at risk for a long list of undesirable outcomes. There is a relationship between mothers' social relationships and many aspects of maternal health and child well-being,

*Parents with Intellectual Disabilities: Past, Present and Futures*   Edited by Gwynnyth Llewellyn, Rannveig Traustadóttir, David McConnell, and Hanna Björg Sigurjónsdóttir   © 2010 John Wiley & Sons, Ltd

as follows: pre- and postnatal depression (Collins, Dunkel-Shetter, Lobel, & Scrimshaw, 1993; Cutrona & Troutman, 1986); parenting stress and sense of competence (Adamakos et al., 1986); maternal warmth and responsiveness (Burchinal, Follmer, & Bryant, 1996; Crnic, Greenberg, Ragozin, Robinson, & Basham, 1983; Pascoe, Loda, Jeffries, & Earp, 1981); risk of child abuse and neglect (Bishop & Leadbeater, 1999; Garbarino & Crouter, 1978; Kotch, Browne, Dufort, & Winsor, 1999; Wandersman & Nation, 1998); and child cognitive, emotional, and social development (Melson, Ladd, & Hsu, 1993; Pianta & Ball, 1993; Sameroff, Siefer, Baldwin, & Baldwin, 1993). Despite these findings, the literature offers little guidance for policy makers and practitioners about how to develop and strengthen the participation of mothers with intellectual disabilities in the community and broaden their social networks.

In 2004, the Australian Supported Parenting Consortium was funded by the Australian government to build systems capacity to support parents with intellectual disabilities and their children. Information about this ongoing national strategy, called *Healthy Start*, is available at www.healthystart.net.au. One component of this strategy was the development, trialing, and dissemination of a program to assist mothers with intellectual disabilities broaden their social networks and increase their community participation. This component, called the Australian Supported Learning Program (ASLP), is the focus of this chapter. We begin by briefly describing the ASLP and its development. We then discuss the theory and thinking behind the ASLP and report findings from our initial work with this program.

## Developing the Australian Supported Learning Program

We used an action-based research process to inform the development of the ASLP. This required information gathered during the development process and piloting to be incorporated into further development (Dick, 2000; Kemmis & McTaggart, 1988). Following our analysis of the literature, we formed a Critical Reference Group (CRG) to begin planning the framework for the ASLP. This group included experts in parenting, adult education, family support, and community development, and practitioners with expertise in working with disadvantaged groups. Once the broad framework was established by the CRG and the Healthy Start Project Team, we established a Critical Action Group (CAG). CAG members were family support practitioners who were keen to pilot the ASLP, once developed. We held a workshop with CAG members to develop the content of the ASLP and complementary resources. Following this, the ASLP was piloted across four sites in two Australian states, New South Wales

**Table 13.1.** Session themes

| | |
|---|---|
| Week 1 | Places I know and love |
| Week 2 | Different kinds of places in my community |
| Week 3 | Places for children and families |
| Week 4 | Outing (family-friendly place) |
| Week 5 | Doing *things for me* in my community |
| Week 6 | Outing (place for me) |
| Week 7 | Helping out in my community |
| Week 8 | Outing (place to help out in my community) |
| Week 9 | Meeting people and making new friends |
| Week 10 | Review: bringing it all together |

(NSW) and Victoria (VIC). The ASLP was then revised based on feedback from the participants as recommended in the action research process, and the revised program was implemented at two sites, one in Sydney, a large metropolitan city, and the other in regional NSW.

The Australian Supported Learning Program has three main components. These are: a weekly group-work program completed over 10 weeks; facilitator-provided individual support for participating mothers; and, self-directed "homework/challenges" for the mothers to carry out at home. The latter are designed to reinforce mothers' learning during the group-work phase and to encourage them to further reflect and internalize the strategies for negotiating the community they have learned about and practiced in the group program. Each group-work session, conducted by the facilitator, is approximately two hours in duration. Session themes are listed in Table 13.1 and the basic session structure is presented in Table 13.2. Individual support commences from the first contact between the ASLP facilitator and the mother. In the pre-group phase the facilitator meets with each mother to identify her goals. Once the group-work phase begins, the facilitator provides ongoing support by working

**Table 13.2.** Basic session structure

| Structure | Notes |
|---|---|
| Icebreaker (15 mins) | Some suggestions are included in the session plans. ASLP facilitators are encouraged to use their own favorites. |
| Activity 1 (30 mins) | Focused on experience and reflection: (1) what happened? and (2) why does this happen? |
| Coffee break (20 mins) | |
| Activity 2 (40 mins) | Focused on problem solving and action: (3) what can we do about it? |
| Wrap-up (15 mins) | Summary, preview of next week, and home challenge |
| Home challenge | "Homework" related to session themes |

with each mother on her goals. In the post-group phase, the facilitator meets with each mother individually to reflect on her experience and progress toward achieving her goals.

The ASLP comes with a Facilitator Guide and the ASLP Participant Workbook. The Facilitator Guide provides background information about the ASLP. It covers topics such as recruiting potential participants, setting goals with individual mothers, preparing for the group, and strategies for maximizing participation (see Table 13.3). The Facilitator Guide also incorporates session plans for each week of the group-work program and structured session evaluation forms. The Participant Workbook includes forms for goal-setting and evaluation; the home challenges to be completed during the group-work phase of the ASLP; and space for mothers to paste in any photos from the group-work sessions. Copies of the complete program materials for the ASLP are available from the second author at cost.

## Theory and Thinking Behind the ASLP

The three cornerstones of the ASLP are (1) Booth and Booth's (2003) groundbreaking "Supported Learning Project" for mothers labeled with intellectual disability in Sheffield, UK; (2) theory and research by Sheldon Cohen (2004) on social relationships and Arie Zimmerman (Zimmerman, 1995; Zimmerman & Rappaport, 1988; Zimmerman, Israel, Schulz, & Checkoway, 1992) on psychological empowerment; and (3) the work of Brazilian educational philosopher Paulo Freire (1998) and his problem-posing approach to adult learning. Building on this tripartite foundation, the ASLP is designed to provide opportunities for mothers with intellectual disabilities to broaden their social networks and strengthen their community participation and, in turn, reduce psychological distress. The conceptual framework for the ASLP is presented in Figure 13.1. The ASLP focuses on the mother's own agency and builds on her capacity to enhance her social and community engagement. The model also shows the association between psychological well-being and social relationships and theorized "downstream" effects on, for example, parent–child interactions and child outcomes. Within this framework we acknowledge that there are a number of structural variables that also influence social networks and community participation, including resources (such as adequate finances, childcare, access to transport) and constraints (such as lack of community safety and social stigma). Structural barriers, however, are not directly addressed by the ASLP. Finding ways to effectively overcome or change the structural barriers that face mothers with intellectual disabilities participating more fully in society is an ongoing challenge.

**Table 13.3.**  Tips for maximizing participation

*Before group commences*

- Establish trust and rapport. Find out what each mother is interested in, identify things you have in common, and take a special interest and delight in her child or children.
- Openly discuss the purpose and process of the ASLP, ensuring that participation is fully informed and voluntary.
- Discuss what "being in the community" means to each mother, and identify their concrete, individual goals, that is, what they want to achieve during the ASLP.
- Look for opportunities to introduce mothers to each other before group starts. Mothers may feel more confident if they know someone other than the facilitator.

*During the group phase*

- Use "icebreakers" and refreshments to create a fun and friendly atmosphere.
- Keep instructions simple, and whenever possible demonstrate what is expected.
- Role-model "participation," using appropriate stories from your own experience.
- Create opportunities for participants to experience success.
- Take turns leading discussions so that participants are not always responding to the facilitator. Use "question prompt sheets" to help participants with this.
- Create opportunities for participants to use visual/creative media to express themselves and share their stories: Sharing does not always have to be in words.
- Use reflective listening to summarize and validate what participants have shared.
- Do not rush, and respect silence! Silence gives participants time to reflect.
- Encourage mothers to use their workbook to "record their own voice" so they can review their own story at their leisure.
- Provide positive reinforcement regularly – lather praise generously.

*Creating opportunities for mothers to experience success*

- Small successes can boost self-esteem and then some problems do not seem so overwhelming. Celebrate every small achievement with verbal praise, certificates at final meeting, prizes, etc.
- Remember that little things matter. Don't attempt more complex issues first. Try simple issues first. Simple issues are not so overwhelming and are more likely to be resolved in a timely manner. Small successes will lead to increased motivation and confidence.
- People often say they can't when they can, particularly when they have low self-esteem. Show the mothers you have faith in their ability.

## Cornerstone 1. The Sheffield Supported Learning Project

The potential of an adult learning approach to provide opportunities for mothers with intellectual disabilities to build and strengthen their social relationships

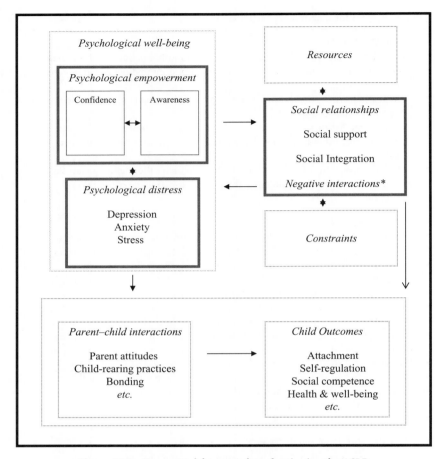

**Figure 13.1.** Conceptual framework underpinning the ASLP.

was demonstrated by Booth and Booth (2003) in partnership with the Sheffield Women's Multicultural Center in the Supported Learning Project (SLP). The SLP is a person-centered approach, in which the mothers make their own decisions about what to learn and how; an adult approach, which recognizes and respects the mothers' prior learning and life skills; a flexible approach, which allows the mothers to participate on their own terms; and an *in vivo* approach, which helps mothers develop self-advocacy skills by tackling issues arising in their own lives. The SLP was implemented over a two-year period. It involved a weekly learning support group and individual assistance in accessing learning and leisure opportunities in the community. Outcomes were evaluated qualitatively, through narrative interviews and review of the learning portfolios kept by the participating mothers. Reported outcomes for the 31 mothers involved in the trial included greater personal and practical skills, greater sense of control over their lives, a better self-image and more confidence in their own abilities, greater assertiveness, more awareness of their own needs and how to get help, a larger support network, and more enjoyment out of life. The SLP demonstrated great promise. However, it was not developed for widespread dissemination, and the lengthy period of intervention, we thought, was likely to be a significant barrier to family support agencies adopting and implementing the model in Australia. Therefore, we saw a need to develop a theoretically robust program that could both capture the promise demonstrated by the SLP and be used easily by practitioners.

## Cornerstone 2. Social relationships and empowerment

The second cornerstone of the ASLP is the association between social concerns and mothers' sense of agency and empowerment. The concept of social relationships and networks is a multi-faceted one. Cohen (2004) distinguished between social support, social integration, and conflict in interpersonal relationships. Each facet is believed to influence health and well-being in a different way. Social support, which can be instrumental, informational, and/or emotional, is thought of as a resource that comes from the social network and is believed to have stress-buffering effects. Social integration is thought of as participation in meaningful social activities, roles, and relationships. Social integration is believed to affect health and well-being quite directly by promoting positive psychological states including, for example, sense of identity, purpose, and self-worth. Conflict in interpersonal relationships, on the other hand, is identified as a source of stress leading to behaviors and physiological responses that increase risk of poor health outcomes.

Syme (1998) suggests that the relationship between social support and stress is mediated by personal sense of control or, as he puts it, "power over destiny." This is often thought of as empowerment. Empowerment is not regarded as something to be taught or imposed on an individual. In Syme's (1998) formulation, empowerment comes about via social support. Social support leads individuals to develop capacity to influence their environment and circumstances with a consequent reduction in stress. Personal control or psychological empowerment is also important for social integration. Without some degree of psychological empowerment people are unlikely to engage in the community (Itzhaky & Schwartz, 1998; Peterson, Lowe, Aquilino, & Schneider, 2005; Speer, Jackson, & Peterson, 2001; Zimmerman et al., 1992; Zimmerman & Rappaport, 1988). An example of this is a study by Zimmerman et al. (1992) in which the researchers interviewed a probability sample of 916 adults to find that groups who were more engaged in organizations and participated in community activities scored more highly on measures of psychological empowerment.

Zimmerman (1995) identified three components of psychological empowerment. These are intra-personal, inter-actional, and behavioral. Intra-personal empowerment or confidence includes the individual's perceptions of self-efficacy, competence, and mastery (Zimmerman & Rappaport, 1988). These perceptions enable people to engage in the proactive behaviors that are necessary for goal attainment (Rappaport, 1984). Inter-actional empowerment is the critical awareness of factors that hinder or facilitate efforts to exert control over one's environments and circumstances. It includes individuals knowing what the options are in a given context. Inter-actional empowerment is understood as the bridge that links intra-personal empowerment to the actions that individuals take to directly influence outcomes.

## Cornerstone 3. The problem-posing approach to adult learning

The ASLP employs a problem-posing approach to adult learning. This means that it is not a curriculum of skills to be learned or information to be imparted by an expert. Instead, in this program we are concerned to provide opportunities for mothers, in the company of other mothers with intellectual disabilities, to develop their awareness and confidence in participating in their community. This means that the problem-posing approach begins with each mother's real-life concerns. This approach also emphasizes group dialogue in which mothers participate as equals and co-learners to create knowledge that they can use in broadening their social networks and increasing their participation in the community. The cyclical process central to the ASLP involves mothers reflecting on their own experiences, past and present, followed by working together to plan a course of action to overcome obstacles and achieve their goals, and then putting these plans into action. It is through this ongoing and cyclical process over the course of the 10-week program that participants develop awareness of opportunities and confidence in seeking out these opportunities in their community. The ASLP employs three main devices to facilitate this process. These are the creation of a discussion object, a three-step questioning strategy, and a stepping stones activity for action planning.

The concept of a discussion object comes from Freire (1998), who proposes creating codes or codifications to give focus to a problem-posing dialogue when groups of people come together to develop awareness and confidence about their community or a particular concern they have in common. A code is a concrete physical representation of an issue, for example, a role play, photos, or collage. Each code re-presents the community reality back to discussion participants. It enables them to project their emotional and social responses into this object for a focused discussion. In the ASLP, we realize the concept of the discussion object by mothers creating a mural of their community. This mural

**Table 13.4.** Questions in problem-posing education 1

| Questions | Process |
| --- | --- |
| What happened? | The facilitator elicits "description," and common or shared experiences are identified |
| Why does this happen? | The facilitator elicits reflection, and the group together generates "hypotheses" or potential reasons why "this" happens |
| What can be done about it? | The facilitator elicits potential solutions: Group members identify strategies they have used to deal with situations |

is used throughout the group-work program as a discussion object. The mural represents specific places of interest or challenge to mothers in a tangible way through the use of pictorial representations such as photos, drawings, and clippings. In each session, mothers bring photographs or images of themselves and put these on different parts of the mural to indicate, for example, places in the community that make them feel either secure and happy or uncomfortable and threatened.

The discussion object alone, however, is not sufficient to facilitate a critical, reflective dialogue between mothers. In the ASLP, we facilitate the weekly group work by a three-step questioning strategy. In the first step of this strategy, we invite mothers to share their experiences in detail, to describe what happened, for example, when they went along to a playgroup or to enroll their child in preschool. Mothers with intellectual disabilities, like mothers everywhere, talk about their individual and common experiences. Once the mothers start to share their stories we invite them to critically reflect on these experiences. This helps them move beyond simply describing what happened to come to an understanding of why things happen the way they do. Once some understanding has been reached about what happened and the reasons why, we assist the mothers to think about what could be done, what they would like to do, and how might they go about it as a group or as individuals. Together, the mothers identify strategies that will help them work toward achieving their goals. They have a proposed plan of action to now put into action. In Tables 13.4 and 13.5 we present the questions that we use to facilitate the description, reflection, problem-solving, and planning process.

Action and reflection upon action are integral aspects of problem-posing education initially described by Freire (1973) and elaborated by many educators since that time (e.g., Freire, 1998; Wallerstein & Bernstein, 1988). It is not enough to develop plans of action; these plans must be put into action and then reflected upon, discussed, and further developed if necessary in an ongoing, iterative way. Throughout the 10-week ASLP program we support the mothers to go out in their community, put their plans into action, and begin working on their goals.

**Table 13.5.** Questions in problem-posing education 2

| Questions | Process |
|-----------|---------|
| What would you like to do? | The facilitator elicits "description," and common "aspirations" are identified |
| What is stopping you? | The facilitator elicits reflection, and the group together identifies barriers to participation |
| How can you achieve it? | The facilitator elicits potential solutions: Group members identify strategies for achieving their goals |

Personal goals vary between participants but may, for example, include enrolling in an adult literacy course, joining a special interest group, volunteering at their child's preschool, or identifying places in the community that they could enjoy with their children. All of these examples come from our initial pilot and subsequent implementation of the ASLP in NSW. Each week the mothers bring back to the group their stories about how things went as they carried out their plans. There is much discussion that takes place as they share and reflect together on what happened and why. Wallerstein and Bernstein (1988) suggest that this process of reflection, action, and reflection upon action leads to deeper awareness and understanding. We have found that to do this successfully with mothers with intellectual disabilities, we need to use the task-analysis approach shown to be effective in parent education programs for parents with intellectual disabilities (Feldman, 1994; Wade, Llewellyn, & Matthews, 2008). We use a stepping stones activity to break down strategies into concrete, feasible, and readily achievable steps. Together the mothers identify each of the steps they can take and these are written down on cardboard stepping stones. Placed in sequence, these stepping stones create a path (easily seen as a visual object) to be followed to achieve the desired community participation goal.

## How We Have Used the ASLP

The first time we used the ASLP was with the members of the CAG who had participated in developing this program. These professionals were all experienced group-work facilitators with qualifications in psychology and/or social welfare. Their experience in the disability field varied from one new entrant to 20+ years. Their active participation in developing the ASLP promoted integrity in its implementation across the six pilot sites: one pilot in metropolitan NSW, three in regional NSW, one in metropolitan VIC, and one in regional VIC. One site was a government service provider; the other five were in the not-for-profit community sector. At two sites the ASLP was piloted with preexisting groups of mothers with intellectual disabilities. New groups were established at each of the other four sites. The number of participating mothers at each site varied from 5 to 10.

A total of 42 mothers with intellectual disabilities commenced the program in this initial pilot phase. Complete program data were available for only 32 of these mothers due to a variety of reasons frequently found when implementing programs over a period of time with parents with intellectual disabilities (Australian Supported Parenting Consortium, 2008). Several mothers moved out of town during the pilot phase, some became too busy with other family commitments, while others found it difficult to come regularly to the group and on time over a three-month period.

In each of the sites and approximately one fortnight prior to the first group-work session, the ASLP facilitator met with each mother to discuss her expectations of the program, document her goals, and complete a demographic questionnaire. In this pre-program session we also included standard measures of social relationships and psychological well-being (empowerment and distress). This was because we were evaluating the contribution of the ASLP to the program aims of broadening social networks and increasing community participation and in turn mother well-being. Within one month of completing the group-work program, each facilitator met individually with the mothers from her group to review and rate their progress toward achieving their goals and to readminister the standard measures.

We employed three standard measures that we had used successfully in previous studies involving mothers with intellectual disabilities (McConnell, Mayes, & Llewellyn, 2008). These measures, all with good psychometric properties, are easy to administer and to score. They are therefore useful for practitioners who are keen to understand the contribution of the programs they implement to achieving change in the mothers' social relationships, feelings of mastery and control, and their psychological health and well-being. We also developed Program Goal Achievement and Personal Goal Attainment Scales to evaluate group and individual outcomes.

## Social relationships

The Tilden Interpersonal Relationships Inventory (IPRI) – Short Form (Tilden, Nelson, & May, 1990) is a self-report measure of social relationships. This measure has 26 items yielding two sub-scale scores, one for perceived social support and the other for conflict in interpersonal relationships. We developed a Personal Goal Attainment Scale to obtain a rating on how well the ASLP promoted the mothers' social integration (program efficacy). In the pre-group phase the mothers were asked how they would like to be (more) involved in their community and to specify up to five personal goals, which they then ranked in order of priority. Following the group-work phase of the program the mothers were asked to rate their progress toward achieving each of their personal goals on a three-point scale from "not close at all" to "I (fully) achieved this goal."

## Psychological empowerment

The Scales of Mastery and Constraints (Lachman & Weaver, 1998) are a measure of psychological empowerment. The Mastery Scale includes four items that tap sense of efficacy or effectiveness in achieving goals. These items include, for example, "I can do just about anything I really set my mind to" and "What happens to me in the future mostly depends on me." The Constraints Scale includes eight items that tap the extent to which there are obstacles or factors beyond one's control that interfere with reaching goals. Examples include: "I often feel helpless in dealing with the problems of life" and "Other people determine most of what I can and cannot do." Respondents indicate on a seven-point scale the extent to which they agree with each item. Higher scale scores reflect greater perceived mastery or constraints.

We developed the ASLP Program Goal Achievement Scale to obtain a measure of psychological empowerment specifically related to program learning objectives. This scale has 10 items that tap confidence and awareness. The items came from three sources: the network of psychological empowerment developed by Zimmerman (1995); findings reported by Booth and Booth (2003) from their evaluation of the Supported Learning Project; and ASLP program content. We asked mothers in the pre-program phase to indicate the extent to which they wanted to achieve each goal on a three-point scale from "not at all" through to "a lot." Post-program, mothers evaluated their progress using a three-point scale, from "not close at all" through to "I fully achieved this goal."

## Psychological distress

The Depression, Anxiety, and Stress Scales (DASS-21) (Lovibond & Lovibond, 1995) are a well-validated 21-item self-report measure for which Australian norms have been published (Antony, Bieling, Cox, Enns, & Swinson, 1998; Brown, Chorpita, Korotitsch, & Barlow, 1997; Nieuwenhuijsen, de Boer, Verbeek, Blonk, & van Dijk, 2003). The DASS-21 taps the negative emotional states of depression, anxiety, and stress.

# What We Found

Prior to the 10-week program commencing, mothers' scores on each of the standard measures (baseline data) demonstrated low levels of psychological

**Table 13.6.** Effects of ASLP

| Measure | Pre-ASLP mean (std) | Post-ASLP mean (std) | Cohen's d |
|---|---|---|---|
| **Mastery and Constraints** | | | |
| Mastery | 5.31 (1.20) | 5.62 (1.03) | 0.25 |
| Constraints | 4.64 (1.00) | 4.36 (1.30) | 0.25 |
| **Depression, Anxiety, and Stress** | | | |
| DASS (total) | 47.29 (31.52) | 33.87 (21.76) | 0.50 |
| Depression | 16.90 (12.61) | 11.38 (7.37) | 0.54 |
| Anxiety | 11.73 (9.48) | 8.32 (7.61) | 0.40 |
| Stress | 18.13(11.36) | 13.81 (9.05) | 0.43 |
| **Interpersonal Relationships** | | | |
| Social Support | 49.22 (9.27) | 52.09 (7.07) | 0.35 |
| Perceived Conflict | 44.77 (11.42) | 43.91 (9.78) | 0.08 |

well-being by comparison with test norm and large probability sample data sets (Lovibond & Lovibond, 1995; Tilden et al., 1990). The mothers had little confidence in their ability to achieve the goals that mattered to them, and perceived that there were obstacles outside their control that interfered with their achieving these goals. On average, the mothers reported high levels of depression, anxiety, and stress compared with population norms (Antony et al., 1998; Brown et al., 1997; Nieuwenhuijsen et al., 2003).

Table 13.6 shows the mean and standard deviation for baseline and post-program measures of psychological empowerment, psychological distress, and social relationships and Cohen's d for standardized effect size. The observed effect sizes ranged from a negligible 0.08 for "conflict in interpersonal relationships" to a high of 0.54 for depression. As the ASLP was not designed to address conflict in interpersonal relationships, a nil or small effect was expected. For depression, however, there was an average decrease of 33% from baseline to post-program on the Depression sub-scale of the DASS. Substantial effect sizes were also calculated for Social Support, Mastery, and Constraints. These were large by comparison with established benchmarks.

One established benchmark comes from a large meta-analysis of family support programs (Layzer, Goodson, Bernstein, & Price, 2001). This analysis found that the average effect size of family support programs on parents' social networks and psychological well-being was a negligible 0.14. A second benchmark comes from the Cochrane review of the effects of parent training programs on maternal psychosocial health (Barlow, Coren, & Stewart-Brown, 2007). This meta-analysis found that parent training approaches had an average effect size of 0.26 for depression and 0.42 for stress and anxiety with a virtually non-existent effect of 0.04 for social support/social relationships. The measured effects of implementing the ASLP were therefore between twice (for depression) and eight times (for social support) larger than is typically found in family support and parent training programs.

## Personal goal attainment

The mothers set a range of personal goals with only one-third (34%) directly related to community participation. Some were likely to be achieved within the program timeframe, others not so likely, such as to eat well, or smoke and gamble less. Some examples of personal goals set by the mothers are "to get out more often (e.g., to the movies, local shops)"; "to meet with other mums and mix socially outside of group"; "to help other people through volunteering"; "to meet other people and feel OK"; "to do a course (e.g., sign language, literacy, computer skills, handicrafts)"; "to join the library for myself and my child"; "to join a gym"; and "to get a job." Most mothers fully or partially achieved their personal goals. More importantly, 84% partially or fully achieved their priority one goal.

## Program goal attainment

Almost all the mothers wanted to achieve each of the pre-specified 10 program goals. The most popular goals were "getting more enjoyment out of life" and "learning more about my own strengths and things that I am good at," with 87.5% wanting to achieve these goals "a lot." Table 13.7 shows the number and percentage of mothers wanting to achieve each goal "a lot," as well as the number and percentage of mothers who reported either partially or fully achieving each goal after the ASLP. Following implementation of the ASLP, a very large proportion of mothers (between 90.6% and 100%) fully or partially achieved their goals. Many mothers were still keen to learn more. Half the mothers (50%) indicated that they wanted to "learn more about my strengths and things that I am good at" and more than half (59%) wanted to "learn more about things I can do to help out in my community."

## Mothers' and facilitators' reflections on the ASLP

Mothers and facilitators were positive about the ASLP. Almost all the primary components of this program, including the three-step questioning strategy, the discussion objects, the stepping stones activities, and support to mothers individually to achieve their goals, worked well. Mothers thought the icebreaker activities were fun; facilitators thought these activities were effective in helping the mothers to feel at ease with one another as many of the mothers did not know each other prior to the implementation of the ASLP. Mothers really enjoyed the outings to a family-friendly place in the community. Most were sorry there were not more outings and suggested more be included in the next version of the program. The group mural, which mothers created to represent their own

**Table 13.7.** Program goal-setting and achievement

| | Goal | I want this a lot* | Partially or fully achieved* | Want to achieve more* |
|---|---|---|---|---|
| 1 | Meet people and make new friends | 22 (68.8%) | 28 (97%) | 9 (31%) |
| 2 | Feel more confident about participating in groups | 20 (64.5%) | 31 (100%) | 5 (16%) |
| 3 | Learn more about places I can go to for help | 23 (71.9%) | 29 (97%) | 10 (33%) |
| 4 | Learn more about places my whole family can go together | 26 (81.3%) | 30 (93%) | 10 (33%) |
| 5 | Find out where I can go to do things I like doing | 24 (75%) | 29 (97%) | 12 (40%) |
| 6 | Learn more about my own strengths and things I am good at | 28 (87.5%) | 29 (90.6%) | 16 (50%) |
| 7 | Learn more about things I can do to help out in my community | 16 (52.0%) | 29 (100%) | 17 (59%) |
| 8 | Feel more confident about going places in my community | 18 (56.3%) | 29 (97%) | 10 (33%) |
| 9 | Learn some things that will help me get out | 21 (66%) | 29 (100%) | 10 (34%) |
| 10 | Get more enjoyment out of life | 28 (87.5%) | 29 (94%) | 9 (29%) |

*Excluding missing cases

community, was a great success with each group and really worked well to bring out points for discussion and to help keep the discussion focused on particular topics of interest to individual mothers and to the group. Facilitators and the mothers commented on how the stepping stones activity really helped to break down big ideas and action plans into something that could be achieved through a sequence of steps. Completing one step at a time gave mothers more confidence in their ability to overcome obstacles and get involved in their community.

The least popular part of the program from both the mothers' and the facilitators' perspectives was the home activities. Many of the mothers had difficulty completing these activities without individualized support and encouragement. There were reasons why this was so. For some mothers it was because they simply could not read or follow the instructions. For others it was because there was no support at home, or even active opposition. Most of the groups also found two hours were really not long enough for a well-paced and relaxed group activity; the suggested activities were just too difficult to always complete in the two-hour timeframe allocated to group-work sessions. Everyone wanted more time to work on the community mural, which was a very popular activity. The facilitators found that co-facilitators were needed to effectively implement the ASLP. This was for two main reasons. The first was because they needed an assistant to support the mothers with less ability so they too could fully participate in the group and within the rather tight session time. The second was to provide the mothers with the individualized support that they wanted or needed to work on their personal goals. The demand for this support and the level required varied within each group and also across the groups. Overall, however, this level of involvement by facilitators had not been allowed for in the program.

## Conclusion

Developing the Australian Supported Learning Program was an ambitious undertaking given that very few programs have been able to successfully broaden social networks and increase the community participation of isolated mothers, such as mothers with intellectual disabilities. We approached this task by bringing together knowledge from research with the experience of practitioners and mothers with intellectual disabilities through several cycles of program development. The outcome of this collaborative and iterative process, the ASLP, is a group-work program supplemented by individual support which applies a problem-posing approach to adult learning. We were pleased to find that, with a rigorous evaluation and robust baseline and post-program measures, participating in the ASLP produced positive effects on mothers' psychological well-being and the strength of their social relationships. The measured effects on the psychological well-being and social relationships of mothers were greater than the reported benchmarks for parent training and family support programs (Barlow et al., 2007; Layzer et al., 2001). We were also pleased to find that most of the mothers partially or fully achieved the goals they set at the beginning of the program. The mothers are now more confident about getting out and about within their respective communities and are more aware of the opportunities and resources available. Some are taking advantage of this, for example by joining other groups and enrolling in special interest courses.

The positive findings of this evaluation are encouraging; however, a larger and more powerful research design is needed to confirm the findings before we can argue conclusively for the effectiveness of the ASLP. In future research it will be important to have a comparison group and to have an independent person complete the outcome measures with each mother. We investigated the short-term effects of program completion and these are very promising.

However, it is also important to investigate medium- and longer-term effects for the mothers. The ASLP approach is designed to provide opportunities for mothers to build on their own agency and to develop awareness and confidence in their capacity to further broaden their social networks and increase their community participation. We would expect, therefore, a cumulative effect over time as mothers' social relationships go from strength to strength. But this hypothesis needs to be tested.

# References

Adamakos, H., Ryan, K., Ullman, D. G., Pascoe, J., Diaz, R., & Chessare, J. (1986). Maternal social support as a predictor of mother–child stress and stimulation. *Child Abuse and Neglect, 10*(4), 463–470.

Antony, M. M., Bieling, P. J., Cox, B. J., Enns, M. W., & Swinson, R. P. (1998). Psychometric properties of the 42-item and 21-item versions of the depression anxiety stress scales in clinical groups and a community sample. *Psychological Assessment, 10*, 176–181.

Australian Supported Parenting Consortium. (2008, June). *Final evaluation report: Healthy Start.* Melbourne: Australian Supported Parenting Consortium.

Barlow, J., Coren, E., & Stewart-Brown, S. S. B. (2007). Parent-training programmes for improving maternal psychosocial health [Systematic review]. *Cochrane Database of Systematic Reviews, 2*, 2.

Bishop, S. J., & Leadbeater, B. J. (1999). Maternal social support patterns and child maltreatment: Comparison of maltreating and non-maltreating mothers. *American Journal of Orthopsychiatry, 69*(2), 172–181.

Booth, T., & Booth, W. (2003). Self-advocacy and supported learning for mothers with learning difficulties. *Journal of Learning Disabilities, 7*(2), 165–193.

Brown, T. A., Chorpita, B. F., Korotitsch, W., & Barlow, D. H. (1997). Psychometric properties of the Depression Anxiety Stress Scales (DASS) in clinical samples. *Behaviour Research and Therapy, 35*(1), 79–89.

Burchinal, M. A., Follmer, A., & Bryant, D. M. (1996). The relations of maternal social support and family structure with maternal responsiveness and child outcomes among African American families. *Development Psychology, 32*(6), 1073–1083.

Cohen, S. (2004). Social relationships and health. *American Psychologist, 59*(8), 676–684.

Collins, N. L., Dunkell-Shetter, C., Lobel, M., & Scrimshaw, S. C. (1993). Social support in pregnancy: Psychosocial correlates of birth outcomes and postpartum depression. *Journal of Personality and Social Psychology, 65*(6), 1243–1258.

Crnic, K. A., Greenberg, M. T., Ragozin, A. S., Robinson, N. M., & Basham, R. B. (1983). Effects of stress and social support on mothers and premature and full-term infants. *Child Development, 54*(1), 209–217.

Cutrona, C. E., & Troutman, B. R. (1986). Social support, infant temperament, and parenting self-efficacy: A mediational model of postpartum depression. *Child Development, 57*(6), 1507–1518.

Dick, B. (2000). *A beginner's guide to action research* [Online]. Available at www.scu.edu.au/schools/gcm/ar/arp/guide.ht.

Feldman, M. A. (1994). Parenting education for parents with intellectual disabilities: A review of outcome studies. *Research in Developmental Disabilities, 15*(4), 299–332.

Feldman, M. A., Varghese, J., Ramsay, J., & Rajska, D. (2002). Relationships between social support, stress and mother–child interactions in mothers with intellectual disabilities. *Journal of Applied Research in Intellectual Disabilities, 15*(4,)314–321.

Freire, P. (1973). *Education for critical consciousness.* New York: Seabury Press.

Freire, P. (1998). The adult literacy process as cultural action for freedom. *Harvard Educational Review, 68*(4), 480–498.

Garbarino, J., & Crouter, A. (1978). Defining the community context for parent–child relations: Correlates of child maltreatment. *Child Development, 49*(3), 604–616.

Itzhaky, H., & Schwartz, C. (1998). Empowering the disabled: A multidimensional approach. *International Journal of Rehabilitation Research, 21*(3), 301–310.

Kemmis, S., & McTaggart, R. (1988). *The action research planner* ( 3rd ed.). Geelong: Deakin University Press.

Kotch, J. B., Browne, D. C., Dufort, V., & Winsor, J. (1999). Predicting child maltreatment in the first four years of life from characteristics assessed in the neonatal period. *Child Abuse and Neglect, 23*(4), 305–319.

Lachman, M. E., & Weaver, S. L. (1998). The sense of control as a moderator of social class differences in health and wellbeing. *Journal of Personality and Social Psychology, 74*(3), 763–773.

Layzer, J. I., Goodson, B. D., Bernstein, L., & Price, C. (2001). *National evaluation of family support programs. Final report Volume A: The meta-analysis.* Cambridge, MA: Abt Associates.

Llewellyn, G., & McConnell, D. (2002). Mothers with learning difficulties and their support networks. *Journal of Intellectual Disability Research, 46*(1), 17–34.

Llewellyn, G., & McConnell, D. (2004). Mothering capacity and social milieu. In S. A. Esdaile & J. A. Olsen (Eds.), *Mothering occupations: Challenge, agency, and participation* (pp. 174–192). Philadelphia: F. A. Davis.

Llewellyn, G., McConnell, D., Cant, R., & Westbrook, M. (1999). Support network of mothers with an intellectual disability: An exploratory study. *Journal of Intellectual and Developmental Disability, 24,* 7–26.

Lovibond, S. H., & Lovibond, P. F. (1995). *Manual for the Depression Anxiety Stress Scales* ( 2nd ed.). Sydney: Psychology Foundation of Australia.

McConnell, D., Mayes, R., & Llewellyn, G. (2008). Prepartum distress in women with intellectual disabilities. *Journal of Intellectual and Developmental Disability, 33*(2), 177–183.

Melson, G. F., Ladd, G. W., & Hsu, H. (1993). Maternal social support networks, maternal cognitions, and young children's social and cognitive development. *Child Development, 64*(5), 1401–1417.

Nieuwenhuijsen, K., de Boer, A. G. E. M., Verbeek, J. H. A. M., Blonk, R. W. B., & van Dijk, F. J. H. (2003). The Depression Anxiety Stress Scales (DASS): Detecting anxiety disorder and depression in employees absent from work because of mental health problems. *Occupational and Environmental Medicine, 60*(Suppl. 1), i77–i82.

Pascoe, J. M., Loda, F. A., Jeffries, V., & Earp, J. A. (1981). The association between mothers' social support and provision of stimulation to their children. *Journal of Developmental and Behavioral Pediatrics, 2*(1), 15–19.

Peterson, M. A., Lowe, J. B., Aquilino, M. L., & Schneider, J. E. (2005). Linking social cohesion and gender to intrapersonal and interactional empowerment: Support and new implications for theory. *Journal of Community Psychology, 33*(2), 233–244.

Pianta, R. C., & Ball, R. M. (1993). Maternal social support as a predictor of child adjustment in kindergarten. *Journal of Applied Developmental Psychology, 14*(1), 107–120.

Rappaport, J. (1984). Studies in empowerment: Introduction to the issue. *Prevention in Human Services, 3*(2/3), 1–7.

Sameroff, A. J., Seifer, R., Baldwin, A., & Baldwin, C. (1993). Stability of intelligence from preschool to adolescence: The influence of social and family risk factors. *Child Development, 64*(1), 80–97.

Speer, P. W., Jackson, C. B., & Peterson, N. A. (2001). The relationship between social cohesion and empowerment: Support and new implications for theory. *Health Education and Behavior, 28*, 716–732.

Stenfert-Kroese, B., Hussein, H., Clifford, C., & Ahmed, N. (2002). Social support networks and psychological wellbeing of mothers with intellectual disabilities. *Journal of Applied Research in Intellectual Disabilities, 15*(4), 324–340.

Syme, L. S. (1998). Social and economic disparities in health: Thoughts about intervention. *Milbank Quarterly, 76*(3), 493–505.

Tilden, V. P., Nelson, C. A., & May, B. A. (1990). The IPR Inventory: Development and psychometric characteristics. *Nursing Research, 39*(6), 337–343.

Wade, C., Llewellyn, G., & Matthews, J. (2008). Review of parent training interventions for parents with intellectual disabilities. *Journal of Applied Research in Intellectual Disabilities, 21*(4), 351–366.

Wallerstein, N., & Bernstein, E. (1988). Empowerment education: Freire's ideas adapted to health education. *Health Education Quarterly, 15*(4), 379–394.

Wandersman, A., & Nation, M. (1998). Urban neighborhoods and mental health: Psychological contributions to understanding toxicity, resilience, and interventions. *American Psychologist, 53*(6), 647–656.

Zimmerman, M. A. (1995). Psychological empowerment: Issues and illustrations. *American Journal of Community Psychology, 23*(5), 581–599.

Zimmerman, M. A., Israel, B. A., Schulz, A., & Checkoway, B. (1992). Further explorations in empowerment theory: An empirical analysis of psychological empowerment. *American Journal of Community Psychology, 20*(6), 707–727.

Zimmerman, M. A., & Rappaport, J. (1988). Citizen participation, perceived control, and psychological empowerment. *American Journal of Community Psychology, 16*(5), 725–750.

# 14

# Advocacy for Change: "The Final Tool in the Toolbox?"

## Linda Ward and Beth Tarleton

[The parents' advocacy service is] the final tool in the toolbox. (Professional, Mencap, 2007, p. 33)

She is a tower of strength, a godsend . . . I wouldn't be where I am now without the advocacy manager backing me up and helping me along. (Parent with an intellectual disability, Mencap, 2007, p. 31)

## Introduction

Article 9 of the United Nations (UN) Convention on the Rights of Children says that every child has the right not to be separated from his or her parents, unless separation is necessary to meet the child's best interests. If this is the case, then, under Article 18, the state is supposed to provide "assistance to parents . . . in the performance of their child-rearing responsibilities" (United Nations, 1989). The Convention was ratified by the United Kingdom government in 1991 and came into force in the UK in 1992.

Under the European Convention on Human Rights (ECHR) (Council of Europe, 1950), everyone – including adults with intellectual disabilities and their children – has the right to respect for their family life. This is reinforced in the UK by the provisions of the Human Rights Act 1998.

Yet despite these internationally adopted conventions, research and experience show that parents with intellectual disabilities (or "learning

*Parents with Intellectual Disabilities: Past, Present and Futures*   Edited by Gwynnyth Llewellyn, Rannveig Traustadóttir, David McConnell, and Hanna Björg Sigurjónsdóttir   © 2010 John Wiley & Sons, Ltd

disabilities/difficulties" in the UK) throughout the world are much less likely than other parents to be allowed to bring up their own children, and far more likely to have them removed from the family home (Llewellyn & McConnell, 2005; McConnell & Llewellyn, 2002). Among the parents with intellectual disabilities interviewed as part of a national survey in England, 48% did not have their children living with them (Emerson, Malam, Davies, & Spencer, 2005). The survey did not collect data on why this was so. Many are likely to have had their children taken into care, but in some cases relatives may have been caring for them or the children had grown up and left home (Cleaver & Nicholson, 2007).

Previous chapters in this book, and the wider research literature, suggest some of the reasons why parents with intellectual disabilities are at such high risk of having their children removed from them. Key factors include low socioeconomic status, social isolation and exclusion, negative attitudes and assumptions on the part of others (including professionals), a lack of accessible information, advice, and appropriate services and support, compounded by broader issues such as poverty, inadequate housing in poor neighborhoods, the experience of harassment and bullying, and the failure of adults and children's social care services to work together (Cleaver & Nicholson, 2007; McGaw & Newman, 2005; Social Care Institute for Excellence, 2005; Tarleton, Ward, & Howarth, 2006).

We know much more now than we did hitherto about the kinds of support that can help parents to look after their children satisfactorily (see, e.g., McGaw & Newman, 2005; Tarleton et al., 2006) so that they *are* able to stay together as a family. But what kind of additional help, or advocacy, is needed to bring about the changes necessary to increase the chances of parents with intellectual disabilities being enabled to bring up their own children?

This chapter focuses on the key role played by independent advocacy in supporting parents with intellectual disabilities going through child protection proceedings, and in improving professional awareness of what needs to be done to improve their chances of keeping hold of their children. Although advocacy may also be undertaken by extended family members, and potentially by parents who themselves have parents with intellectual disabilities, neither of these have been the subject of research in the UK and so are not discussed in any detail in this chapter.

## A Life Like Any Other?

The UK has recently been the scene of a parliamentary inquiry into the human rights of adults with intellectual disabilities. The inquiry – and ensuing report – was the work of the Joint Parliamentary Committee on Human Rights, a Committee made up of members of both the House of Lords and House of Commons, supported by specialist advisers and staff. The focus of the inquiry was far reaching – but the issue of parents' access to a family life with their children was a recurring feature in the nearly 200 items of evidence received. As a result, Chapter 9 of the final report, *A Life Like Any Other?*, focuses entirely on "Parenting and family life" (Joint Committee on Human Rights, 2008).

In its report, the Committee reminds readers that compulsory removal of a child from the care of his or her parents poses a significant infringement of the rights of both the child and the parents under Article 8 of the European Convention – unless it can be justified as a proportionate and necessary response to a risk to the child. It also cites the European Court of Human Rights, which stressed (in a case in 2002) that any decisions to remove a child from his or her parents and family home must take into account what help is available to support the family, and whether it would be more appropriate to provide more help, rather than remove the child. The Court made clear that removing a child from his or her biological parents could not be justified simply on the grounds that the child could be placed in an environment that was more "beneficial" for his or her upbringing, as there was a positive obligation on the state to enable ties between parents and their children to be preserved (*Kutzner* v. *Germany*, 2002, cited in Joint Committee on Human Rights, 2008, p. 59).

Despite this, the inquiry reported receiving significant evidence to the effect that decisions about the future placement of children of parents with intellectual disabilities were:

> regularly taken without adequate information, arrangements or support being put in place to allow parents to demonstrate that they can look after their children satisfactorily. (Joint Committee on Human Rights, 2008, p. 60)

Other factors working against parents keeping their children with them included:

- inaccessible assessments that did not test parents' abilities or support needs effectively;
- negative or stereotyped attitudes on the part of professionals about adults with intellectual disabilities and their parenting ability;
- a failure to provide the kind of information that is routinely made available to non-disabled parents in a format that is easy to understand by parents with intellectual disabilities;
- lack of availability of the support parents need to help them look after their children satisfactorily, due to the increasingly tight "eligibility criteria" for services operated by local authorities in the face of insufficient resources. (Joint Committee on Human Rights, 2008, p. 61)

## Good Practice Guidance on Working with Parents with a Learning Disability

*A Life Like Any Other?* draws attention to the fact that there is now government *Good Practice Guidance on Working with Parents with a Learning Disability* for professionals and others working in this area in England (Department of Health/Department for Education and Skills, 2007). The *Guidance* provides examples of good practice on how professionals in adult and children's services should work together to improve support to parents and their children. It confirms that adults with intellectual disabilities can be "good parents" and have the right to be supported in their parenting role "just as their children have the right to live in a safe and supportive environment" (Department of Health/Department for Education and Skills, 2007, p. 1). Children's needs, it says, are best met by providing support to their parents to look after them.

The *Guidance* sets out five features of good practice in working with parents with intellectual disabilities:

1.  Accessible information and communication.
2.  Clear and coordinated referral and assessment processes, care pathways, and eligibility criteria.
3.  Support designed to meet the needs of parents and children based on assessment of their needs and strengths.
4.  Long-term support where necessary.
5.  Access to advocacy.
    (Department of Health/Department for Education and Skills, 2007, p. 7)

The *Guidance* identifies three different kinds of advocacy to which parents need access if their chances of parenting successfully are to be maximized:

1.  Self-advocacy – to help parents build confidence and self-esteem.
2.  Advocacy and self-advocacy – to help parents access and engage with services.
3.  Independent advocacy – where children are the subject of a child protection plan and/or care proceedings are instituted.

First, the *Guidance* argues that self-advocacy support should be made available to parents as it can "help to build confidence and self-esteem," the lack of which may otherwise exacerbate parenting difficulties; for example, a parent may not go to a parenting class because she lacks the confidence to do so (Department of Health/Department for Education and Skills, 2007, p. 22). The *Guidance* suggests that a self-advocacy group may help boost self-esteem and confidence and thus encourage the development of parenting skills; it may also help parents develop strategies for coping with harassment and bullying.

Experience in the UK, however, suggests that, on the whole, parents are not likely to belong to regular self-advocacy groups, and that involvement in groups with other *parents* with intellectual disabilities (rather than just other *adults* with intellectual disabilities) may be more useful. In the research by Tarleton and colleagues, for instance, parents' groups (rather than self-advocacy groups as such) were seen as a valuable resource by parents because they enabled them to share helpful tips and hints with each other (Tarleton et al., 2006).

In the UK, CHANGE, an organization of and for disabled people, runs a Parents' Network specifically for parents with intellectual disabilities as part of a wider Working Together with Parents Network (www.right-support.org.uk). CHANGE's experience is that parents with intellectual disabilities are rarely members of ordinary self-advocacy groups. So parents in CHANGE are actively engaged in reaching out to individual parents with an intellectual disability and their groups, sharing information with them through a newsletter, organizing events to bring them together, involving them in training courses (designed to better train professionals in how to meet parents' support needs), and making them aware of the existence and content of the easy-read version of the *Good Practice Guidance* produced by them for the government (CHANGE, 2006).

Second, the *Guidance* identifies the need for advocacy and self-advocacy to help parents access and engage with services. Parents' lack of engagement with children and family services was identified as a key issue in the research conducted by Tarleton and colleagues. Parents in that study, *Finding the Right Support?*, felt that services generally:

- did not understand parents with learning difficulties;
- did not listen to them;
- expected them to fail;
- did not give them clear messages regarding what was expected of them;
- treated them differently from other parents who needed support;
- used their need for support, or any difficulties with their child, against them as evidence that they could not parent;
- used their previous history of having children removed, when they had not had adequate support, against them;
- provided no support once their children had been taken from them.
  (Tarleton et al., 2006, p. 26)

These kinds of experiences could lead parents to adopt a negative stance against services and workers they felt were threatening their family – especially if they had had children removed in the past. Taking an adversarial position like this, and disengaging from children and family services, could then reinforce and exacerbate those services' concerns about their parenting skills and ability.

The *Guidance* acknowledges that there may be a long history of difficult relationships between parents and children's social care services, particularly where previous children have been removed from them, and that hostility, feelings of powerlessness, and a reluctance to engage with services may ensue. It argues that advocacy, and support for self-advocacy, can help parents to understand professionals' concerns, while at the same time giving parents knowledge about their rights and the confidence to state their needs. Parents may also benefit from advocacy support in their dealings with other services. For example, the *Guidance* highlights the fact that parents with intellectual disabilities may well have difficulties in relation to accessing suitable housing. Advocacy support – and/or support to develop self-advocacy skills – may help them in their dealings with housing providers. In the same way, parents may also need advocacy support to ensure they receive all the welfare benefits to which they are entitled.

Finally, the *Guidance* is clear that "independent advocacy should always be provided where children are the subject of a child protection plan and/or care proceedings are instituted" (Tarleton et al., 2006, p. 22), though there is no statutory obligation on any agency in the UK to ensure this happens.

The *Guidance* goes on to say that any parent involved in a child protection conference and/or care proceedings "should be informed about local and national sources of independent advocacy" as it is particularly important for parents to have access to independent advocacy in these situations (Tarleton et al., 2006, p. 22). In the UK, however, independent advocacy is not always readily available. The *Guidance* acknowledges this and argues that local planning or commissioning strategies need to address this issue. Parents need access to independent advocacy at an early stage in proceedings, while advocates need the appropriate skills and knowledge of both child protection and intellectual disability issues (Department of Health/Department for Education and Skills, 2007).

## Independent Advocacy for Parents

There is only a limited amount of research literature on the provision of independent advocacy to support parents with intellectual disabilities, and even less on its impact and outcomes.

In the UK the most widely cited source of information on advocacy for parents with an intellectual disability has, until recently, been the work undertaken by Tim and Wendy Booth in the 1990s, which reported on an advocacy support project and group for parents that they set up (Booth & Booth, 1998, 1999).

More recently, the study by Tarleton et al. (2006) included questionnaire responses from, and interviews with, some independent advocates as part of an overall scoping study on issues and positive practice in supporting parents with intellectual disabilities and their children, rather than a systematic review of advocacy provision for them as such. Chapter 7 of their report has a section focused specifically on "The role of advocates," who included both paid professionals and unpaid volunteers, operating like "citizen advocates" in supporting and speaking up on behalf of the parents with whom they were involved. The parents in that study who had had access to an advocate spoke warmly of the help they had received, saying they were "good at problem solving and keeping social services on their toes," and giving as examples of the support received assistance with "writing letters" and help to "argue their points across" (Tarleton et al., 2006, p. 67).

The advocates involved in this study appeared to use a range of strategies in their mission to empower the parents concerned, including:

- organizing parents' groups and meetings between parents (so they could support each other);
- helping parents to write reports as necessary or typing one up for them, so they too had a report to hand out at meetings with professionals;
- ensuring parents were prepared for meetings with professionals, by meeting up with them beforehand to read through reports and paperwork;
- asking for reports to be made accessible, or putting them into easy-to-understand formats themselves;
- going with parents to meetings, and ensuring those meetings were run in such a way that parents could participate;
- supporting parents to take part in meetings and/or speaking up for them, as required.

(Tarleton et al., 2006, pp. 68–69)

The *Finding the Right Support?* study noted, however, the shortage of advocates generally. In their absence, a kind of advocacy role was adopted by some professionals, despite the need for advocates ideally to be independent of services and their staff, just to ensure that parents did have "a voice" in meetings. But professionals were aware that the provision of advocacy support could conflict with their role in, for example, parental assessments and child protection proceedings and was not, therefore, a wholly desirable or realistic long-term option (Tarleton et al., 2006).

## Independent Advocacy and Child Protection Proceedings

There is no statutory provision for independent advocacy for parents with intellectual disabilities in the UK, even when their children are subject to safeguarding procedures. Nonetheless, there is increasing recognition of the vital role advocates can play here. For example, the government-funded *Protocol on Advice and Advocacy for Parents* (which relates to all parents involved in child protection proceedings, not just those with intellectual disabilities) states that: "although parents do not as yet have a statutory right to involve an advocate on their behalf in a child protection case, there is nevertheless a strong presumption that they should be able to" (Lindley & Richards, 2002, p. 3). So what is the role of independent advocates in relation to supporting parents during child protection proceedings? One advocate in the Tarleton et al. (2006) study explained it like this:

> Advocates have a direct role in explaining what is happening in court. The judicial system is wholly inaccessible, and a great deal of time and effort is expended in explaining what is going on, what is going to happen, who the different parties are, and what their roles are. A lot of time gets taken up in explaining outcomes and what people have to do – which may be detailed inaccessibly in conditions or agreements set by the court or social services. (p. 83)

Advocates need a good understanding of the child protection process. The specific activities undertaken by them and noted in *Finding the Right Support?* include all or some of the following:

- Ensuring everyone involved uses accessible language.
- Making sure issues are clearly explained.
- Helping parents to speak or speaking on their behalf as required.
- Making sure parents have access to reports and time to understand their contents and put forward their own views on them.
- Keeping a diary of meetings, phone calls, and conversations for the parents.
- Engaging solicitors where necessary and supporting parents to meet them.
- Reinforcing to parents important messages from the legal team.
- Visiting the court with parents before the hearing to help them familiarize themselves with the location and the procedures.
- Attending court during the hearing, explaining what is going on.
- Explaining the advocates' role to the court, and seeking any special measures that may be helpful to the parents in question, for example, a break in sessions or permission for parents to enter court only when their presence is explicitly required.
- Providing parents with emotional support.
  (Adapted from Tarleton et al., 2006)

Clearly, the welfare of the child is paramount at all times but the needs of the parents also have to be addressed. One advocate interviewed in the study by Tarleton et al. (2006) stressed that they were always scrupulously honest about the possible outcomes of the proceedings. If the solicitor involved thought that it was likely that the child would be taken into care, then the parents were warned of this so that they could be prepared for this eventuality.

A report published by Mencap (the major British voluntary organization working on behalf of people with intellectual disabilities) provides more detailed information on the role of the independent advocate for parents with intellectual disabilities, based on an evaluation of two parent support/advocacy services in England carried out by Beth Tarleton, an external researcher. Both services were funded initially, either in whole or in part, from charitable sources for a fixed-term period, though one received a quarter of its funding from the local authority where it was located. Although one of the services had been established initially to provide general support services to parents with intellectual disabilities (with a view to encouraging the development of appropriate services locally to meet parents' needs), by the time the evaluation was conducted, both were focusing primarily on advocacy to parents going through child protection proceedings.

So what kind of services did the schemes provide? In both services parents could access one-to-one support in order to prepare for, attend, understand, and contribute to child protection meetings. The advocates helped parents to understand often lengthy and complex reports about their parenting and to articulate their views. In addition, they supported the parents when they met with their solicitors.

The support provided was both practical and emotional, for example, help to access community facilities and to deal with housing problems and the parents' often traumatic experiences. The report notes that going through the complexities of the child protection system is a hugely confusing and upsetting time for parents, who often have little other social support of their own. Workers may come to be seen as "friends," but the relationship is more complicated than that as these "friends" have an ultimate responsibility to safeguard the children as well as to support their parents (Mencap, 2007).

One of the services had established a parent support group, which gave parents the opportunity to share experiences and get practical advice from invited speakers. Such groups clearly have a great deal to recommend them, but they also raise a number of complex issues of their own, which the Mencap group was grappling with. For example, should the group be open to parents who are *not* involved in child protection procedures? How do you address the development of relationships outside the group between parents about whom there are child protection concerns when their children are still living in the family home (given that some men may target vulnerable women in order to form abusive relationships with their children)? How can you ensure that parents in the group keep information shared there confidential?

The advice and support provided by the two services went beyond direct help to the parents themselves. One scheme was working with local professionals to ensure they adhered to the protocol for involving parents in child protection proceedings. They were also supporting a local (generic) advocacy service in their work with parents with intellectual disabilities. The other scheme worked at sharing good practice with the professionals responsible for the assessment of parents at a local family center, reinforcing the need to communicate in ways that the parents could make sense of and to use easy-to-understand information. The advocate in this service also had been involved in advising local professionals on good practice in supporting parents with intellectual disabilities generally.

# What Is the Impact of Independent Advocacy?

The Mencap evaluation drew on interviews in both areas with parents, advocacy workers, and external professionals involved with parents' cases, as well as with workers from a community support service providing in-home support to parents in one area. On the basis of these interviews, it concluded that the impact of the services was positive in a variety of ways, as illustrated below, with comments taken from that report (Mencap, 2007).

## Greater respect

The parents, for example, reported that they were now treated with greater respect: "They [social workers] know we have the advocacy manager behind us, and that he is an ex-social worker. They know he tells us the score so basically they treat us better" (Mencap, 2007, p. 46). Previously their experiences had been more like a "war between myself and the social worker."

## More information

The parents also said they got more information now about the child protection process in general and about the perceived issues with their parenting in particular. They were appreciative of the efforts by advocates to provide them with information in ways they could understand, and for noticing when parents had lost track of what was going on in meetings. As one parent explained:

> Beforehand [I] used to just nod my head to everything . . . like a puppet or a robot . . . the advocacy manager picked up on that, now I look straight at her and I know she will explain . . . if I am looking strange, she'll say "did you understand that?" or afterwards will go through the meeting again explaining. (Mencap, 2007, p. 47)

The professionals, for their part, respected the advocacy services for giving the parents' realistic information and understanding about their situation. This contrasted favorably with their contact with other, generic, advocacy services, which did not have such familiarity with the child protection system. Such services were, in the professionals' experience, more likely to encourage unrealistic expectations on the parents' part, for example, that their children might be returned to them when the evidence suggested clearly that this was unlikely to happen.

## Emotional and practical support

For parents, having an advocate meant that their voices were heard, with the result that a number of parents reported feeling more confident about speaking up for themselves when their advocate was alongside them. Other parents were aware that they were at risk of becoming upset and angry in a way that could work against them, so were happy to let their advocate speak up and ask questions on their behalf, with the result that they were more appropriately involved in the child protection process in a way they might not have been otherwise. "He's [the advocate] there for me, could see fire in my eyes – if he hadn't been there [I] would have said something vulgar" (Mencap, 2007, p. 51).

Parents were also grateful for the emotional support their advocates gave them outside meetings and court appearances. Going to the parents' group also boosted their morale. They also talked about the practical support they received, like help with benefits, housing, and shopping.

## Impact on other professionals' practice

An impact on the practice of local professionals was also reported. Professionals involved in carrying out assessments expressed their appreciation of the time taken by advocates to share resources and help them develop their skills. Another professional said, "The advocacy manager knows exactly what should and shouldn't be done; he's up to speed on all rules and regulations that social workers should be abiding by" (Mencap, 2007, p. 52). Another described how the local advocacy manager had intervened in a case, saying, "this [child protection case] conference isn't taking place because the client hasn't had the opportunity to read the report" (Mencap, 2007, p. 53).

## Increased awareness on the part of other professionals

The advocacy services were also credited for increasing the awareness of local professionals about the needs of parents with intellectual disabilities, for example, by raising their consciousness of the need to follow guidelines on the involvement of parents in child protection proceedings. Advocacy workers had supported local professionals to design more accessible and appropriate versions of documents to use with the parents they worked with. At a more strategic level, the consultancy work undertaken by one service had resulted in a local authority plan to improve practice around parents with intellectual disabilities in the area. Elsewhere, a local judge had asked the advocacy manager to help develop guidelines for the role of advocates in court (Mencap, 2007).

## Advocacy for Parents – What Are the Issues?

This evaluation of two Mencap parent support and advocacy services in England, albeit limited in scope, suggests that advocacy can have a critical role to play in improving the situation of parents with intellectual disabilities. But some caveats are clear.

First, the success of the services appears to stem in large measure from the professionalism and commitment of the advocacy workers involved, with the result that, at least in one service, the manager was regarded as "always available" to respond to parents' concerns, including at evenings and weekends. The impact of this on the staff concerned cannot be positive for them or sustainable in the longer term.

Second, the impact on the day-to-day practice of local professionals was limited, at least in one area, by the constraints under which they operated. These professionals were greatly reassured by the existence of the advocacy service, and grateful for the support and advice offered by its workers. But they were clear that they themselves lacked the time to reconfigure how they worked with parents on a routine basis. They relied on the advocacy service for this. As one professional said: "I know I can tap into the advocacy manager. I've no time to change my practice; no time to change anything at all" (Mencap, 2007, p. 54). Such an admission clearly poses fundamental issues about the wider prospects of spreading better practice in supporting parents and securing advocacy, given that both the advocacy services reviewed were funded from charitable sources and/or for a fixed-term period.

Third, there is the critical issue of the extent to which the provision of independent advocacy actually results in a different outcome for the parents concerned. Are they more likely to hold on to their children if they have access to independent advocacy, or is it largely the case that they simply understand the child protection process better, that they are more aware of the likely outcome of the case, and that they have emotional support during and after it? Is the definition of "success" here not that parents are supported sufficiently to hold on to their children, but that they are supported to understand what is going on, however negative that is for them? One professional, for example, suggested that in their view: "I would say the service is a success if parents understand why what is happening is happening. A lot of the time it's not going to change the outcome" (Mencap, 2007, p. 48).

What seems to be clear from the research and literature about the experiences of parents with intellectual disabilities is that advocacy is only "one tool in the toolbox." What parents need is access to a full range of "tools," or support, from an early stage, at the times that they need it, so they can show that they can successfully "parent with support" (Tarleton et al., 2006) – and so that the need for independent advocacy in child protection proceedings later on may be minimized. Where it is still needed, it is clear that independent advocates have a vital role to play in helping parents, for whom the stakes are so high, to understand the ins and outs of what is going on, and to support them through the process, whatever the eventual outcome may be.

For that to happen, funding is needed to develop and sustain independent advocacy services. There have been some promising signs recently in this regard. *Valuing People Now*, the government's new three-year strategy for people with learning disabilities in England (Department of Health, 2009a), contains a commitment to "work to develop advocacy services which include support for parents with a learning disability" (Department of Health, 2009b, p. 40). Meanwhile, the Office for Disability Issues (a cross-government agency spanning all government departments whose work impacts on people with disabilities) has commissioned a preliminary study on access to independent advocacy as part of its overall strategy for independent living for people with disabilities (Office for Disability Issues, 2008). The study is designed to assist the development of subsequent research "to assess the need for, and costs and benefits of providing, independent advocacy" for disabled people in four situations where they are most at risk of losing choice and control in their lives. One of the four situations specified is where "the children of disabled people are subject to safeguarding procedures" (Office for Disability Issues, 2008, p. 66). Parents with intellectual disabilities have been specifically highlighted as a key vulnerable group here (Townsley, Marriott, & Ward, 2009).

## Conclusion

The evidence from the research literature is that independent advocacy may well be "the final tool" needed in the toolbox. However, in order to bring up their children safely and successfully, and in a way that allows their children to develop and thrive, many (if not most) parents with intellectual disabilities will also need access to a range of other tools first: accessible information (see, e.g., Affleck & Baker, 2004; Hawkins & Lynch, 2006), a change in attitudes and ways of working, and a range of support, services, and advocacy of different kinds. They will also need the help of others, including other parents and professionals committed to working cooperatively with others in other agencies to deliver the kind of joined-up support parents need (Social Care Institute for Excellence, 2007). They will need services to deliver on government commitments to ensure equality of opportunity for all people with disabilities under UK disability discrimination legislation. In addition, they will need all those concerned with improving the situation of parents with intellectual disabilities to work together to promote and disseminate the policy and practice changes that are required along the lines of the Working Together with Parents Network in the UK. Only with all these changes can we be more confident of parents becoming enabled to live "a life like any other" family, alongside their children, as international conventions and national legislation and policies in the UK suggest should be their right.

## Principles for Practice

- Many parents with intellectual disabilities will need self-advocacy support to help build their confidence and self-esteem as parents.
- Most parents with intellectual disabilities do not belong to ordinary self-advocacy groups for people with intellectual disabilities. Better support will be offered by a parents' or mother and baby group.
- Parents with intellectual disabilities often need advocacy support to deal with other problems in their lives (like housing, harassment, or money and debts) that affect their ability to parent their children successfully.
- Parents often need advocacy to ensure they get the support services they need, so they can show they can look after their children satisfactorily. Although they may have a legal entitlement to such support services in some countries, they may well need an advocate to ensure they receive those services in practice.
- Parents whose children are at risk of being removed from them need advocacy support to understand what is going on, what the concerns are, and what they need to do to address them.
- Any parent involved in child protection proceedings should be told where he or she can get access to independent advocacy.
- Advocates for parents whose children are at risk of being removed from them need to have a good understanding and experience of the child protection system if they are to be of real help.
- Advocates working with parents with intellectual disabilities will always have the welfare of the child as their top priority. A key task for them is to explain clearly to parents anything they need to do differently in order to keep their children at home with them – and to help them get the support they need to do this.
- For more information and links to many of the resources referred to in this chapter, go to the Working Together with Parents Network website at www.right-support.org.uk.

# References

Affleck, F., & Baker, S. (2004). *You and your baby.* Leeds: CHANGE.

Booth, W., & Booth, T. (1998). *Advocacy for parents with learning difficulties.* Brighton: Pavilion Publishing/Joseph Rowntree Foundation.

Booth, T., & Booth, W. (1999). Parents together: Action research and advocacy support for parents with learning difficulties. *Health and Social Care in the Community, 7*(6), 464–474.

CHANGE. (2006). *Supporting parents with learning disabilities – Good practice guidance.* Retrieved July 2009, from www.changepeople.co.uk/uploaded/good_practice_guidance_easy_read.pdf.

Cleaver, H., & Nicholson, D. (2007). *Parental learning disability and children's needs: Family experiences and effective practice.* London: Jessica Kingsley.

Council of Europe. (1950). *The European convention on human rights.* Rome: Author.

Department of Health. (2009a). *Valuing people now: A new three-year strategy for people with learning disabilities.* London: Author.

Department of Health. (2009b). *Valuing people now: The delivery plan.* London: Author.

Department of Health/Department for Education and Skills. (2007). *Good practice guidance on working with parents with a learning disability.* London: Author.

Emerson, E., Malam, S., Davies, I., & Spencer, K. (2005). *Adults with learning difficulties in England 2003/4.* London: Office of National Statistics.

Hawkins, D., & Lynch, S. J. (2006). *The court and your child: When social workers get involved.* Leeds: Wake Smith and BankHouse.

Joint Committee on Human Rights. (2008). *A life like any other? Human rights of adults with learning disabilities.* London: The Stationery Office.

Lindley, B., & Richards, M. (2002). *Protocol on advice and advocacy for parents (child protection).* Cambridge: Centre for Family Research.

Llewellyn, G., & McConnell, D. (2005). You have to prove yourself all the time: People with learning disabilities parenting. In G. Grant, P. Goward, M. Richardson, & P. Ramcharan (Eds.), *Learning disability: A life cycle approach to valuing people* (pp. 441–467). Buckingham: Open University Press.

McConnell, D., & Llewellyn, G. (2002). Stereotypes, parents with intellectual disability and child protection. *Journal of Social Welfare and Family Law, 24*(3), 296–317.

McGaw, S., & Newman, T. (2005). *What works for parents with learning disabilities?* Ilford: Barnardo's.

Mencap. (2007). *Providing the right support for parents with a learning disability: Evaluating the work of the north-east parents' support service and the Walsall parents' advocacy service.* London: Author.

Office for Disability Issues. (2008). *Independent living: A cross-government strategy about independent living for disabled people.* London: Author.

Social Care Institute for Excellence. (2005). *Helping parents with learning disabilities in their role as parents.* London: Author.

Social Care Institute for Excellence. (2007). *Working together to support disabled parents.* London: Author.

Tarleton, B., Ward, L., & Howarth, J. (2006). *Finding the right support? A review of issues and positive practice in supporting parents with learning difficulties and their children.* London: Baring Foundation.

Townsley, R., Marriott, A., & Ward, L. (2009). *Access to independent advocacy: An evidence review.* London: Office for Disability Issues.

United Nations. (1989). *Convention on the rights of the child.* Geneva: Author.

# Conclusion: Taking Stock and Looking to the Future

*David McConnell, Gwynnyth Llewellyn, Rannveig Traustadóttir and Hanna Björg Sigurjónsdóttir*

## Introduction

This book includes contributions from researchers and practitioners from seven different countries. Most are members of the International Association for the Scientific Study of Intellectual Disability (IASSID) and its Special Interest Research Group (SIRG) on Parents and Parenting with Intellectual Disabilities, which has been a meeting point for many of those who compose the growing field of research and scholarship aimed at families headed by parents with intellectual disabilities. This scholarship is expanding and there is now a wealth of research demonstrating that many parents with intellectual disability do succeed while others struggle and lose custody of their children. As a group, parents with intellectual disabilities face predictable but regrettable challenges. These include poverty, prejudice, and limited access to the resources that most other parents can take for granted, including, for example, respect, moral support, information, good guidance, and practical assistance. Our hope is that this volume strengthens the case for doing more to translate the principles of normalization, anti-discrimination, and the findings from empirical research into policy and practice to support parents with intellectual disabilities and their children.

This concluding chapter begins with final remarks from the four editors of this book. This is followed by a brief description of the SIRG on Parenting and its members. The bulk of the chapter, however, is an edited version of "Parents Labeled with Intellectual Disability: Position of the IASSID SIRG on Parents

*Parents with Intellectual Disabilities: Past, Present and Futures*   Edited by Gwynnyth Llewellyn, Rannveig Traustadóttir, David McConnell, and Hanna Björg Sigurjónsdóttir   © 2010 John Wiley & Sons, Ltd

and Parenting with Intellectual Disabilities," prepared by the SIRG on Parenting and endorsed by IASSID in 2008.[1]

## Concluding Remarks from the Editors

May 1927 was a particularly dark time in history for persons with intellectual disabilities. That year in the United States of America, Justice Oliver Wendell Homes, Jr. infamously declared that "three generations of imbeciles are enough" as he handed down the United States Supreme Court majority decision upholding the compulsory sterilization of Carrie Buck (and, by extension, "the mentally retarded") "for the protection and health of the state" (*Buck* v. *Bell*, 274 US 200). This determination was based on an assumption that the very existence of people with intellectual disabilities was a threat to the human species. At that time, over eight decades ago, people with intellectual disabilities were segregated from society and in many places they were sterilized to prevent them from having children. Times have changed for the better in many places around the globe, but not in all.

As this book was nearing completion in July 2009, the United States of America became the latest nation to formally endorse the UN Convention on the Rights of Persons with Disabilities (United Nations, 2006). As signatories to this landmark convention, states recognize the rights of persons with disabilities across all areas of life, and are held to uphold and make progress toward the many articles in the Convention. The Article of particular relevance to the topic of this book is Article 23, which states the right to marry and found a family. To enforce this right, the Convention goes on to require that nation-states are obligated to root out discrimination against parents with disabilities and to render appropriate assistance to disabled persons, including those with intellectual disabilities, in the parenting role.

It remains to be seen whether the nations of the world act on their obligations under the UN Convention. Turning words into actions – rhetoric into reality – will be the real test of our humanity. The challenge is great. As many of the contributors to this book attest, when parents with intellectual disabilities talk about their own lives, they tell stories of discrimination against them found across and within all systems in society and particularly in the social care and welfare sector. Their stories also reflect that services are ill-equipped to accommodate the support needs of parents or those of their children. Other contributions

[1] IASSID Special Interest Research Group on Parents and Parenting with Intellectual Disabilities. Parents labeled with intellectual disability: Position of the IASSID SIRG on Parents and Parenting with intellectual disabilities. *Journal of Applied Research in Intellectual Disabilities*, *21*, 296–307. Reproduced by permission of Wiley-Blackwell.

reflect the efforts of positive practice and how parents and professionals strive to bring about changes. However, clearly there is still a long way to go before people with intellectual disabilities achieve their right to parent and to do so feeling secure in the knowledge that their rights will be protected.

Since the 1990s, research about parents with intellectual disabilities, their lives, and their support needs has increased exponentially, and there is now a critical mass of research literature to guide and support the reforms that are necessary. Importantly, there is also an international community of researchers and practitioners who are committed to translating this knowledge into best practice and better outcomes. There can be no reasonable excuse for any failure to act across a nation, collectively or as individuals.

## The SIRG on Parents and Parenting with Intellectual Disabilities

The IASSID's SIRG on Parents and Parenting with Intellectual Disabilities includes researchers and practitioners from the United States, Canada, United Kingdom, Germany, the Netherlands, Sweden, Denmark, Iceland, Japan, Australia, and New Zealand. Members come from a range of academic and professional disciplines, including sociology, psychology, education, nursing, social work, and occupational therapy. In 2008, the SIRG members developed a position paper that was endorsed by IASSID Council and published in a special issue of the *Journal of Applied Research in Intellectual Disabilities* (IASSID SIRG on Parents and Parenting with Intellectual Disabilities, 2008). Based on international scientific consensus, the position paper presents a robust review of the current state of knowledge in the field and identifies some important directions for future research. The position paper synthesized messages from research about the challenges that parents labeled with intellectual disability face, and how they can be assisted in their parenting role. As we take stock and look to the future, an edited version of this authoritative position paper provides a fitting conclusion to this book.

## The IASSID Position Paper on Parents and Parenting with Intellectual Disabilities

In one of the first scientific studies in the field, Mickelson (1947) investigated the adequacy of care and outcomes for 300 children of "feeble-minded" parents. Over 50 years later there are now more than 400 refereed journal articles in the field (abstracts available at www.healthystart.net.au). Although researchers have employed somewhat diverse systems for classifying and labeling people with intellectual disability, in line with the practice in their country of origin, the findings from this body of literature are remarkably consistent. This position paper begins by addressing the question, "Who are parents with intellectual disabilities?" This is followed by a brief discussion of challenges or barriers that parents with intellectual disabilities typically face. We then present findings about the capacity of parents with intellectual disabilities to raise children and the outcomes for their children. Findings from intervention studies are reviewed with some promising developments briefly described. The paper concludes with recommendations for policy and practice.

## Who are parents with intellectual disabilities?

Most parents with intellectual disabilities have mild to borderline cognitive limitations. In high-income countries, where almost all of the research on the topic has been conducted, these parents fall into one of three groups. Firstly, there are those who, previously institutionalized, now live in the community and have had children. Then there are parents who, although never institutionalized, have received services for people labeled with intellectual disability more or less continuously for most of their lives. Third, there are those whom Edgerton (2001) refers to as the hidden majority. These are parents who, when at school, were usually labeled as "slow," having developmental delay, learning difficulties, or intellectual disabilities. On leaving school, they live in the community with few, if any, specialized supports. It is only when they become parents that their general cognitive ability is questioned again. Historically, these three groups have been "pooled" together for the purposes of research, with potential between-group differences remaining under-explored.

Several factors make it difficult to estimate the number of parents with intellectual disabilities. These include the lack of a common definition of intellectual disability, variable population screening and diagnostic practices, inconsistent record-keeping, and the invisibility of many parents to official agencies. Consequently, mothers and fathers with intellectual disability constitute a hidden population whose size is hard to estimate (Booth, Booth, & McConnell, 2005a). There is evidence, however, that referral of parents with intellectual disabilities and their children for social and protective services is rising steadily in developed countries. Most health and social welfare practitioners such as health visitors and midwives, community nurses, community disability team personnel, and child welfare officers now have parents with intellectual disabilities on their caseloads (English, 2000; Genders, 1998; Guinea, 2001; McConnell, Llewellyn, & Bye, 1997).

## Barriers to participation in the parenting role

People with intellectual disabilities now enjoy a historically unprecedented opportunity to become parents, yet significant barriers persist. One barrier is continuing opposition from others to their childbearing. Llewellyn (1994), for example, reported that the announcement of pregnancy was often met with disbelief or dismay from family, friends, and the community more broadly. Similarly, Booth and Booth (1995) observed that becoming pregnant was often viewed by others as a mistake never to be repeated rather than an event to be celebrated. More recently Mayes, Llewellyn, and McConnell (2006) also found that women with intellectual disabilities encounter significant opposition to their childbearing. This opposition may take the form of pressure to have an abortion (Booth & Booth, 1995; Mayes et al., 2006; Sigurjónsdóttir & Traustadóttir, 2000). Opposition often intensifies once the child is born. Some parents with intellectual disabilities are not allowed to take their child home from the birthing center or hospital. Others face ongoing scrutiny and live with an ever-present fear that "the welfare is coming" to take their child away. All too often that fear is realized. The removal of children from parents with intellectual disabilities is discussed further below.

Parents with intellectual disabilities often lack the resources that most other parents count on, for example safe and suitable housing and an adequate subsistence base. Although the level of income support and accommodation assistance for parents with intellectual disabilities varies from country to country, most are impoverished relative to other parents in their community. Poverty is a significant barrier to good parenting. Good health is another vital resource for parenting. Mickelson (1947) found that poor mental health was prevalent in a sample of 90 "feeble-minded" mothers, and was a primary influence on the quality of care given to their children. More than 50 years later, Llewellyn, McConnell, and Mayes (2003) investigated the self-reported mental health status of 50 mothers with intellectual disabilities using the MOS SF-36 health survey and found that they reported significantly poorer mental health than their similarly socioeconomically disadvantaged peers. Overall, parents with intellectual disabilities, as a group, report higher levels of stress, depression, and generally poorer mental health than their peers (Feldman, Leger, & Walton-Allen, 1997; Llewellyn, McConnell, Honey, Mayes, & Russo, 2003; Mickelson, 1947; Tymchuk, 1994). Further research is needed to identify the processes underlying these health inequalities. A number of conditions may contribute, including higher exposure to poverty, stigma and social exclusion, and limited access to health-promoting services.

Still another barrier is the lack of access by parents with intellectual disabilities to the learning opportunities and support that other parents can take for granted. Most other parents have positive parenting role models, but this is not the case for some parents with intellectual disabilities, particularly those who have grown up in institutions or in out-of-home care. Most other parents can access popular literature and educational materials on pregnancy and parenthood. Parents with intellectual disabilities may have great difficulty sourcing, understanding, and applying this information. Most other parents have a network of people to whom they can turn for reassurance, practical help, and guidance. Research into the support networks of parents with intellectual disabilities has found that, on average, they tend to have smaller support networks compared to other parents in the community, and they report lower levels of perceived social support (Feldman, Varghese, Ramsay, & Rajska, 2002; Llewellyn, McConnell, Cant, & Westbrook, 1999; Llewellyn & McConnell, 2002; Stenfert-Kroese, Hussein, Clifford, & Ahmed, 2002).

Further barriers are presented by the fact that, while most other parents can access formal or professional services when needed, these services are rarely equipped to support parents with intellectual disabilities (Goodinge, 2000; Tarleton, Ward, & Howarth, 2006). Health and human service professionals often lack time, training (knowledge and skills), and material resources (e.g., evidence-based parenting programs) to work effectively with these parents (McConnell et al., 1997). Center-based and/or group-based parent training programs in the community often exclude parents with intellectual disabilities because they are not able to accommodate their special learning needs. Even those services that are more welcoming may inadvertently disadvantage parents with intellectual disabilities by being time-limited when these parents need flexible support, varying in intensity, over a longer time (McConnell et al., 1997; Tarleton et al., 2006).

## Capacity of parents with intellectual disabilities to raise their children

With respect to parenting capacity, above an IQ of 60 parental intelligence (IQ) is not systematically correlated with parenting capacity or child outcomes. Researchers have employed a variety of research designs and methods to assess adequacy of parental care. Early research employed review of welfare records and professional (third-party) observation and opinion (e.g., Ainsworth, Wagner, & Strauss, 1945; Berry & Shapiro, 1975; Floor, Baxter, Rosen, & Zisfein, 1975; Mattinson, 1970; Mickelson, 1947; Scally, 1973). Subsequent research used more systematic methods including standardized measures and behavioral checklists (e.g., Feldman, Case, Towns, & Betel, 1985; Feldman, Towns, Betel, Case, Rincover, & Rubino, 1986; Keltner, 1992, 1994; Llewellyn, McConnell, Honey et al., 2003; Tymchuk, 1990a, 1990b; Unger & Howes, 1988). This body of research demonstrates that few generalizations can be made about the parenting abilities of parents with intellectual disabilities. Professionals must therefore regard each parent as an individual rather than as a member of a category (Budd & Greenspan, 1984; Taylor, 1995, 2000).

There is little robust data to explain why some parents with intellectual disabilities "succeed" while others struggle. That said, several factors are thought to offer some parents a general advantage. One factor is informal and formal social support, although how parents think about the support they receive is critical to support being helpful (e.g., Aunos, Goupil, & Feldman, 2003; Tucker & Johnson, 1989; Tymchuk, 1992). Tucker and Johnson (1989) observed that support which is competence-promoting helps parents to learn and achieve by themselves. Support, however, can also be competence-inhibiting when others criticize or "do for" the parents, thus undermining the parents' confidence and denying them opportunities to learn. Another factor is the absence of comorbidity, including mental illness and physical disability (e.g., McGaw, Shaw, & Beckley, 2007; Mickelson, 1947). Other factors believed to contribute to a general advantage profile include no personal history of maltreatment or childhood trauma, positive parenting role model/s, a supportive and healthy partner, an intelligence quotient above 60, fewer children, and children without special needs (Andron & Tymchuk, 1987; Feldman, 2002; McGaw et al, 2007; Tymchuk, 1992).

The frequently seen focus on individual parent knowledge and skills as the determinant of parenting capacity has been called into question by social-ecological theories of child development which promote parenting as a social rather than a solo activity (Booth & Booth, 2000). These theories, in contrast to assuming that only parents affect child outcomes, propose that many people and circumstances influence children's life chances (Llewellyn & McConnell, 2004). This social-ecological conceptualization regards parenting as the work of many to meet the needs of a child for preservation (physical care needs), nurturance (emotional and intellectual needs), and socialization (learning to "fit in" to society). From this perspective, parenting capacity is a quality of the child's environment or social milieu rather than a quality possessed by any one individual (i.e., a mother or father). A social-ecological assessment of parenting capacity considers the complex interplay between children and their parents, home and community environments, and family and human service systems (Feldman, 2002; McConnell & Llewellyn, 2005).

## Outcomes for children of parents with intellectual disabilities

There are two distinct periods of research into outcomes for children of parents with intellectual disabilities. Pre-1980s research discredited the earlier eugenic fear that if people labeled with intellectual disability were allowed to "breed," they would infect the human gene pool by reproducing "imbeciles" in untold numbers. Research findings demonstrated that people with intellectual disabilities typically did not produce a higher than average number of children and that, on average, their children had significantly higher IQs and most have IQs above 70 (and within one standard deviation of the mean) (Brandon, 1957; Laxova, Gilderdale, & Ridler, 1973; Mickelson, 1947; Penrose, 1938; Reed & Reed, 1965; Scally, 1973; Shaw & Wright, 1960). Brandon (1957) assessed the intellectual status of 108 children of 73 mothers who were "certified mental defectives" (mean IQ~73.5) and who were former patients at the Fountain Hospital in London, UK. Various measures of intelligence were employed and four statistical methods were used to synthesize the results. These four methods produced mean IQ scores ranging from 91.2 to 94.5. Only 3.7% of the children were identified as "mentally defective." In another early study, Ainsworth et al. (1945) followed up 50 women (mean IQ~68.2) who were former residents of the Wayne County Training School in Detroit, USA. These 50 women had 115 living children between them, aged 7 years and 4 months on average. This study assessed the general behavior and social maturation of the children. The general behavior of 94% of these children was rated as "fair" or "no problem" on the basis of their mothers' descriptions. In addition, the children were assessed using an abbreviated version of the Vineland Social Maturity Scale. On this measure, 89% of the children were graded as developing in accord with or above age expectations.

From the 1980s onwards, researchers have expanded the range of child outcomes examined. A major limitation is that most of the studies are conducted with mothers who attend clinics, which introduces a clinical population bias to the findings. That said, the research as a whole suggests that children of parents with intellectual disabilities, as a group, are at risk for poor development outcomes. In the USA, for example, Keltner, Wise, and Taylor (1999) examined the developmental status of 70 2-year-old children, 38 born to low-income mothers with intellectual "limitations" (IQ < 75) and 32 born to low-income mothers without such limitations matched for age, race, and the number of viable pregnancies. Using the Bayley Scales for Infant Development, 42% of the children of parents with intellectual limitations and 12% of children in the comparison group were assessed as developmentally delayed. In Canada, Feldman and Walton-Allen (1997) looked at outcomes for children 6–12 years of age. Twenty-seven children of mothers with "mental retardation" (IQ < 70) were compared with 25 children of mothers without mental retardation, recruited from the same low-income neighborhoods, on measures of intelligence, academic achievement, and child behavior. Although the outcomes for the children of mothers with intellectual disabilities were diverse, with many exhibiting no problems, on average their performance on measures of IQ, reading, spelling, and math was poorer than the comparison group, and more behavioral problems were observed.

Qualitative methods have been used to investigate life experiences and outcomes for children of parents with intellectual disabilities. In Denmark, Faureholm (2007) interviewed 20 young-adult children of mothers with intellectual disability. Overall, these young people recounted stressful childhoods. They recalled at times being bullied, ostracized, and rejected by other children, attributed in part to the stigma of having a mother with disability. Despite the difficult circumstances of their growing up, most of the young people had an underlying personal strength that enabled them to overcome this experience, and all but one maintained a close and warm relationship with their parents. In England, Booth and Booth (2000) also interviewed adult children of parents with intellectual disabilities. The majority recalled happy, if not necessarily carefree, childhoods. Only three regarded their childhoods as wholly unhappy. Significantly, most (24 out of 30) of the interviewees expressed positive feelings of love and affection toward their parents with intellectual disabilities. All of the adult children maintained close contact with their parents and most said that they were particularly close to their mothers. Those who had been removed by child welfare authorities had subsequently reestablished and maintained contact with their surviving parents. In both studies, family bonds endured despite time and circumstance intervening. This led Booth and Booth (2000) to observe, "(t)he general conclusion seems to be the obvious one: people love their parents despite and not because of who they are" (p. 28).

Research is only just beginning into the factors that predict child outcomes and in particular to determine which children fare better and under what circumstances. For example, Feldman and Walton-Allen (1997) have reported an association between maternal social support and child outcomes. Feldman et al. (2002) found an association between social support and maternal stress, and in turn, Aunos et al. (2003) report significant correlations between maternal stress, parenting style, and child behavior problems. Another small sample study has drawn attention to the potential influence of pregnancy and birth outcomes. McConnell, Llewellyn, Mayes, Russo, and Honey (2003) investigated the developmental status of 37 preschool-aged children of mothers with intellectual disabilities. Between 1/3 and 1/2 of these children demonstrated delay of at least three months in one or more developmental domains. The relationships between developmental status and selected child, maternal, and home/environment characteristics were examined. Only pregnancy and birth outcomes explained the observed variation.

## Child welfare intervention and family outcomes

Parents with intellectual disability are more likely than any other group of parents to have their children removed by child welfare authorities and permanently placed away from their home (Booth et al., 2005a, 2005b). In the United States, analysis of the 1994/5 National Health Interview Survey data identified 430,257 adults with intellectual disabilities (MR/DD) who had a living child (28% of all adults with intellectual disabilities in non-institutional settings) (Larson, Lakin, Anderson, & Kwak, 2001). Of these, 219,357 (51%) had a child who lived with them. Although child removal is only one possible reason why 49%

of the identified parents with intellectual disabilities were not living with their child/ren, this figure is consistent with earlier reports from the United States by Accardo and Whitman (1990) in St. Louis and the New York State Commission on Quality of Care for the Mentally Disabled (1993) on the proportion of children removed from parents with intellectual disabilities/mental retardation. In England, the first national survey of adults with "learning difficulties" found that 48% of parents with cognitive limitations interviewed were not living with their children (Emerson, Malam, Davies, & Spencer, 2005). Again, other factors, such as children growing up and leaving home, may contribute to this figure, but a similar figure was earlier reported by Nicholson (1997), who found that 48% of children of parents with cognitive limitations in his Nottinghamshire study had been adopted, fostered, or placed with kin. Studies in other European countries, including Denmark, Sweden, Norway, Germany, and Belgium, report figures ranging from 30% to 45% of children permanently placed away from their family home (Faureholm, 1996; Gillberg & Geijer-Karlsson, 1983; Mørch, Skar, & Andersgard, 1997; Pixa-Kettner, 1998; Van Hove & en Wellens, 1995). In Australia and New Zealand respectively, Bowden (1994) and Mirfin-Veitch, Bray, Williams, Clarkson, and Belton (1999) report similar figures of 30% and 45%.

A substantial proportion of all matters in children's welfare courts appear to feature parents with intellectual disabilities. In the USA, Taylor et al. (1991) examined 206 consecutive cases before the Boston Juvenile Court. In approximately 15% of cases one or both parents were identified as intellectually impaired (IQ < 79). Llewellyn, McConnell, and Ferronato (2003) reviewed 407 consecutive Children's Court cases in Sydney, Australia, and found that parents with intellectual disabilities featured in 9% of cases initiated by the child welfare authority. And in England, Booth et al. (2005a,b) reviewed 437 cases involving public law applications by local authorities under the Children Act 1989, and found that parents with intellectual disabilities featured in 22.1% of these cases. All three studies found that children of parents with intellectual disabilities were more likely than any other group, including children of parents with mental illness and/or drug and alcohol issues, to be permanently placed away from their family home.

When a child's welfare is at stake, child removal is a necessary last resort. However, there is evidence that the removal of children from parents with intellectual disabilities is often based on two prejudicial and empirically invalid assumptions. These have been documented by legal scholars and disability researchers in several countries including Australia, the United States, the UK, and Iceland. In the first assumption parental intellectual disability *per se* is mistakenly taken for *prima facie* evidence of parental incapacity or risk of harm to the child. In some instances this is sanctioned or "legitimized" by state statute. Lightfoot and LaLiberte (2006) in their recent audit of US state statutes, found that 32 US states still include parental intellectual or developmental disability (mental deficiency is the most frequently used synonym) in their grounds for the termination of parental rights. In other countries, states, and jurisdictions, this false assumption is legitimized by the routine use of IQ assessment as a proxy measure of parenting capacity. In New South Wales, Australia, for instance, McConnell, Llewellyn, and Ferronato (2002) found that standardized measures of IQ were the most common assessment tools used by court-appointed "experts" in their assessment of parenting capacity. The assumption of incapacity leads to two likely outcomes. One is when the risk of harm is imputed despite there being no evidence of parental deficiencies. The other is when any perceived parenting deficiencies are automatically attributed to the parent's intellectual disability without due consideration of other relevant factors such as poverty, ill-health, and/or limited social supports.

The second assumption is of irremediable deficiency in the parent such that any parental incapacity cannot be overcome or corrected. This occurs when any parenting deficiencies are thought to be part of an irreversible "condition" of intellectual disability. This leads to the assumption that no matter what interventions are undertaken, it is unlikely that parents are able to change. In this situation, the state authority "naturally" holds little hope of improving the child's situation, resulting in the permanent placement of the child away from his or her family home (Booth, McConnell, & Booth, 2006; McConnell, Llewellyn, & Ferronato, 2006). Both the assumption of parental intellectual disability as indisputable evidence of risk of harm to a child and the assumption of parenting deficiencies being irreversible are incorrect and invalid.

## Teaching and supporting parents with intellectual disabilities

A consistent research finding is that many parents with intellectual disabilities can learn, apply new knowledge, and maintain new skills (Budd & Greenspan, 1985; Feldman, 1994; Tymchuk, 1990a; Tymchuk & Feldman, 1991). Maurice Feldman in Canada, Alexander Tymchuk in the USA, and Susan McGaw in the UK pioneered the use of applied behavioral methods in teaching skills to parents with intellectual disabilities. Their studies and others since, including a randomized controlled trial (Llewellyn, McConnell, Honey et al., 2003), have demonstrated positive parent skill gains through appropriate training in childcare such as bathing, changing diapers, and cleaning baby bottles (e.g., Feldman, Case, & Sparks, 1992); child health and home safety (e.g., Llewellyn, McConnell, Honey et al., 2003; Tymchuk, Andron, & Hagelstein, 1992; Tymchuk, Hamada, Andron, & Anderson, 1990a,b); parent–child interaction and play (e.g., Feldman et al. 1986; Feldman, Case, Rincover, Towns, & Betel, 1989; Keltner, Finn, & Shearer, 1995); decision making (e.g., Tymchuk, Andron, & Rahbar, 1988); responding to common problematic parenting and social situations (e.g., Fantuzzo, Wray, Hall, Goins, & Azar, 1986); and menu planning and grocery shopping (Sarber, Halasz, Messmer, Bickett, & Lutzker, 1983).

Successful parent education programs for parents with intellectual disabilities contain certain attributes. The program needs to be individually tailored to the parent's learning needs; it should address topics of interest to the parent, where there is a high degree of motivation to learn; the skills need to be taught in the environment in which they are to be applied; and all training needs to be systematic and concrete. Training must also incorporate modeling and simplified verbal and visual techniques and allow opportunities for practice with feedback and positive reinforcement. Periodic maintenance training sessions may be required and more self-directed approaches may also be effective (Feldman & Case, 1999).

## Strengthening social relationships

Over the past decade intervention studies have begun to address other challenges to successful parenting, including the social isolation of parents with intellectual disabilities. In Sheffield, England, Booth and Booth (2003) prospectively evaluated the Supported Learning Project (SLP), a group-based intervention designed to enhance the support networks of mothers with intellectual disabilities and foster their self-advocacy skills. Reported outcomes for the 31 participating mothers included greater personal and practical skills, greater sense of control over their lives, a better self-image and more confidence in their own abilities, greater assertiveness, more awareness of their own needs and how to get help, and a larger support network. McGaw, Ball, and Clark (2002) report similar findings from their evaluation of a group intervention for parents with mild intellectual disabilities conducted in Cornwall, England. In this study, 12 parents were assigned to an experimental parent group and 10 were assigned to a control group. A cognitive-behavioral approach was employed to teaching topics that were intended to raise social awareness and to enhance interpersonal communications and listening in relationships. Major findings included significantly improved self-concept, improved relationships with partners, new friends, and increased confidence in accessing resources for themselves.

## Cultural and cross-country limitations of current knowledge

Research about parents and parenting with intellectual disability comes primarily from high-income countries. While it would be expected that in middle- and low-income countries there are parents with intellectual disabilities, concerns about their parenting do not seem to have attracted attention in service delivery, in policy formulation, or among researchers. This may be attributed in part to how intellectual disability is understood in particular social settings and cultures. In part it may be due to the more pressing concerns of people who present with severe health, daily life, accommodation, or employment needs.

With few exceptions, the body of research is also drawn from the dominant sociocultural group within each country. In some instances, parents from another culture group or indigenous parents may be included in larger population group studies. As yet, there are very few studies that address the needs of parents labeled as intellectually disabled from a minority cultural group within any one high-income country. This is a gap in our understanding which requires urgent and dedicated attention.

## Promising developments

The IASSID SIRG on Parents and Parenting with Intellectual Disabilities strongly emphasizes the need for a concerted international effort to mobilize knowledge from research for policy and practice. There are several recent positive developments. These developments include interventions that target change at organizational and institutional levels of social organization, in addition to the well-tested interventions with parents and their families. One example is the Disability and Parental Rights Legislative Change Project, initiated at the University of Minnesota as a collaborative project in the College of Education and Human Development between the School of Social Work and the Institute on Community Integration (see http://ssw.che.umn.edu/cascw/parentdisability.html). The overall goal of the project is to assist interested parties in eliminating discriminatory statutes from legislation including statutes that equate parental intellectual disability with parental incapacity or risk of harm to the child.

Another example is the development of a statutory code of practice and good practice guidelines on working with parents with learning disability in the United Kingdom. The *Duty to Promote Disability Equality: Statutory Code of Practice* (Disability Rights Commission, 2006) places a duty on all public authorities, when carrying out their function, to have due regard to the need to promote equality of opportunity between disabled persons and other persons; eliminate discrimination that is unlawful; eliminate harassment of disabled persons that is related to their disabilities; promote positive attitudes toward disabled persons; encourage participation by disabled persons in public life; and to take steps that take account of disabled persons' disabilities.

The *Good Practice Guidance on Working with Parents with a Learning Disability*, issued by the Department of Health (DoH) and Department for Education and Skills (DFES), is aimed at improving practice across children and adult services, including greater collaboration between workers in these departments when supporting parents with learning disability, so that the children of parents with a learning disability can live in a positive and supportive environment that meets their needs and reduces the risk of removal from their birth families (Department of Health/Department for Education and Skills, 2007).

A third example comes from Australia where the Parenting Research Centre (www.parentingrc.org.au) and the University of Sydney-based Australian Family and Disability Studies Research Collaboration (www.afdsrc.org) have come together as the Australian Supported Parenting Consortium to implement and evaluate an Australia-wide capacity-building initiative, funded by the Australian government. This initiative aims to build systems capacity, including the commitment, knowledge, skills, and material resources needed to support parents with intellectual disability and promote a healthy start to life for their young children. The *Healthy Start* initiative (www.healthystart.net.au) involves the development of local leaders and practitioner networks and dissemination of knowledge and innovation to support research-informed practice. At the heart of the initiative is the establishment of local cross-disciplinary and intersectoral practitioner networks. These networks are designed to translate knowledge from research into practice and to bring this together with knowledge of the local community as a basis for planning and coordinating local, research-informed service development.

The now substantive body of research on parents and parenting with intellectual disabilities demonstrates that many people labeled with intellectual disability are able to raise children. The opportunity to do so is often limited by enduring prejudice and unequal access to resources, in particular by scarce and inappropriate professional support and services. Equity demands that governments and human service agencies translate the findings from research into policy and practice to support people labeled with intellectual disability as parents, as now required by the UN Convention of the Rights of Persons with Disabilities.

This position paper concludes by highlighting the significant barriers to people with intellectual disabilities being successful parents in high-income countries at this time. The IASSID SIRG on Parents and Parenting with Intellectual Disabilities presents 11 recommendations aimed at overcoming these barriers to achieve greater equity and more opportunities for parents with intellectual disabilities and their children. Recommendation 12 addresses the need for research to advance knowledge about parents and parenting with intellectual disability in low- and middle-income countries.

# Recommendations

**Problem 1.**
Statutes and "expert opinion" give legitimacy to the widespread, prejudicial, and empirically invalid assumption that parents with intellectual disabilities do not have the capacity to raise children.

Recommendation 1. Governments should revise child welfare statutes that equate parental intellectual disability with parental incapacity or risk of harm to the child.

Recommendation 2. Professionals should stop using standardized assessments of parental intelligence (IQ) as a proxy measure of parenting capacity.

Recommendation 3. The assessment of parenting capacity should incorporate valid methods that directly evaluate parenting knowledge and skills, and consider the role of ecological factors that may impede or support positive outcomes.

**Problem 2.**
Parents with intellectual disabilities lack access to resources that most other parents take for granted, such as safe and suitable housing, employment and/or an adequate subsistence base, and good health and quality health care.

Recommendation 4. Governments should invest in prevention, focusing first on meeting the basic survival and maintenance needs of these socially vulnerable families.

Recommendation 5. Health authorities should implement universal psychosocial screening in antenatal care, and provide information and support to vulnerable mothers on the basis of need, not diagnosis.

**Problem 3.**
Policy preferences and/or funding constraints that exclude parents with intellectual disabilities from mainstream services, or limit agencies to providing center-based and/or time-limited support services are discriminatory.

*(continued)*

<u>Recommendation 6</u>. Governments should develop and/or enforce service standards that require mainstream services to include parents with intellectual disabilities and to accommodate their special needs.

<u>Recommendation 7</u>. Governments should fund mainstream agencies to deliver home-based learning and support services that are evidence based, tailored to individual needs, and build on the strengths of each parent and family.

<u>Recommendation 8</u>. Service providers should provide flexible support to families over the long term, recognizing that the intensity of support required increases and decreases as children develop and circumstances change.

**Problem 4.**
Unidisciplinary and one-dimensional models of service provision do not give due consideration to the broad range of factors that may impact children and families, including socioeconomic and other disadvantages such as poor parent health.

<u>Recommendation 9</u>. Health, social, and other community service authorities should promote trans-disciplinary and cross-sector collaboration, for example, by establishing trans-disciplinary and cross-sector networks at the local community level.

**Problem 5.**
Parents with intellectual disabilities are often consigned to the "too hard basket" by health and social service professionals who are ill-equipped both in knowledge and skills to assess and provide confident and competent support to parents with intellectual disabilities.

<u>Recommendation 10</u>. Professional bodies and health and social service authorities should ensure that professionals are taught and implement evidence-based methods and non-discriminatory practices to work with parents with intellectual disabilities.

<u>Recommendation 11</u>. Governments should fund and support the wide dissemination of evidence-based programs and resources for parents with intellectual disabilities.

**Problem 6.**
Little research attention has been paid to parents and parenting with intellectual disabilities in low- and middle-income countries.

Recommendation 12. The International Association for the Scientific Study of Intellectual Disabilities, in partnership with member organizations, should foster cross-national research partnerships and develop strategies to stimulate research about parents and parenting with intellectual disabilities in low- and middle-income countries.

# References

Accardo, P. J., & Whitman, B. Y. (1990). Review: Children of mentally retarded parents. *American Journal of Diseases of Children, 144*, 69–70.

Ainsworth, M. H., Wagner, E. A., & Strauss, A. A. (1945). Children of our children. *American Journal of Mental Deficiency, 49*(3), 277–289.

Andron, L., & Tymchuk, A. J. (1987). Parents who are mentally retarded. In A. Craft (Ed.), *Mental handicap and sexuality: Issues and perspectives* (pp. 238–262). Tunbridge Wells: Costello.

Aunos, M., Goupil, G., & Feldman, M. A. (2003). Mothers with intellectual disability who do or do not have custody of their children. *Journal on Mental Retardation, 10*(2), 65–79.

Berry, J. M., & Shapiro, A. (1975). Married mentally handicapped patients in the community. *Proceedings of the Royal Society of Medicine, 68*(12), 795–798.

Booth, T., & Booth, W. (1995). Unto us a child is born: The trials and rewards of parenthood for people with learning difficulties. *Journal of Intellectual and Developmental Disability, 20*(1), 25–39.

Booth, T., & Booth, W. (2000). Against the odds: Growing up with parents who have learning difficulties. *Mental Retardation, 38*(1), 1–14.

Booth, T., & Booth, W. (2003). Self-advocacy and supported learning for mothers with learning difficulties. *Journal of Learning Disabilities, 7*(2), 165–193.

Booth, T., Booth, W., & McConnell, D. (2005a). The prevalence and outcomes of care proceedings involving parents with learning difficulties in the family courts. *Journal of Applied Research in Intellectual Disabilities, 18*(1), 7–17.

Booth, T., Booth, W., & McConnell, D. (2005b). Care proceedings and parents with learning difficulties: Comparative prevalence and outcomes in an English and Australian court sample. *Child and Family Social Work, 10*(4), 353–360.

Booth, T., McConnell, D., & Booth, W. (2006). Temporal discrimination and parents with learning difficulties in the child protection system. *British Journal of Social Work, 36*(6), 997–1015.

Bowden, K. (1994). Parents with intellectual disability. *CAFHS Forum, 2*(4), 19–24.

Brandon, M. W. G. (1957). The intellectual and social status of children of mental defectives. *Journal of Mental Science, 103*(433), 710–724.

Budd, K., & Greenspan, S. (1984). Mentally retarded mothers. In E. A. Blelchman (Ed.), *Behavior modification with women* (pp. 477–506). New York: Guilford.

Budd, K., & Greenspan, S. (1985). Parameters of successful and unsuccessful interventions with parents who are mentally retarded. *Mental Retardation, 23*(6), 269–273.

Department of Health/Department for Education and Skills. (2007). *Good practice guidance on working with parents with a learning disability.* London: Author.

Disability Rights Commission. (2006). *The duty to promote disability equality: Statutory code of practice* [Online]. www.drc.org.uk.

Edgerton, R. B. (2001). The hidden majority of individuals with mental retardation and developmental disabilities. In A. J. Tymchuk, C. K. Lakin, & R. Luckasson (Eds.), *The forgotten generation: The status and challenges of adults with mild cognitive limitations* (pp. 3–19). Baltimore: Paul H Brookes.

Emerson, E., Malam, S., Davies, I., & Spencer, K. (2005). *Adults with learning difficulties in England 2003/4.* London: Office of National Statistics.

English, S. (2000). Parents in partnership. *Learning Disability Practice, 3*(2), 14–18.

Fantuzzo, J. W., Wray, L., Hall, R., Goins, C., & Azar, S. (1986). Parent and social-skills training for mentally retarded mothers identified as child maltreaters. *American Journal of Mental Deficiency, 91*(2), 135–140.

Faureholm, J. (1996). From lifetime client to fellow citizen. In Danish Ministry of Social Affairs, *Parenting with intellectual disability.* Copenhagen: Danish Ministry of Social Affairs.

Faureholm, J. (2007). *Man må jo kæmpe. Børns opvækst i familier med udviklingshæmmede forældre* [You've got to fight: Children growing up in families of parents with intellectual disabilities]. Unpublished doctoral dissertation, Danish University of Education, Copenhagen.

Feldman, M. A. (1994). Parenting education for parents with intellectual disabilities: A review of outcome studies. *Research in Developmental Disabilities, 15*(4), 299–332.

Feldman, M. A. (2002). Parents with intellectual disabilities and their children: Impediments and supports. In D. Griffiths & P. Federoff (Eds.), *Ethical issues in sexuality of people with developmental disabilities* (pp. 255–292). Kingston: NADD Press.

Feldman, M. A., & Case, L. (1999). Teaching child-care and safety skills to parents with intellectual disabilities through self-learning. *Journal of Intellectual and Developmental Disability, 24*(1), 27–44.

Feldman, M. A., Case, L., Rincover, A., Towns, F., & Betel, J. (1989). Parent education project III: Increasing affection and responsivity in developmentally handicapped mothers: Component analysis, generalization, and effects on child language. *Journal of Applied Behavior Analysis, 22*(2), 211–222.

Feldman, M. A., Case, L., & Sparks, B. (1992). Effectiveness of a child-care training program for parents at-risk for child neglect. *Canadian Journal of Behavioral Science, 24*(1), 14–28.

Feldman, M. A., Case, L., Towns, F., & Betel, J. (1985). Parent education project I: Development and nurturance of children of mentally retarded parents. *American Journal of Mental Deficiency, 90*(3), 253–258.

Feldman, M. A., Léger, M., & Walton-Allen, N. (1997). Stress in mothers with intellectual disabilities. *Journal of Child and Family Studies, 6*(4), 471–485.

Feldman, M. A., Towns, F., Betel, J., Case, L., Rincover, A., & Rubino, C. A. (1986). Parent education project II: Increasing stimulating interactions of developmentally handicapped mothers. *Journal of Applied Behavior Analysis, 19*(1), 23–27.

Feldman, M. A., Varghese, J., Ramsay, J., & Rajska, D. (2002). Relationship between social support, stress and mother–child interactions in mothers with intellectual disabilities. *Journal of Applied Research in Intellectual Disabilities, 15*(4), 314–323.

Feldman, M. A., & Walton-Allen, N. (1997). Effects of maternal mental retardation and poverty on intellectual, academic, and behavioral status of school-age children. *American Journal on Mental Retardation, 101*(4), 352–364.

Floor, L., Baxter, D., Rosen, M., & Zisfein, L. (1975). A survey of marriages among previously institutionalized retardates. *Mental Retardation, 13*(2), 33–37.

Genders, N. (1998). *The role of the community nurse (learning disability): Parenting by people with learning disabilities.* London: Maternity Alliance.

Gillberg, C., & Geijer-Karlsson, M. (1983). Children born to mentally retarded women: A 1–21-year follow-up study of 41 cases. *Psychological Medicine, 13*(4), 891–894.

Goodinge, S. (2000). *A jigsaw of services: Inspection of services to support disabled adults in their parenting role.* London: Department of Health, Social Services Inspectorate Social Care Group.

Guinea, S. (2001). Parents with a learning disability and their views on support received: A preliminary study. *Journal of Learning Disabilities, 5*(1), 43–56.

IASSID Special Interest Research Group on Parents and Parenting with Intellectual Disabilities. (2008). Parents labeled with intellectual disability: Position of the IASSID SIRG on parents and parenting with intellectual disabilities. **Journal of Applied Research in Intellectual Disabilities, 21**(4), 293–307.

Keltner, B. (1992). Caregiving by mothers with mental retardation. *Family Community Health, 15*(2), 10–18.

Keltner, B. (1994). Home environments of mothers with mental retardation. *Mental Retardation, 32*(2), 123–127.

Keltner, B., Finn, D., & Shearer, D. (1995). Effects of family intervention on maternal–child interaction for mothers with developmental disabilities. *Family Community Health, 17*(4), 35–49.

Keltner, B., Wise, L., & Taylor, G. (1999). Mothers with intellectual limitations and their 2-year-old children's developmental outcomes. *Journal of Intellectual and Developmental Disability, 24*(1), 45–57.

Larson, S., Lakin, K., Anderson, L., & Kwak, N. (2001). Characteristics of and service use by persons with MR/DD living in their own homes or with family members: NHIS-D Analysis. *MR/DD Data Brief, 3*(1), 1–12.

Laxova, R., Gilderdale, S., & Ridler, M. A. C. (1973). An aetiological study of fifty-three female patients from a subnormality hospital and their offspring. *Journal of Mental Deficiency Research, 17*(3–4), 193–225.

Lightfoot, E., & LaLiberte, T. (2006). The inclusion of disability as grounds for termination of parental rights in state codes. *Policy Research Brief, 17*(2),http://ici.umn.edu/products/prb/172/default.html.

Llewellyn, G. (1994). *Intellectual disability and parenting: A shared experience.* Unpublished doctoral dissertation, University of Sydney, Sydney.

Llewellyn, G., & McConnell, D. (2002). Mothers with learning difficulties and their support networks. *Journal of Intellectual Disability Research, 46*(1), 17–34.

Llewellyn, G., & McConnell, D. (2004). Mothering capacity and social milieu. In S. Esdaile & J. Olsen (Eds.), *Mothering occupations: Challenge, agency and participation* (pp. 174–192). Philadelphia: F. A. Davis.

Llewellyn, G., McConnell, D., Cant, R., & Westbrook, M. (1999). Support networks of mothers with an intellectual disability: An exploratory study. *Journal of Intellectual and Developmental Disability, 24*(1), 7–26.

Llewellyn, G., McConnell, D., & Ferronato, L. (2003). Prevalence and outcomes for parents with disabilities and their children in an Australian court sample. *Child Abuse and Neglect, 27*(3), 235–251.

Llewellyn, G., McConnell, D., Honey, A., Mayes, R., & Russo, D. (2003). Promoting health and home safety for children of parents with intellectual disability: A randomized controlled trial. *Research in Developmental Disabilities, 24*, 405–431.

Llewellyn, G., McConnell, D., & Mayes, R. (2003). Health of mothers with intellectual limitations. *Australian and New Zealand Journal of Public Health, 27*(1), 17–19.

Mattinson, J. (1970). *Marriage and mental handicap.* London: Duckworth.

Mayes, R., Llewellyn, G., & McConnell, D. (2006). Misconception: The experience of pregnancy for women with intellectual disabilities. *Scandinavian Journal of Disability Research, 8*(2&3), 120–131.

McConnell, D., & Llewellyn, G. (2005). Social inequality, the "deviant parent" and child protection practice. *Australian Journal of Social Issues, 40*(4), 553–566.

McConnell, D., Llewellyn, G., & Bye, R. (1997). Providing services for parents with intellectual disability: Parent needs and service constraints. *Journal of Intellectual and Developmental Disability, 22*(1), 5–17.

McConnell, D., Llewellyn, G., & Ferronato, L. (2002). Disability and decision-making in Australian care proceedings. *International Journal of Law, Policy and the Family, 16*(2), 270–299.

McConnell, D., Llewellyn, G., & Ferronato, L. (2006). Context contingent decision-making in child protection practice. *International Journal of Social Welfare, 15*(3), 230–239.

McConnell, D., Llewellyn, G., Mayes, R., Russo, D., & Honey, A. (2003). Developmental profiles of children born to mothers with intellectual disability. *Journal of Intellectual and Developmental Disability, 28*(2), 122–134.

McGaw, S., Ball, K., & Clark, A. (2002). The effect of group intervention on the relationships of parents with intellectual disabilities. *Journal of Applied Research in Intellectual Disabilities, 15*(4), 354–366.

McGaw, S., Shaw, T., & Beckley, K. (2007). Prevalence of psychopathology across a service population of parents with intellectual disabilities and their children. *Journal of Policy and Practice in Intellectual Disabilities, 4*(1), 11–22.

Mickelson, P. (1947). The feeble-minded parent: A study of 90 family cases. *American Journal of Mental Deficiency, 51*(4), 644–653.

Mirfin-Veitch, B., Bray, A., Williams, S., Clarkson, J., & Belton, A. (1999). Supporting parents with intellectual disabilities. *New Zealand Journal of Disability Studies, 6*, 60–74.

Mørch, W., Skar, J., & Andersgard, A. B. (1997). Mentally retarded persons as parents: Prevalence and the situation of their children. *Scandinavian Journal of Psychology, 38*(4), 343–348.

New York State Commission on Quality of Care for the Mentally Disabled. (1993). *Parenting with special needs: Parents who are mentally retarded and their children.* Albany: New York State Commission on Quality of Care for the Mentally Disabled.

Nicholson, J. (1997). *Parents with learning disabilities: A survey of current services in the Mansfield and Ashfield areas.* Mansfield: Central Nottinghamshire Healthcare Trust.

Penrose, L. S. (1938). A clinical and genetic study of 1,280 cases of mental defect. The Colchester survey. *MRC Special Report Series 229*. London: The Stationery Office.

Pixa-Kettner, U. (1998). Parents with intellectual disability in Germany: Results of a nation-wide study. *Journal of Applied Research in Intellectual Disabilities, 11*(4), 355–364.

Reed, E. W., & Reed, S. C. (1965). *Mental retardation: A family study*. Philadelphia: Saunders.

Sarber, R. E., Halasz, M. M., Messmer, M. C., Bickett, A. D., & Lutzker, J. R. (1983). Teaching menu planning and grocery shopping skills to a mentally retarded mother. *Mental Retardation, 21*(3), 101–106.

Scally, B. G. (1973). Marriage and mental handicap: Some observations in Northern Ireland. In F. F. de la Cruz & G. D. la Veck (Eds.), *Human sexuality and the mentally retarded* (pp. 186–194). New York: Brunner/Mazel.

Shaw, C. H., & Wright, C. H. (1960). The married mental defective: A follow-up study. *The Lancet, 30* (January), 273–274.

Sigurjónsdóttir, H. B., & Traustadóttir, R. (2000). Motherhood, family and community life. In R. Traustadóttir & K. Johnson (Eds.), *Women with intellectual disabilities* (pp. 253–270). London: Jessica Kingsley.

Stenfert-Kroese, B., Hussein, H., Clifford, C., & Ahmed, N. (2002). Social support networks and psychological wellbeing of mothers with intellectual disabilities. *Journal of Applied Research in Intellectual Disabilities, 15*(4), 324–340.

Tarleton, B., Ward, L., & Howarth, J. (2006). *Finding the right support? A review of issues and positive practice in supporting parents with learning difficulties and their children*. London: Baring Foundation.

Taylor, C. G., Norman, D., Murphy, J., Jellinek, M., Quinn, D., Poitrast, F., & Goshko, M. (1991). Diagnosed intellectual and emotional impairment among parents who seriously mistreat their children: Prevalence, type, and outcome in a court sample. *Child Abuse and Neglect, 15*(4), 389–401.

Taylor, S. J. (1995). "Children's division is coming to take pictures": Family life and parenting in a family with disabilities. In S. J. Taylor, R. Bogdan, & Z. M. Lutfiyya (Eds.), *The variety of community experience: Qualitative studies of family and community life* (pp. 23–45). Baltimore: Paul H. Brookes.

Taylor, S. J. (2000). "You are not a retard, you're just wise": Disability, social identity and family networks. *Journal of Contemporary Ethnography, 29*(1), 58–92.

Tucker, M. B., & Johnson, O. (1989). Competence promoting versus competence inhibiting social support for mentally retarded mothers. *Human Organization, 48*(2), 95–107.

Tymchuk, A. J. (1990a). Parents with mental retardation: A national strategy. *Journal of Disability Policy Studies, 1*(4), 43–56.

Tymchuk, A. J. (1990b). Assessing emergency responses of people with mental handicaps: An assessment instrument. *Mental Handicap, 18*(4), 136–142.

Tymchuk, A. J. (1992). Predicting adequacy of parenting by people with mental retardation. *Child Abuse and Neglect, 16*(2), 165–178.

Tymchuk, A. J. (1994). Depression symptomatology in mothers with mild intellectual disability: An exploratory study. *Australia and New Zealand Journal of Developmental Disabilities, 19*(2), 111–119.

Tymchuk, A., Andron, L., & Hagelstein, M. (1992). Training mothers with mental retardation to discuss home safety and emergencies with their children. *Journal of Developmental and Physical Disabilities*, 4(2), 151–165.

Tymchuk, A., Andron, L., & Rahbar, B. (1988). Effective decision-making/problem-solving training with mothers who have mental retardation. *American Journal on Mental Retardation*, 92(6), 510–516.

Tymchuk, A., & Feldman, M. A. (1991). Parents with mental retardation and their children: Review of research relevant to professional practice. *Canadian Psychology*, 32(3), 486–494.

Tymchuk, A. J., Hamada, D., Andron, L., & Anderson, S. (1990a). Emergency training with mothers who are mentally retarded. *Child and Family Behavior Therapy*, 12(3), 31–47.

Tymchuk, A. J., Hamada, D., Andron, L., & Anderson, S. (1990b). Home safety training with mothers who are mentally retarded. *Education and Training of the Mentally Retarded*, 25, 142–149.

Unger, O., & Howes, C. (1988). Mother–child interactions and symbolic play between toddlers and their adolescent or mentally retarded mothers. *Occupational Therapy Journal of Research*, 8(4), 237–249.

United Nations. (2006). *Convention on the rights of persons with disabilities* [Online]. www.un.org/esa/socdev/enable/rights/convtexte.htm#convtext.

Van Hove, G., & en Wellens, V. (1995). Ouders met een mentale handicap: Realitet en begeleiding. *Orthopedagogische Reeks Gent*, 5, 4–7.

# Index

*Parents with Intellectual Disabilities: Past, Present and Futures*  Edited by Gwynnyth Llewellyn, Rannveig
Traustadóttir, David McConnell, and Hanna Björg Sigurjónsdóttir  © 2010 John Wiley & Sons, Ltd